RUSKIN
LACE & LINEN
WORK

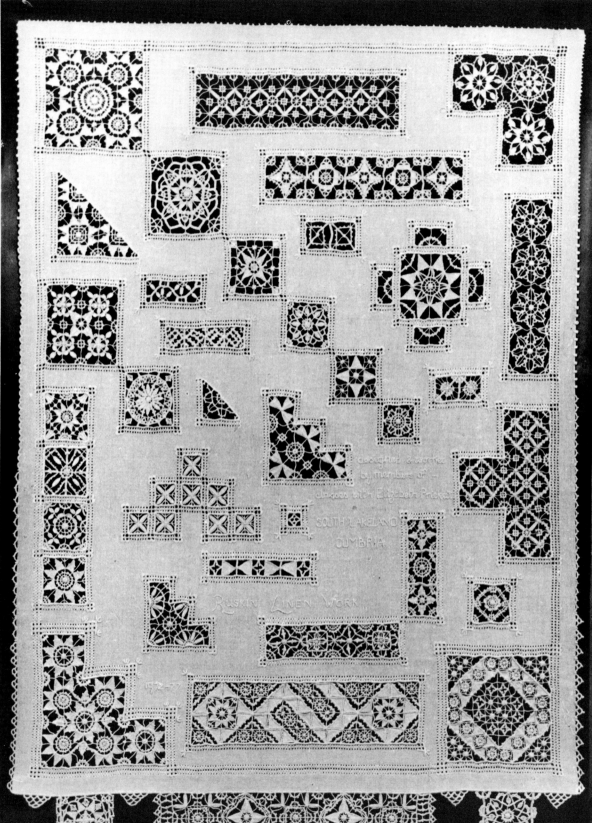

RUSKIN LACE & LINEN WORK

Elizabeth Prickett

B.T. Batsford Ltd, *London*

Acknowledgment

I would like to acknowledge with gratitude each and every student who has attended classes and courses, without whom I would not have developed the skill and confidence to attempt to record a craft that until recent years has remained unique to the Furness and Lake District areas of England. I would like to thank in particular Mrs Lucy Jones who suggested to Mrs Winifred Raby M.B.E. that I may be capable of maintaining the standard she had spent many years establishing. A very sincere thank you to Mr L. Patch who has done the photography for this book and for the hundreds of prints he has produced over the years; also to Mr I. D. Taylor who kindly produced the colour photograph on the cover, to Greta who located the poem by John Ruskin and to Doris who researched the origin of the other verse.

Without the diligence of Mrs K. Steel, who came to live in this area, and Carolyn MacKenzie, I may not have received the invitation to write this book. Finally, a special thank you to my family for their forebearance, especially Rachel for her interest and encouragement.

Figure 1 (frontispiece) *Sampler at the Victoria and Albert Museum, London. This was a group effort involving 60 students, and took five winters to complete at Further Education classes 1972–7. It was presented to the V & A in July 1978 (Index No. T18–1979). It is worked on handspun, handwoven linen approximately 60 years old, donated by Miss Shuttleworth and Mrs J. Butterworth of Coniston, and was designed by the author.*

ISBN 0 7134 4561 0

Typeset by Latimer Trend & Company Ltd, Plymouth and printed in Great Britain by
R.J. Acford
Chichester, Sussex
for the publishers
B.T. Batsford Ltd
4 Fitzhardinge Street
London W1H 0AH

Contents

Introduction

Put a pin in,
Draw a thread
Do 'four-sided'
'Til you're dead.
Petal here and picot there
Everything must fit the square.
Work a 'bug' and roll bar too,
Pyramids you all must do!
Come at two and leave at four
Back next week and do some more.
Join a class and take your place
Finish up with RUSKIN LACE!

Mrs K. White

It is now more than 100 years since the establishment of the Ruskin Linen Industry in 1883, though the production of linen ceased many years ago. One type of needlework that was originated to apply to that linen still survives, happily, today in the form of Ruskin linen or lace work. Ruskin work embraces three forms of needlework: drawn thread, cut linen and needlepoint lace. The tradition is to work directly on to the linen, producing a distinctive result with many typifying features.

This book is intended to be fully instructional and functional, in the hope that the best of the tradition will be continued and enjoyed to the full and that it will provide those who are not fortunate enough to be within the reach of tuition with the opportunity to enjoy this unique craft. I began as a young Mum looking for an absorbing interest I could pursue at home; little did I realise how this was to change the course of our lives. I now hope that my efforts will help further the creativity of those who read this book.

AND SPINNING
NGDALE LINEN INDUST...
ROVED BY PROF...

History

The real good of a piece of lace, then, you will find, is that it should show, first, that the designer of it had a pretty fancy; next, that the maker of it had fine fingers; lastly, that the wearer of it has worthiness or dignity enough to obtain what is difficult to obtain, and common sense enough not to wear it on all occasions.

John Ruskin

John Ruskin was instrumental in the revival of linen fabric production as a cottage industry.

This came about when he came to live at Brantwood, Coniston, in the Lake District, in 1872. He showed great concern for the well-being of the local people and the need for a pastime that could supplement their income. In some parts of the Lake District and surrounding areas in Cumbria a condition of tenancy to some of the farms was to grow and process flax into a fabric called 'harden sark'. 'Hards' are the coarse fibres of hemp or flax and 'sark' was a shirt, though not a shirt as we know it today; it was used as an outer garment.

With this in mind, John Ruskin was successful in enthusing others who were able to further this venture. One such person was Albert Fleming, who at that time lived at Neaum Crag, Skelwith Bridge, a village within six miles of Coniston. Albert Fleming and John Ruskin were both companions to the Guild of St George which had been formed to help the furtherance of country life in the best traditions of agriculture, education and handiwork.

But it is to Marion Twelves, Albert Fleming's housekeeper, that I owe the privilege of recording this history. Having managed, eventually to procure an old spinning wheel, she

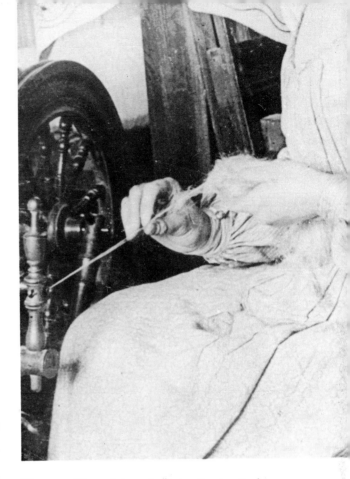

Figure 3 *The technique of spinning flax practised in the Langdale Linen Industry* (reproduced by kind permission of James Atkinson, Ulverston)

set about teaching herself to spin, with the help of an elderly local lady resident who had been taught to spin as a child. A local carpenter was then commissioned to produce more spinning wheels to the same pattern.

From here, Marion Twelves became the prime instigator. A cottage at Elterwater in the Langdale Valley was acquired by the Guild of St George and renamed 'St Martins'. Here the local women could learn to spin and, when proficient, were allowed to take a spinning wheel home. The spinsters were rewarded at the rate of 2/6 (12½p) per pound of thread. A spinning wheel bobbin would hold approximately 2 oz (56 g) of thread and some 500 yd (460 m) of the thickness that was eventually spun for the finer linens.

The need for a loom soon became evident, and this came as a gift, in pieces, from a

Figure 2 *A spinner at work: Mrs Nelson, daughter of Mrs Elizabeth Pepper, using one of the original spinning wheels* (reproduced by kind permission of James Atkinson, Ulverston)

9

HAND WEAVING.
LANGDALE LINEN INDUSTRY, CONISTON.
APPROVED BY PROF RUSKIN.

ATKINSON

Figure 4 *Mrs Elizabeth Pepper at her loom* (reproduced by kind permission of James Atkinson, Ulverston)

weaver in Kendal who no longer needed it. But no one at St Martins knew how to assemble it until they were lent a photograph of Giotto's 'Campanile' in Florence where the Italian cottage weaver was depicted on a mural in the Duomo Tower.

A retired weaver from the Kendal establishment was persuaded to live and work at St Martins for the princely sum of 16/- (80p) per week.

The first linen, 20 yd in length, came off the loom at Easter 1884. Albert Fleming wrote to John Ruskin:

I own it seems terrible stuff, frightful in colour and of dreadful roughness with huge lumps and knots meandering up and down its surface. But we took heart of grace and refreshed ourselves by reading the beautiful passage in the *Seven Lamps*, which convinced us that these little irregularities were really honourable badges of all true handiwork. Better still an elect lady called one day and even without preliminary refreshment of the passage, she pronounced the stuff delightful and bought a dozen yards at 4/- (20p) per yard.'

In 1889 Marion Twelves moved to Keswick to join Mrs Canon Rawnsley at the Keswick Arts Industry in the hope of enjoying more independence, leaving Mrs Elizabeth Pepper in charge at St Martins, Elterwater. The Guild of St George helped Marion Twelves purchase 'Porch Cottage' and, in 1894, she established her industry of spinning and weaving linen there as she had done at Elterwater. There she continued to work until the 1920s, giving 35 years of her life to this end.

Before leaving Elterwater Marion Twelves

10

Figure 5 *A square mat worked by the author, using linen spun and woven by hand by Mrs Coward of Coniston. The pattern is based on a ½ in. (1.3 cm) unit which has no basic grid; the original threads are worked in double buttonhole stitch.*

had realised that if the linen was made up into garments, it would provide work for even more local women, and so she began to teach many forms of embroidery to be applied to various domestic and personal articles, demand for which seemed to be greater than supply.

One of these forms of embroidery was known as Greek lace, though this was a misnomer. In an article that Marion Twelves wrote for the magazine of the National League of Handicraft Societies in America there is reference to a class of 'Greek lace workers in Coniston village who were taught some five years since under my supervision, expenses over and above a fee of 5/- [25 p] each paid by the students was defrayed by the Guild of St George'. This must have been a forerunner of further education as we know it today.

On 8 February 1894 on his birthday, John Ruskin gave Marion Twelves a signed authority to use his name and his motto 'Today' as a trademark. In the same article as above she says 'a photographed copy of which [authority] I send to be used with this article if desired, and I here set down once and for all that my industry is the only one of any description having authority from Mr Ruskin to use his name, and that no other industry in the Lake District or elsewhere has any connection with it, except a class of Greek lace workers in Coniston.'

When John Ruskin died in 1900, Marion Twelves and her workers at Keswick made a pall of natural-coloured linen to cover his coffin. It was embroidered with silk floss thread, with a central wreath of wild roses enclosing the words 'Unto this last, J.R.', with petals and leaves scattered over the surface and lined with rose pink silk. This pall is now in the Ruskin Museum, Coniston, Cumbria.

In 1907, Marion Twelves travelled to Ambleside to take a month's course of daily lessons in Greek lace, now known as Ruskin lace or Ruskin linen work, followed in 1909 by a course of ten days' duration. The latter was followed by an exhibition with names appearing in the catalogue from Grasmere, Langdale, Coniston, Windermere as well as Ambleside.

Possibly hearing of the earlier classes held in Coniston, Mrs Alan Coward of Coniston found her way to the sessions at Ambleside, along with other ladies of the area. Mrs Coward was also a proficient spinner and weaver, possibly having acquired her skill through connections with Mrs Elizabeth Pepper at Elterwater and later at Tilberthwaite.

Many ladies were involved as out-workers for Marion Twelves at Keswick, Elizabeth Pepper at Elterwater, Annie Garnett at Windermere, Mrs Coward at Coniston and Miss Butterworth at Flax Home, Grasmere, as well as others in the area, and there was plenty of demand for their work.

Mrs Coward was the sister-in-law of the schoolmaster at Broughton-in-Furness who had to organise Adult Education Classes and, in 1932 Mrs Coward was duly invited to take a class for Greek lace. Time has proved that this action secured the continuation of the craft as

we know it today. Unfortunately Mrs Coward died quite suddenly shortly before the 1934 session was due to begin.

One of Mrs Coward's pupils at Broughton-in-Furness, Mrs Winifred Raby, stepped into the breach for what she thought would be a temporary situation. Little did she realise that this temporary situation was to last for 36 years, during which time many changes were to take place.

The production of handspun, handwoven linen ceased in the late 1930s. A manufactured linen was introduced in the form of Glenshee Evenweave, a line linen we still use today, with 29 threads to the inch, as compared to the 30–36 threads to the inch of the earlier handwoven linen, and from which threads can be withdrawn easily. Thread sources and types have changed and, during the Second World War years, supplies of both linen and threads were often scarce and difficult to obtain.

Mrs Winifred Raby was able to establish classes in the Furness areas at Kirkby and Dalton, Grange-over-Sands and Broughton-in-Furness. Through the 1940s transport was difficult; it took her most of the day to travel to Grange-over-Sands from her home at Broughton-in-Furness, take the class and get home again – a return journey of approximately 50 miles. Partly for her efforts and stalwart determination to keep the craft alive and partly for her work in other organisations, she was awarded the M.B.E. when she retired in 1970.

Three winters prior to Mrs Raby's retirement, I had attended the class at Broughton-in-Furness and had become besotted with the craft. Little did I realise that the acceptance of the invitation to continue the furtherance of this craft would be so satisfying, rewarding and fulfilling.

In the face of mass-production there are still many ladies eager and happy to learn the traditional skills, producing articles that are beyond the constraints of commercial viability in which the craft had its beginning. Now, a century later, Ruskin lacemaking is going from strength to strength as a very satisfying leisure activity.

Figure 6 *Brush and comb bag. This bag was purchased in Coniston in approximately 1916. Made of handspun handwoven linen, it was worked with Silk Floss thread and lined with silk fabric.*

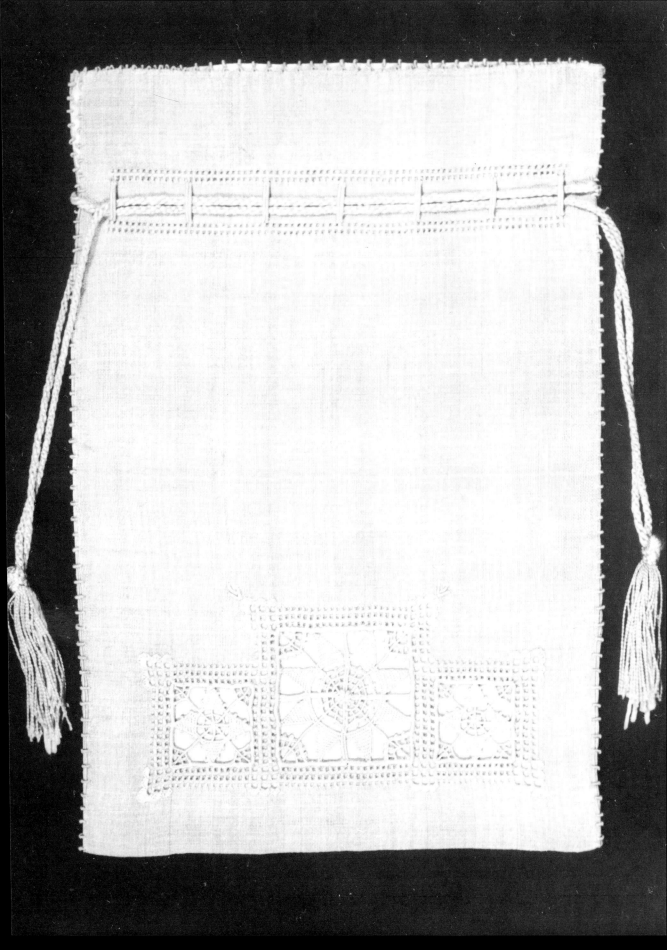

Part I

MATERIALS & TECHNIQUES

One of the advantages of this craft is that the equipment and materials are few. Any fabric can be used, so long as a thread can be withdrawn easily, though traditionally an evenweave linen fabric is used. The most suitable linen is Glenshee evenweave at 29 threads to the inch.

The lace-work area is mounted on to leather-cloth or a rexene-type material that has a woven backing. This is to maintain the shape of the lace-work area while the inside area of linen is cut away and the lace-work pattern worked.

Linen lace thread is used whenever possible, of a weight or thickness equal to that of the fabric. For use with Glenshee Linen Barbour, Campbell's No. 50 or Bocken's No. 35 are suitable threads.

For the best results a round-eyed needle is used in the form of a Sharps or Betweens, usually a No. 6; this prevents the thread from becoming softened and fluffy. This type of needle is used throughout, except for the four-sided stitch when a tapestry needle No. 22 is used.

A thimble will be found to be invaluable – this work converted me to the use of one – a clearly marked tape-measure useful and a pair of sharp-pointed embroidery scissors essential.

Preparation of linen

A thread is withdrawn to ascertain measurement. Often linen will appear to be distorted; this is because it is baled folded. If it is cut using a drawn thread and hems are folded according to the following instructions, there will be no need to pull and tug the linen into shape.

To lay a hem

Make all measurements along the grain of one thread. Measure from the outside edge of the linen, twice the depth of the required finished hem, plus $\frac{1}{4}$ in. (6 mm) for the first turn. For example, for $\frac{1}{2}$ in. (1.3 cm) hem, measure $1\frac{1}{4}$ in. (3.2 cm) from the outside edge and pick up on a pin the next two threads beyond the measurement.

The only exception is in the event of a $\frac{1}{4}$ in. (6 mm) hem, when we allow twice the depth of the finished hem, but only $\frac{1}{8}$ in. (3 mm) for the first turn. For example, measure $\frac{5}{8}$ in. (15 cm) from the outside edge and pick up on a pin the next two threads beyond the measurement. When locating these two threads, make sure they are picked up well away from the point where the two threads on the two adjacent sides will eventually meet. *Threads are not withdrawn completely to the outside edge.*

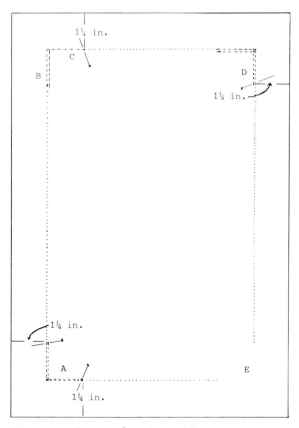

Diagram 1 *Laying a $\frac{1}{2}$ in. (1.3 cm) hem*

17

The most convenient order of working is to begin at one corner of the fabric, take measurements on each side of the corner well away from the point where the two pairs will meet (diagram 1 [A]).* Cut threads where picked up and unpick back to form a right angle, working clockwise, or to the left. Pull the outer thread of the two cut and trace along towards the next right angle or corner at B, pick up and cut this thread and the one innermost, well away from the next right angle, and withdraw these two threads. Turn the fabric a quarter turn to the right and make the third measurement at C, and repeat as for the previous side from *. Turn the fabric as before and measure the fourth side, at D, repeat from * to *. Draw the two threads from the right angle back to meet the threads from the fourth side at E, cutting well away from the point of merging.

Picking up threads on a pin, then checking them will help prevent cutting wrong threads and having to repair or replace them.

To repair or replace a wrongly cut or withdrawn thread

Use a Sharps needle and a length of withdrawn thread, longer than required. Unless the thread has just been withdrawn too far, it is better to use another length of thread rather than try to replace the offending end, as it is advisable to overlap the wrongly cut ends. Introduce the new thread approximately $\frac{1}{2}$ in. (1.3 cm) before it is actually needed by passing the needle through the unders and overs and placing the new thread on *top* of the old one. Leave an end of thread protruding; then, weaving along the spacing in the position in which the thread is intended to remain, overlap the other end as in the beginning. Cut off the old threads and the replacement close to the fabric.

To fold a hem

Turn the fabric over, with the wrong side uppermost and lay it on a flat surface. The long sides of an oblong article are folded first or, in the case of a square, the opposite sides are folded.

Begin by folding over $\frac{1}{4}$ in. (6 mm) centrally along one side (diagram 2). By working on a

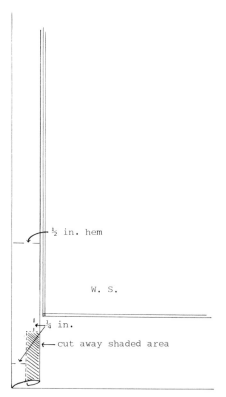

Diagram 2 *Folding a hem*

flat surface it will be easier to fold along the grain of one thread. Fold out to each end. Turn the fold to lie just outside the two withdrawn threads, making sure the grain is straight (this will rectify any distortion of the fabric). Square corners are a traditional feature of Ruskin work, so we need to remove excess bulk from the corners. To do this on hems of $\frac{3}{8}$ in. (1 cm) or deeper, cut away $\frac{1}{4}$ in. (6 mm) from the outer edge, as in diagram 2, cutting back along the folded edge – this removes the first turn and part of the second fold – and stop $\frac{1}{4}$ in. (6 mm) away from the two threads withdrawn on the next side. For a $\frac{1}{4}$ in. (6 mm) hem, only the depth of the first turn is removed, otherwise the corner would be weakened. Fold the other two sides in the same way to form square corners. Tack.

Slip-stitching

If self thread can be used for the slip-stitching, which is a necessary means of securing the hem, the stitching will be least noticeable. (Self thread is that which has been withdrawn from the article or frayed from surplus fabric.) Any self thread which is two-fold, as in Glenshee linen, is perfectly adequate for this purpose; otherwise it will be necessary to substitute a thread of matching colour to the fabric.

The most successful method of slip-stitching is as follows: with the wrong side of the fabric facing, hold the hem in the left hand and prepare to work right to left. Begin the thread by passing the needle through the hem and bringing it out at the inner fold; make a small back stitch into the inner edge of the hem. Hold the needle horizontally to the hem, picking up a small amount of fabric at the inner edge of the hem then cross to the space where threads have been withdrawn. Pick up a small amount of vertical thread, as in diagram 3, in the drawn-out space and repeat frequently so as not to leave a long thread between contacts. Work a number of repeats before withdrawing the needle.

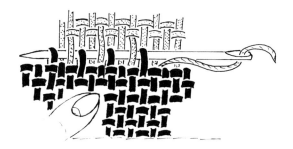

Diagram 3 *Slip-stitching a hem*

To draw threads for a four-sided stitch border

This is another typifying feature of Ruskin work (diagram 4). This stitch is always worked as a border immediately inside the hem and also surrounds the pattern areas. This stitch can be worked as a single row or in multiples.

Single four-sided stitch border
When this is worked immediately inside the hem, with the right side of the fabric uppermost, two threads have already been withdrawn to ensure a straight hem. Leave four threads, draw the next two inside threads. The

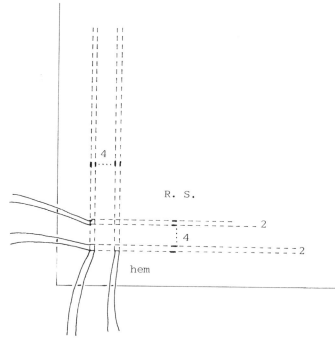

Diagram 4 *Drawing threads for four-sided stitch border*

second two threads are withdrawn to the outside of the initial two threads, as in diagram 4. Whenever possible, cut the threads well away from the junction of the corner; this is so that they can be held back out of the way whilst working the four-sided stitch. They will be reduced and utilised later.

Double and multiple rows of four-sided stitch
Draw threads as above, * then leave another four threads, draw two threads *. For multiple rows, repeat from * to * as required. Refer to diagram 7 (see p. 21), for a similar example.

Working four-sided stitch

Use a tapestry needle, bringing it up from underneath at A (diagram 5a). Leave an end on the under-side and lay along under the four threads being worked over, to be included. Begin in the far right-hand corner of the article or pattern area. This is so that, in case of the outer border especially, the bulk of the work will be resting on the worker's lap – life is easier that way. There are two stitches worked on each side of a block of four threads.

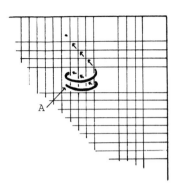

Diagram 5a *To begin four-sided stitch*

Take the needle down at B and out at A; again in at B and out diagonally underneath at C; in at D and out at C; again in at D and out diagonally down to A; in at C and out at A again; in at C again and out diagonally at E to begin another block repeating from A as in diagram 5b. Continue in this manner until the next corner is approaching. At approximately $\frac{1}{2}$ in. (1.3 cm) away, count the last few threads and divide into blocks of four or three; never two or five, as the area will have been measured, therefore threads will not be in multiples of four. Take care not to pull the stitch

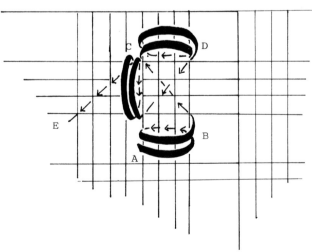

Diagram 5b *To work four-sided stitch*

tight but allow the thread to wrap round the fabric threads closely without being loose. A tight ridge should not form along the border, otherwise the surrounding area or hem will be fluted and the inside area, especially over a small pattern area, will be distorted.

To finish and restart a thread
Take the needle down to the underneath at any stage of the stitch and pass it through approximately three blocks of crosses, back stitch around one thread and continue under three more blocks. Restart another length of thread reversing the previous procedure and bringing the needle up into the next position to continue.

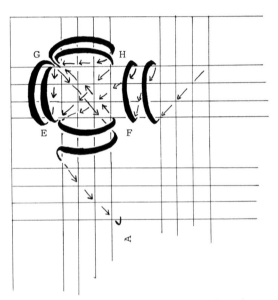

Diagram 6 *To turn a corner in four-sided stitch*

To turn a corner
Work to E, then refer to diagram 6. There is only one stitch around the bottom of the block at this stage. Take the needle in at F and out diagonally at G; in at H and out at G; again in at H and out diagonally at E; turn work a quarter turn to the left so that the next side is lying horizontally; in at G and out at E; in at G and out diagonally at F; in at E, to put the second stitch over and diagonally out at A, to continue along the next side.

Working multiple rows of four-sided stitch

There must still be two stitches on each side of the block. To achieve this, when working the outer row make only one stitch at the bottom of the block. If only a double row of four-sided stitch is required then there will be one stitch around the top of the block on the inner row. If more than two rows are required then there will be one stitch around the top and bottom of the block on intervening rows.

It will be observed that the more rows of threads withdrawn, the more spaces appear at the corners; these can be made into a feature later. When working the four-sided stitch do not encroach into the spaces; therefore finish at D, in diagram 5b. (Refer to diagram 7.)

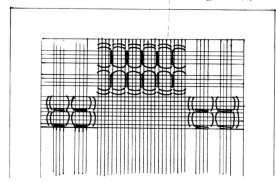

Diagram 7 *Double four-sided stitch, leaving corners unworked*

Woven corners

These are decorative features that can be worked into the spaces which appear at the corners when double or multiple rows of four-sided stitch have been worked.

Using a Sharps needle, begin by running the thread through the crosses on the side as described on page 20. Bring the needle up between one pair of the four threads and one thread back from the corner. One foundation thread needs to be added to lie on top of each pair of the original threads, as in diagram 8. Bring the needle up between the two columns of (now) three threads, * take the needle around the right-hand column and up through the middle of the two columns, take the needle to the left and up through the middle again,

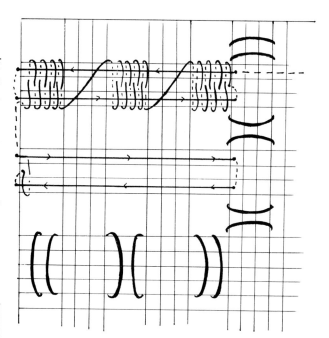

Diagram 8 *Woven corners, stage one*

repeat from * three times more. Do not be tempted to work more than four rows. After completing the fourth row, take the needle under and across to the right, pass diagonally over the junction to the left and, from underneath, bring the needle up between the two columns of three threads *. Repeat from * to *

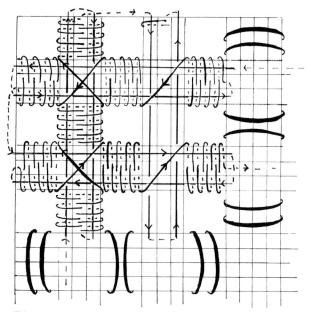

Diagram 9 *Woven corners, stage two*

as required, to end of row. If the thread in the needle is long enough to work another row, slip through the fabric close to the inside edge to lay the extra foundation threads for the next row and repeat in the exact sequence as before.

When all rows in one direction are completed repeat as above for the opposites, except that the foundation threads are passed under the half crosses which now appear over the junctions. The crosses will then be completed over the junctions, as in diagram 9. The thread is now finished off in the same way as it began.

Drawing threads for pattern areas

There are various methods of doing this depending on the shape and situation of the article. A four-sided stitch border is worked around all pattern areas. Where one begins to draw threads for a square, which can be of any size, will be determined by the size of article or its relation to the pattern layout as a whole.

Squares attached to a border
If a square is to be positioned centrally on an article then plot from the centre of the square outwards, as in diagram 10. First find the centre of the article or area. Decide on the size of square to be worked, then mark half the measurement on each side of the centre, fol-

lowing the grain of the fabric so that the measurement will stay accurate if the fabric is not completely straight. Pick up on a pin the two outermost threads at each end of the measurement, leave the next four threads and pick up the next two outermost threads. Repeat in the opposite direction. It will be noted that threads are picked up well away from the corners of the square; this needs to be practised whenever threads are to be withdrawn and will result in long ends at all corners. This makes working easier, as the long ends can be held back out of the way when working. Cut the outer two threads on all sides and draw any two adjacent sides back to the point where four threads merge, resulting in a square of two drawn-out threads. Cut the inner two threads on all sides and draw back to the outside of the outer threads, forming an isolated block of four threads in each corner. Four-sided stitch is now worked over this border.

Detached square
In this instance the square is close to another border or relative to another part of the layout. The margin between this and the square must be decided. The minimum margin should be eight threads; less than this interferes with the neatening of corners at a later stage.

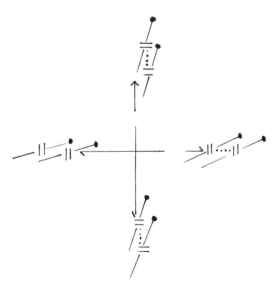

Diagram 10 *Plotting a square, from the centre*

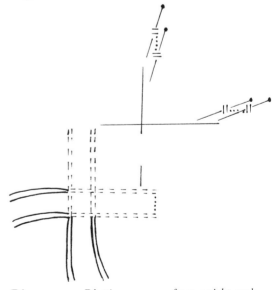

Diagram 11 *Plotting a square, from a right angle*

Once the margin has been decided, follow diagram 11. Pick up on a pin two threads well away from where the junction of the corner is expected to fall, leave four threads and pick up the next two innermost threads. Repeat on the next side to form a right angle to the side just plotted. Cut the outer two pairs of threads on each side and draw back to the point where all four threads merge. Cut the inner two pairs of threads and draw back to the outside of the previously withdrawn threads; this forms an isolated block of four threads at the corner. Measure from the innermost of the inner two threads, along the grain of the fabric or along the line of one thread, for the required pattern measurement, pick up two threads beyond the measurement, leave four threads, pick up two in both directions to complete the plotting of the square. Cut the outer two threads and draw back to meet the threads from the initial right angle, draw the other cut ends back to form the fourth right angle, thus completing the outer circuit and draw the inner cut ends back to complete the inner circuit of the square. This is now ready for four-sided stitch to be worked as described on pages 19 and 20 and in diagrams 5 and 6.

Squares can be positioned obliquely or diagonally; this positioning can be applied to tablecloths, lampshades, wall hangings and samplers. This arrangement can be repeated as required, area permitting. By referring to photographs in this book where this arrangement occurs it will be noted that two sides of the previous square automatically form two sides of the next square. The size of the squares set diagonally can vary in size as the worker desires.

Plotting the inside area of a square

Following diagram 12, leave the four threads innermost of the four-sided stitch border, pick up on a pin the next thread innermost and, horizontally to the border, at about the centre of each side of the square, cut and unpick back to the point where two cut ends from adjacent sides meet.

* Find the centre three threads of the inner area of the square. To do this, pick up on a pin

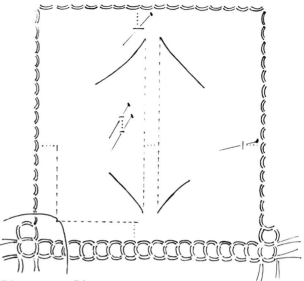

Diagram 12 *Plotting inside square area*

at random three threads centrally in one direction. Count the threads in each half of the square and adjust the three threads picked up on the pin accordingly. If it proves there is an odd thread in one half, adjust the three threads picked up so that it is least noticeable. Cut one thread in the middle on each side of the centre three threads, and unpick each cut end back towards the one previously taken out on all sides, stopping just inside this thread. Repeat from * in the opposite direction which will then form a cross of three outlined threads. These three threads are retained and used later to form part of the basic foundation.

Mounting on to leathercloth

This is to maintain the size and shape of the cut-out area, regardless of how small this area is to be, whilst working the pattern.

A piece of leathercloth larger than the intended pattern area by about 1 in. (2.5 cm) all round, is placed to the underside of the pattern area with the vinyl side uppermost to the fabric. Begin to attach the leathercloth to the fabric at a corner of the shape, using a sharp needle and strong thread, such as double tacking thread or, if working on linen, then surplus withdrawn self thread is ideal. Work a form of back stitch: instead of taking the needle back to where it came out previously, go only halfway back; in this way more con-

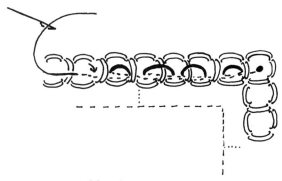

Diagram 13 *Mounting pattern area on to leathercloth, back stitch*

tacts between the two fabrics can be made to help prevent contraction of the pattern area as it is being worked. Make the stitches through the middle of the four threads used in the four-sided stitch, as in diagram 13. Stretch slightly, hold fabric taut along the length of the border stitch and pull stitches tight. Fix each side straight to form a good right angle with the previous side attached. When complete, the inner pattern area should be taut and the centre cross of three threads square. Patience will be justly rewarded in the end result; weakness here cannot be rectified once the next two stages have been worked.

When multiple or double rows of four-sided stitch have been worked, the back stitch attachment must be made along the innermost row nearest to the pattern area.

Spaced whipping

This stitch is worked over the inner margin of the four threads on the inside of the four-sided stitch. Using a Sharps needle and working thread, begin by running the thread into these four threads and work a back stitch (to anchor the thread) before coming out at the bottom left-hand corner, as at A (diagram 14) at the outside diagonal point of the corner, to work from left to right or anticlockwise. Take the needle diagonally over the corner to the inside junction of the four threads, out at the next space along towards the right, created by the four-sided stitch, and in above the next space along – this will usually be four threads along. There will be a left-to-right slanting stitch on the upper side of the work with a straight stitch on the under-side.

Organise the whip stitch so that the centre three threads that are to be retained are in one block or group, as in B, and that a diagonal stitch falls over each corner, as in C. This is a marker for the next stage. Continue to complete the circuit. If there is more than 6 in. (15 cm) of thread remaining in the needle, make a tiny back stitch into the four threads before bringing the needle out finally at the outside of the corner, as in the first instance. Otherwise, finish the thread off as it was begun. Rejoin thread, if need be, as before but in another corner.

Padded roll

This is worked over the four whipped threads as a close whip stitch incorporating a padding cord of three threads.

To make padding cord. With the working thread, make a generous continuous measurement of the four thread whipped border. Make the cord three times this length, knot together at one end and cut any loops there are at the other end, so that there are now three separate threads knotted together at one end.

Lay the padding cord over the four whipped threads with the knotted end extending just beyond the bottom left-hand corner, as in diagram 15. Make the first whip stitch lie diagonally over the corner: as the needle is taken underneath, pick up a small amount of fabric (with running stitch action) and pull tight. The diagonal stitches over each corner are the only stitches to be pulled up tight; all others must just wrap closely without being

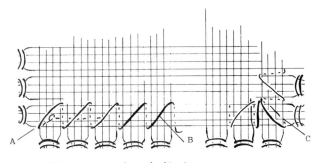

Diagram 14 *Spaced whipping*

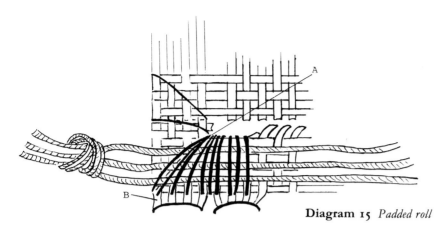

Diagram 15 *Padded roll*

loose, overlapped or given an extra tug to fix. The stitches must be upright and just close enough so that one cannot see the cord running beneath, but can still identify each stitch individually. During later stages, many connections are made into the roll so, if the roll is worked tight at this stage, it is possible that distortions will occur in the completed work. * Take the next stitch into the space at A, round underneath the four whipped threads and out into the first thread of the fabric to the right of the diagonal stitch at B. Repeat from * approximately three times. In order to maintain a closely whipped roll it may be necessary to go into the fabric threads more than once. Aim to spread the threads from the four-sided stitch out to the spacing they originally occupied before being worked.

It is now necessary to cut away the fabric from the inside area as the work progresses in advance of whipping. With embroidery scissors, cut no more than four threads at any one time along the line of the one drawn-out thread. Before cutting, push the fabric towards the centre; this will expose vertical threads that should then be cut as long as possible. These cut ends will then turn over in the direction of working and be incorporated into the roll to give added strength. Only one stitch must come out into the space between the four-sided stitch blocks; all others must make contact with the fabric as at B.

To finish and restart a whipping thread. At this stage move the padding cord to one side and make running stitches through the four threads still to be whipped. Begin a new length of thread by running in reverse along the same threads and make a back stitch before coming out in the lower side where the next stitch has to register.

Continue to the centre three threads; *these must not be cut.* Work through these threads by working into the threads on the inside as well as the outside, keeping the roll continuous. Beyond these three threads begin to cut again, towards the next corner. Continue to whip until the needle comes out at the outside point of the diagonal stitch in the previous stage. In order to do this, stitches will pile up on the inside edge, but ignore this. Take the needle under and make contact with the fabric underneath, as at the beginning of this stage, before drawing the needle out and pulling this stitch up tight. Turn the cord at right angles and begin on the next side. Only one stitch actually forms the corner. When all sides are complete and the last group of cut ends worked in, cut off the knotted end of cord diagonally with the corner so as to form a mitre and continue until the last stitch lies close to the first. Cut off the cord ends diagonally, work one final stitch to settle over the top of the cut ends, pick up the fabric underneath as before and pull the thread up tight to draw the cut ends down out of sight.

To finish and restart a thread

To finish the thread in the previous example and any other thread from now on, take the needle through the roll at right angles to it, as in diagram 16, three times. Do not draw the

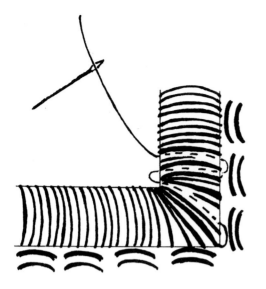

Diagram 16 *Finishing the thread at the end of the padded roll*

To remove surplus fabric from the inside area

Cut along the line of one drawn-out thread that outlines the centre three threads, taking care not to cut the opposite three threads. Repeat once in the opposite direction. Now the four sections of fabric will easily pull free, leaving three threads in both directions. It will be noted that the original threads are now considerably looser than they were when the fabric was first mounted. This is because of the withdrawal of the opposite threads and this extra looseness must be maintained.

To whip square foundation bars

Whenever working over original threads one working thread is added. * Begin the thread as diagram 17. To lay an extra thread over the three originals, hold the leathercloth convexed so that the extra thread will be laid at the same tension as the originals, take the needle over to the other side of the square, out through the padded roll and back again. Hold the threads being worked at tension and horizontal to the worker. Now, work whip stitch, taking the needle under the foundation threads (now four) from above and working from left to right, as in diagram 18. Stitches will be at right angles to the four foundation threads, lying close without overlapping or being drawn up tight. Other threads will need to pass through this bar later so if worked tight it will cause

thread up tight but just close enough to prevent a loop of thread showing.

To begin a thread beyond this stage of the procedure, take the needle at right angles though a roll or bar in such a direction that the end of the thread, approximately $\frac{1}{4}$ in. (6 mm), will lie over or along the threads to be worked immediately. Take the needle back through, splitting the end of the thread in so doing, as shown in diagram 17. This anchors the thread sufficiently, so long as the end is worked in during the next operation.

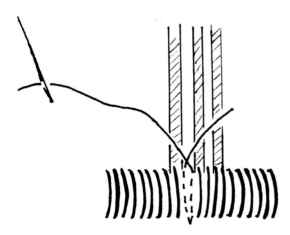

Diagram 17 *Beginning a thread*

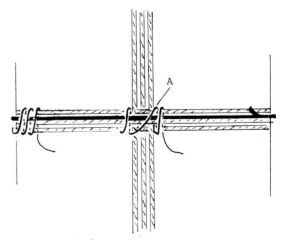

Diagram 18 *Whip-stitching square foundation bar*

difficulties and distortions. Continue towards the centre and up to the three opposite original threads. This junction must be fixed centrally. Maintain the natural spacing of the opposite original threads, take the thread diagonally over the centre junction, as at A in diagram 18, and continue to the end. Finish thread as in diagram 16 *. Repeat from * to * on the opposite original threads, taking the added thread under the half cross stitch at the centre junction. The cross will be completed as the second square bar is worked. Take care in centralising the centre junction.

To whip diagonal foundation bars

Begin the thread as before in a corner of the square and, as in diagram 19, lay the thread towards the opposite corner, taking the needle through the centre junction and holding the leathercloth slightly convexed so laying these foundation threads at the same tension as those of the square bars. Bring the needle through the padded roll at the opposite corner, take the needle back through the padded

roll and repeat until three threads are laid. Whip stitch as for square foundation bars, forming another cross stitch at the centre junction.

To work diamond foundation bars

These are not worked in all patterns but, when they are, they are worked at this stage of the procedure. Begin the thread as before, at the right-hand side of a square bar and into the padded roll, as at A in diagram 20. Lay the thread over to the next square bar in an anticlockwise direction. Take the needle through at the point where the thread passes over the diagonal bar, then to the left of the next square bar and out through the padded roll at B. Take the needle back through the padded roll, holding the leathercloth convexed so that the tension will be equal to the other foundation bars. Repeat to full circuit and then lay two more circuits and whip stitch, keeping diagonal foundation bars straight.

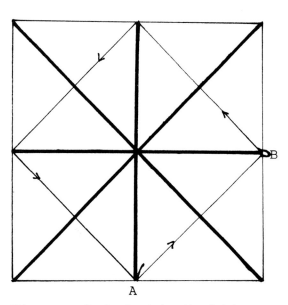

Diagram 20 *Laying threads for whip-stitched diamond bar*

To work woven square bars

This feature is usually worked over the three original threads when little or no part of the pattern occupies the square bars. This stage is

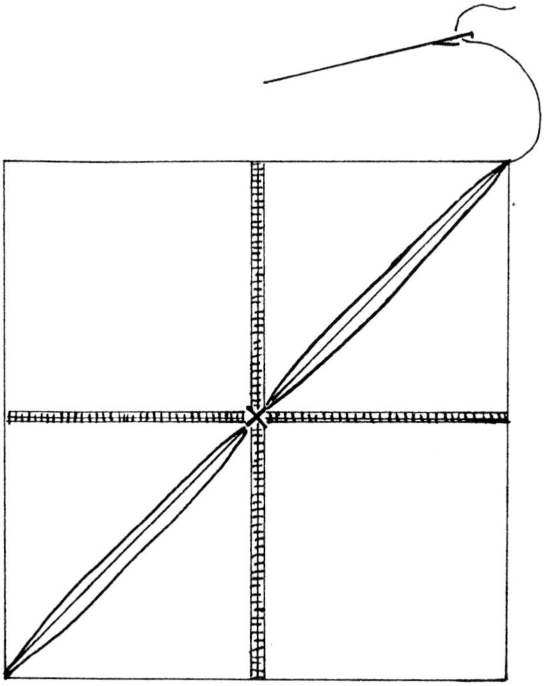

Diagram 19 *Laying threads for whip-stitched diagonal bar*

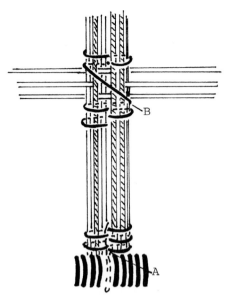

Diagram 21 *Woven foundation bar*

worked after the completion of the padded
roll. The weaving is worked over six foundation threads, so a further three threads need to
be added.

Begin the thread as before in order to lay
the extra threads parallel to the originals; two
threads are laid on top of one original thread
and one thread is laid on top of the other two
original threads, taking care not to spread the
width that the originals occupy, as in diagram
21. Bring the needle back through the padded
roll and between the two columns of now
three threads, as at A. Hold the threads to be
worked over next in a vertical position.
* Take the needle to the right, around behind
and up through the middle of the two
columns. Take the needle to the left, around
behind and up through the middle again.
Wrap the threads closely and pack stitches
depthwise just close enough to cover the
foundation threads*. Repeat from * to *,
towards the centre and the opposite three
threads, making sure they are central. Take the
needle to the right, as before, and then to the
left but, instead of coming up through the
middle, take the needle straight across behind
the six threads, as at B. Coming out at the
right, take the needle diagonally over the
centre junction to the left, behind the left-hand
column and up through the middle. The

thread is now lying towards the right. Proceed
as before to the end. Finish the thread as in
diagram 16 (*see p. 26*). Lay the threads in the
opposite direction, as before, but taking them
under the half cross stitch at the centre junction: otherwise repeat as for the first bar.

To work double buttonhole-stitched bars

This feature can be applied to a variety of
situations and is sometimes worked over an
already whipped bar when this feature is not
required over the full length or circuit of
foundation threads. The type of buttonhole
stitch used throughout this craft is also known
as button stitch or blanket stitch, therefore it is
the type without a twist, as is shown in
diagram 22.

If this feature is worked over the three
original threads, then one working thread is
added. Begin thread as before, add an extra
thread as before and hold threads to be
worked in a horizontal position and at tension.
Work the buttonhole stitch slightly spaced, as
at A, to allow a buttonhole stitch to fit in
between from the other side. Continue to the
end, secure thread as at B and return along the
other side as illustrated. Finish the thread as
before.

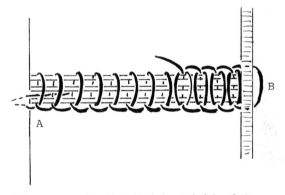

Diagram 22 *Double buttonhole-stitched foundation bar*

Drawing threads for an insertion

All the pattern areas in this craft are based on a
square. There is no limit to the multiple so
long as the shape follows the grain of the

fabric. In the case of an insertion the total length of the pattern will be a multiple of the depth. This can be an odd or even number of repeats, depending on the type of pattern or patterns to be worked. If an alternate pattern repeat is to be worked, then an odd number of repeats will be required. If one or a running pattern are to be worked then either an odd or an even number of repeats can be worked – the area for plotting will probably determine which. There are three methods of plotting this shape, depending on their situation.

Insertion as an independent shape

This is usually widthways as at A in diagram 23, to fit between two outer borders, when the shape will be plotted from the centre to the ends. First find the centre of what is going to be the length of the insertion. The repeat is called a unit. The unit measurement will be

Figure 7 *Traycloth or place mat using linen spun and woven by hand by the author. It illustrates an insertion plotted as an independent shape, using the same pattern as a running repeat.*

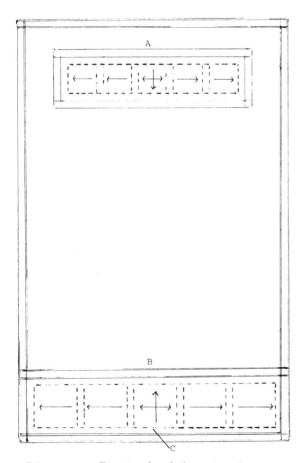

Diagram 23 *Drawing threads for an insertion*

determined by the number of repeats required within the given distance. It will often take several attempts at plotting before a unit size that will fit is determined, therefore do not get scissor-happy. If an odd number of units is required, as in diagram 23A, centralise the unit measurement over the centre mark on the fabric. Pick up on a pin the first and last thread of the unit, * leave three, pick up one, plotting towards one end of the insertion. The next unit begins with the last one thread picked up. Pick up the last thread in the unit *, repeat from * to * as required. Leave four threads (for the padded roll) pick up two, leave four, pick up two (for the four-sided stitch border). If the first plotting is not satisfactory, then alter the unit measurement accordingly. The minimum margin between the end of a shape and any other border is eight threads. Now plot the other half, to make sure the initial centring was correct. Decide on the depth of margin from the end of the article. This need not be the same as that at the ends of the shape; the eye will help to decide a good balance for the size of the article being made. Pick up two, leave four, pick up two, leave four, pick up one, plot unit as before, pick up one (being the last thread in the unit), leave four, pick up two, leave four, pick up two. If an even number of units is required, then three threads form the initial centre. Pick up one thread on each side of the same, this thread being the beginning of the unit; otherwise continue as above.

Cut the one thread picked up from next to the border on all sides, and draw back to form a rectangle. This outlines the inside pattern area. Cut the one thread on either side of the three which separate the units and draw back to just inside the one forming the rectangle. Now cut and draw threads for the four-sided stitch border around this rectangle as for the square. This is now ready for the four-sided stitch to be worked, as described on pages 19–20 and in diagrams 5 and 6.

Insertion occupying the full width of the area between borders

This must be plotted before the four-sided stitch border is worked. Leave the four threads immediately next to the border at each end, pick up one (this will be included in the unit) and plot from the centre as above. Leave four threads, as in C, diagram 23 and plot the unit as before. Pick up one (this is the last thread included in the unit), leave four, pick up two, leave four, pick up two. The single threads picked up immediately next to the border are now cut and drawn back to form a rectangle. Cut the single threads on either side

of the three which separate the units, draw back to just inside the one forming the rectangle. Cut and draw the threads for the fourth side; these threads are drawn back to interlock with the border on the adjacent sides. Here an isolated block of four threads will occur and will be worked as one block when working the four-sided stitch border. It is possible that blocks immediately before will not be multiples of four threads – refer to the working of four-sided stitch.

This is now ready for the four-sided stitch to be worked, as described on page 19 and diagrams 5 and 6.

Insertion circumjacent to the outer border (Figure 8)

Here the fabric cannot be cut to size until two sides of the article have been plotted. Begin at one corner of the fabric, allowing for the required depth of hem (as in diagram 1 see p. 17) on both sides of the initial right angle. Plot the threads for the depth of border required, then leave four threads for the padded roll. Pick up one thread, as at A in diagram 24, plot the unit as before, picking up the last thread at C; leave four threads (this is because these same four threads will be used for the padded roll on the inside of the insertion — see figure 8) and pick up one. Continue to plot as in the previous insertion (diagram 23 [B], see p. 29. Plot an odd or even number of units as required, until just before the last unit, when four threads are left again. The same situation arises as occurred at the beginning; pick up one as at D in diagram 24, plot the last unit, leave four, then plot the depth of the border and hem allowance and pick up one thread. This is where the piece of fabric can then be cut away. Having plotted in both directions, forming a square or oblong as required, check measurements and number of units plotted, then cut out the piece of fabric.

Return to the initial right angle and cut the border threads as at A in diagram 1 (see p. 17). Cut the next single thread on both sides of the right angle as at A in diagram 24, draw back to form the corner and draw the other cut end back to meet the single thread immediately inside the border, plotting at the other end of

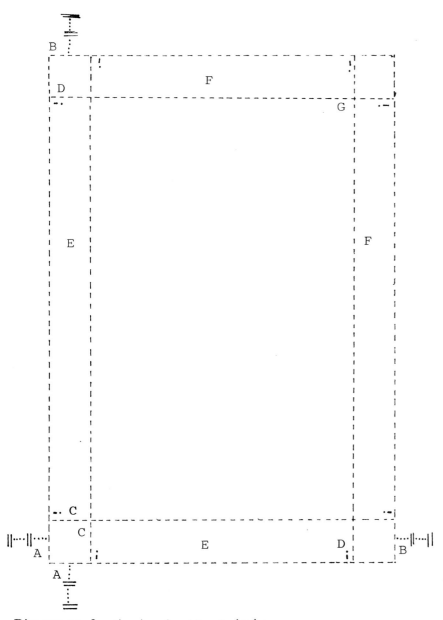

Diagram 24 *Insertion circumjacent to outer border*

the insertion at B in both directions. Cut and draw one end back to form the second and third corner and draw the other end of the thread back to meet the corresponding thread from B; this forms the fourth corner.

Return, again, to the initial right angle, cut the next single thread in both directions at C and draw across to fall just short of the one already taken out at B. From the second and third corners cut the first single thread away from those right angles, as at D.

The threads picked up on pins on sides E can now be cut in the middle of the margin between A and C. Divide areas F into the same number of units separated by three threads. It will be noted that the other threads outlining the four threads are still to be cut. Cut these approximately $\frac{1}{2}$ in. (1.3 cm) inwards from A and D, only unpick towards these points. They are not drawn back in the other direction as it will be noted that these threads are part of the border threads on the inside border.

31

Figure 8 *A traycloth illustrating the plotting of an insertion circumjacent to the border, using Pattern 8.*

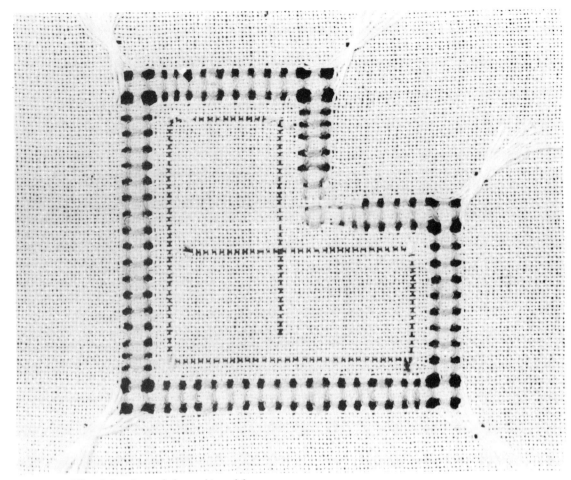

Figure 9 *Thread-drawing and the working of four-sided stitch at an inverted corner*

Now plot the border on the inside of the insertion: leave four threads for the padded roll, pick up two, leave four, pick up two. A single row of borders is advisable; deeper could be worked but it would detract from the pattern and cause an unnecessary weakness in the corners that really is not justified in the end result. When a padded roll is worked through an inverted corner, as at G, the point has to be built out. To make this easier, it is advantageous not to withdraw the border threads back to the corner but rather to leave them in and work the four-sided stitch, as in figure 9, and later the padded roll over the usual threads. This means that when the leathercloth is finally taken off these threads can be remove to expose a neat corner working, as in figure 8.

Work four-sided stitch on all borders. Mount on to the leathercloth, fixing the outer circuit first. Great care is needed here; check by measuring diagonally as well as on the straight to ensure a good shape and tension, as in diagram 13 (*see p. 24*), then fix the inner circuit.

The spaced whipping is worked in two circuits. Work the outer in the usual way, as in diagram 14 (*see p. 24*). The inner circuit is also worked as usual, except at the inverted corners, where the retained border threads are excluded; space whip over the usual threads, making a diagonal stitch over the corner with a block of four threads on each side of it.

There are two complete circuits of padded roll, the outer being worked first. The padding cords must be long enough to go round the

33

full circuit. Work the padded roll as in diagram 15 (*see p. 25*), taking care to retain the four threads where necessary and the three threads elsewhere. The inner circuit is begun in the corner, working from left to right and the stitches worked from the inside to the outside of the pattern area, just as for the outer circuit. Here corners are inverted and must be built up to achieve a right angle. Place the cord over the four whipped threads as before. Place the first whip stitch diagonally over the corner, picking up the fabric as before, but not pulling tight. Split each of the four threads to be retained on the inside of the insertion, bringing the needle out at the same place each time. Do not cut the threads on the inside until the last two threads retained in the opposite direction have been passed. Split the threads on the inside as well as on the outside; avoid making contact with the retained threads that run parallel; continue as usual towards the next inverted corner. Stop cutting on the inside when the first pair of retained threads in the opposite direction is reached; continue the padded roll, splitting the threads on the inside as well as on the outside. When the junction of the corner is reached, as at A in diagram 25, split each of the four threads which are to be retained for the foundation bar adjacent to C and D in diagram 24: work a diagonal stitch over the corner, picking up the fabric underneath (as at other corners) but, as this corner has to be built up, this stitch must not be pulled tight; split the next four threads, easing the cord around the corner to keep the bulk towards the point and bringing the needle out at A each time for the whole of the corner turning; begin to split the threads on the inside and outside again, until the last pair of threads retained in the opposite direction is worked. Begin to cut on the inside again; continue and finish as in the instruction for the padded roll, but without pulling the stitches tight, as in diagram 16 (*see p. 26*).

To remove the surplus fabric from the inside area, the fabric still attached on the inside of the inverted corner must be cut away close to the roll, avoiding, at all costs, the four threads that must remain.

The two bars of four threads in each corner

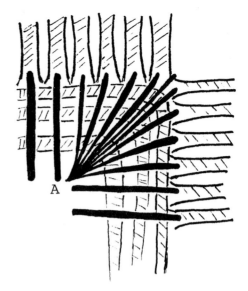

Diagram 25 *Padded roll at an inverted corner*

will both be worked in one operation. One working thread will be added if these threads are to be whipped or double buttonhole-stitched and two threads if they are to be woven. Begin the thread at one of the outer edges. Take the foundation thread in and out of the inverted corner to the other outer edge, return to the first outer edge and, using the same length of thread, whip or buttonhole stitch as required. This gives added strength to the point of the inverted corner.

Follow the order of working for the insertion or as the desired pattern indicates.

On completion of the pattern, it will be noted that there are no cut ends on the inverted corners so, therefore, the only corner neatenings are on the outer corners.

Remove the leathercloth. The threads that were retained at the inverted corners can now be withdrawn. First cut them close to the padded roll and then unpick the loose threads.

Order of working for insertions

Insertions are mounted on to the leathercloth as a whole. The padded roll is also worked as a whole. If the retained original threads that separate the units are to be whipped, a working thread is added, as in diagram 18, though, a feature can be made of these threads. If patterns are to be alternated or any other

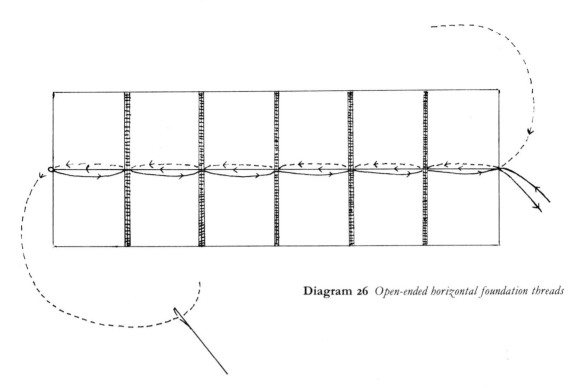

Diagram 26 *Open-ended horizontal foundation threads*

combination of patterns included, these original threads can be woven or double buttonhole stitched, as in diagram 21 or 22 (*see p. 28*). If the units are large enough to be divided into the usual eight sections, then proceed as described below. Each unit will be divided in half vertically (this represents one of the square bars), usually with a three-thread bar, and whip stitched.

To lay the horizontal threads
The aim is to do this in such a way that the threads across each individual unit can be tensioned as required (diagram 26). Measure the full length of the area plus a short length, which will eventually be used to finish off, and double this length – this provides two foundation threads. Using a Sharps needle begin to pass this thread from one end to the other from right to left and in a horizontal direction centrally through the verticals, leaving the end loose. Make the halfway point of the length of thread register at the other edge. Pass the thread through the verticals to the right and unthread the needle, leaving two loose ends. Take another piece of thread which is equal to the length, plus enough to work one complete

unit at the right, plus enough to use as a whipping thread. Take the third foundation thread through from the right, leaving a long end to whip one complete unit later and, with the remaining thread in the needle, begin to whip towards the right. This thread can be finished off and rejoined at any of the junctions. Tension the length through each unit, as with the bars, using the original threads as this foundation represents the other square bar. Finally, finish the whipping thread at the beginning of the last unit, using the longer of the foundation threads from the right to whip through the last junction. In this way, only two threads need to be finished off at any one position.

To lay and work diagonal foundation threads
These threads are estimated in the same way as for the horizontal bar, except that the measurement follows the diagonal through each unit and continues to the end of the insertion. So, again, the first thread provides double the required length plus enough thread to finish each end later. Other exceptions to the horizontal bar are that threads are only threaded through one unit at any one time and that the

35

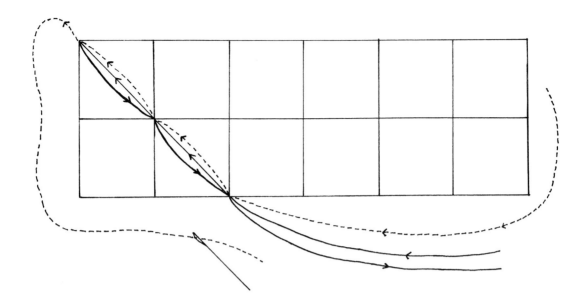

Diagram 27 *Open-ended diagonal foundation threads*

threads are whipped before passing them through to the next unit. In this way each unit can be tensioned as required.

Lay threads as in diagram 25, whip across the one unit and take the needle through the padded roll to maintain the whipping tension. Keep this thread separate from the others if it is long enough to work another unit; otherwise finish it off now. * Thread needle with one of the foundation threads, take it back through the padded roll, coming out to the right of the vertical bar, pass through the centre junction and out diagonally at the other outside edge. Repeat with the other two foundation threads, whip and tension *. Repeat from * to * to last unit. Lay foundations as before, whip to the centre junction and finish off the whipping thread. With the long end of the foundation thread whip to the centre junction, tension and finish off the thread. Finish off the remaining two short ends into the padded roll.

Turn the work around so the other diagonal threads lie in the opposite direction and so that the finishing at the last centre junction will be at the other end of the insertion. If an unusually long insertion is to be worked, then this instruction is, of course, not practicable.

It is looking forward to this stage that urges the worker through the basic foundations; now she is ready to apply the pattern of her choice.

Remove the leathercloth.

Drawing threads for a right angle of units

This shape can be drawn in relation to a border or the right angle of a border, or it can interlock into the outer border or be drawn in complete isolation.

For the right angle to be plotted independently, the margin must be decided – again, this must consist of at least eight threads – and the unit size must also be determined, if only approximately.

** Begin to plot near to A in diagram 28. Locating threads for the four-sided stitch border and the single thread inside the padded roll threads as at A, plot the unit along the grain of

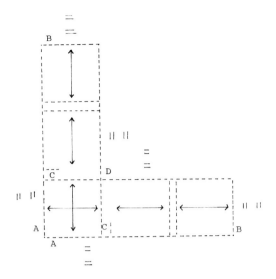

Diagram 28 *Right angle insertion*

the previous shape, or as the desired pattern indicates.

Drawing threads for a multiple unit shape

This shape can be sited in the same situation as the previous example.

Plot the border threads and padded roll and pick up one thread at A in diagram 29. It will be observed that only the unit nearest to the intitial right angle is the correct size and shape and that there are four threads separating each unit.

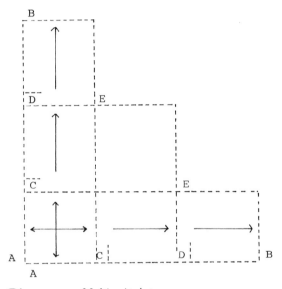

Diagram 29 *Multi-unit shape*

thread to include the one thread picked up. Pick up the last thread in the unit, *leave four threads* (these will be the padded roll threads on the inside border of the right angle – see the photograph on the back cover), * pick up 1, plot the next unit, pick up the last thread, leave 3 *. Repeat from * to * until the last repeat: leave four instead of three for the padded roll, pick up two, leave four, pick up two **. Repeat from ** to ** in the other direction.

Return to the initial right angle. Cut the border threads as at A in diagram 1 (*see p. 17*). Cut a single thread on both sides of the right angle, as at A in diagram 28, draw the short ends back to form the corner and draw the other end back to the single thread at B which is now cut and drawn back to meet A. Return to the initial right angle again, cut the single thread at C, drawing the short end to meet A and the long end to reach B. This now completes the outlining of the inner pattern area. Cut the next thread along $\frac{1}{2}$ in. (1.3 cm) inside A and draw back to meet A. Cut the single thread on each side of the three threads separating the units. Continue to draw the threads around this shape for the four-sided stitch border, but not through the inverted corner at D (refer to the instruction for G in diagram 24 – see p. 31. Work the four-sided stitch border and proceed as for the instructions for

* Plot the unit, pick up one thread, leave four threads, pick up one *. Repeat from * to * twice more, picking up two on the last occasion. Leave four, pick up two, repeat from * to ** in the other direction.

Return to the initial right angle, cut both A threads and draw back to meet the B threads. Cut the B threads and draw back to meet A. Cut threads C and draw back to meet A and B. Cut the next thread $\frac{1}{2}$ in. (1.3 cm) inside A and draw back to meet A. Cut threads D and draw back to meet A and where both D threads meet. This now completes the outlining of the inner pattern area. Draw threads for the four-sided stitch border around this shape, except

37

through the inverted corners at E (refer to the instructions for G in diagram 24 – *see p. 31*).

Work the four-sided stitch border and proceed as for the instructions for the insertion circumjacent to the outer border (*see p. 30*), as far as the working of the four-thread bars, when the threads from C and D in diagram 29 are worked together. Any other foundations will be determined by the pattern being worked.

Laying threads to form a circle

The direction of working in the main is from left to right, which, on a circle, is anticlockwise. When working whip or buttonhole stitch, the direction of the needle is from inside to outside, so as to be working with the arc.

The beginning of the threads in this situation differs slightly from the instruction given previously. Begin the thread as in diagram 30, at the required distance from the centre. Take

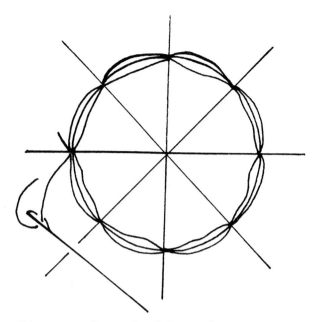

Diagram 31 *Laying threads for a circle*

as in diagram 31. With the same thread, length permitting, continue in the stitch required. Usually circles are worked in either whip stitch or buttonhole stitch; whichever is chosen, a stitch is worked on top of each bar in passing. A whip stitch forms a slanted stitch over the bar as at A in Diagram 18 (*see p. 26*). A buttonhole stitch is worked into and parallel with the bar being passed over.

If a one-thread bar is to connect into the circle, then an even number of whip stitches will be needed in each section to form a central space to accommodate the linkage later, as in diagram 32.

One-thread bars

This usually links a whipped bar to a buttonhole-stitched bar, as the latter is being worked, either as a circle or a straight bar.

The whipped bar usually has a number of whip stitches to accommodate a specific number of one-thread bars – for instance, for one one-thread bar, an even number of whip stitches will have been worked, e.g. four or six. These stitches will be slightly spaced so that the one-thread bar can settle in as another stitch. If more than one bar is to be linked to a whipped section then the number of stitches

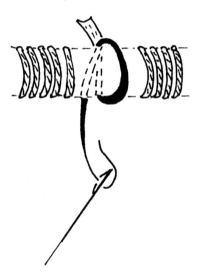

Diagram 30 *Beginning a thread for a circle*

the needle through a bar on the left of the centre junction in the direction of working, leave an end of thread approximately $\frac{1}{2}$ in. (1.3 cm) and take the needle through the bar again in the same place, splitting the end of the thread in so doing. Take the needle through each bar to register a good, full circle – a tight circle will register an octagon – and continue to lay two more circuits on top of each other,

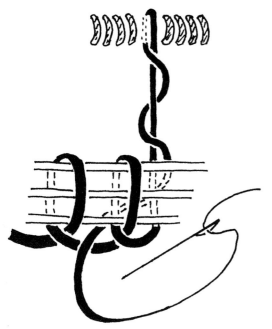

Diagram 32 *A one-thread bar*

Diagram 33 *First stage for a picot*

must be divisable by the number of bars to be added, plus one.

Lay threads for the second circle or bar no more than $\frac{1}{8}$ in. (3 mm) away from the first circle or bar and work in buttonhole stitch to where the one-thread bar is needed.

Take the needle under the buttonhole-stitched bar and bring it out in the space between the two bars, as in diagram 32. From above, bring the needle through the bar, between the whip stitches and towards the worker and draw the thread up to fix the distance between the circles or bars. Take the needle to the right and under the one thread. To the right of the one-thread bar bring the needle back under the buttonhole-stitch bar. From underneath, bring the needle up between the last two buttonhole-stitches. The thread is now back to where it set out. When only connecting a single one-thread bar, at this point work one less stitch than already worked, totalling an odd number of stitches.

Picots

These are only worked in conjunction with buttonhole stitch, often in the same position as a one-thread bar. The one-thread bar is com-

pleted first, followed by the picot between the same two buttonhole stitches. Picots add texture to a pattern or soften what may otherwise be a severe line or shape.

Take the needle down into the space between the last two buttonhole stitches, as in diagram 33, to form a chain stitch (with the thread travelling from right to left). Take the needle down into the chain, as if to make another chain and, before drawing it out, fold the work so that the needle stands upright and wrap the thread coming from the chain stitch round the needle closely three times in an anticlockwise direction. Hold the wraps with the first finger and thumb of the left hand. Withdraw the needle and draw the thread through completely. This makes the picot. To continue, bring the needle from underneath up between the last two buttonhole stitches back to where it set out, as in diagram 34.

Diagram 34 *Second stage for a picot*

Petals

Petals are worked in various positions – on to three foundation threads, over an already worked bar, into a circular shape or on to a straight bar – sometimes having a one-thread bar linking them to another bar, which can be either circular or straight. The first row of a petal can be double buttonhole-stitched eventually, therefore the first row of stitches will need to be slightly spaced in order to take another row of buttonhole stitch from the other side after the petal has been completed: a picot could be worked here as well.

Begin by laying the foundation threads or by beginning the working thread, as necessary, to work from left to right.

First row: * work the required number of buttonhole stitches, working a one-thread bar from the centre stitch if the pattern requires it, in which case there will be an odd number of stitches.

Second row: take the needle to the left and down into the loop to the left of the first stitch at A in diagram 35 (this stitch is not counted), and out over the loose thread which is to be a foundation thread for the next row; this thread must be left loose. Make a detached buttonhole stitch into the loop between each stitch on the previous row. There will automatically be one stitch less than on the previous row, as there is always one less in-between space than there are stitches.

Third and final row: take the needle to the left and attach as before into the loop to the left of the first stitch as at A in diagram 36. Make the first buttonhole stitch between two and three stitches on the previous row; leave the last space unworked to correspond with the beginning of the row. There will be three stitches less than on the previous row; this is the method of decreasing. Bring the needle up from underneath into the last empty space on the previous row at B. Bring the needle up from underneath into the space between the last two stitches on the first row. If the circle of these shapes is to be worked, work a buttonhole stitch on top of and parallel with the bar, to pass to the next section *. Repeat from * to *, length of thread permitting, otherwise finish the thread off as at A in diagram 37, in the bar slightly to the outside of the circle.

Re-join the thread, as at B, slightly to the inside of the circle. Take the thread through the bar so that the new end lies alongside the next section to be worked in, bring the needle back through the bar, splitting the end of thread in so doing, and pick up the buttonhole stitch on top of the bar so that the new thread is in the same position as the old one was before finishing. This method of re-joining will be used frequently.

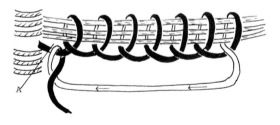

Diagram 35 *Attaching a foundation thread*

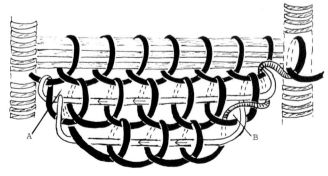

Diagram 36 *Petal*

40

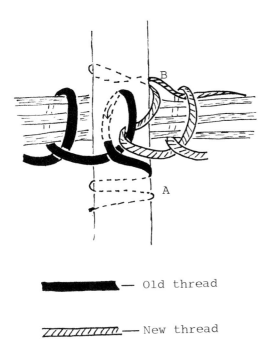

— Old thread

— New thread

Diagram 37 *Finishing and re-starting a thread to continue working*

Pyramids

These shapes are worked in detached buttonhole stitch and are preferably worked directly from three foundation threads; pyramids can be worked from a whipped bar, but are rather bulky. They can be tailored to fit into a specific area by decreasing stitches or by the tension of working, and can also be worked from a circle or a straight bar. Pyramids can also have picots worked on to the long sides: the one on the left is worked as the pyramid is worked, the other one as the right-hand side is whipped back up to the end of the first row. It will be noted that on some patterns picots appear on the inside of the circle from which pyramids have been worked. The stitches on the first row of the pyramid must be slightly spaced to accommodate a row of buttonhole stitches on the inside, when all the shapes are complete. Then work the picots.

Lay the threads, or begin a thread as the pattern requires, to work from left to right. Work the necessary number of buttonhole stitches over the foundation threads or bar. These should not be closely packed but just close enough so that the loop in-between the

stitches can be located easily and so that the next row of stitches will not distort the shape.

Take the needle back to the left and down into the loop to the left of the first stitch, as illustrated in diagram 35. This foundation thread must be left loose, otherwise the shape will be narrow and it will be difficult to identify the space in-between. The tension of the buttonhole stitch will vary from worker to worker. This stitch can be drawn up as close as the worker feels necessary; so long as the foundation loop is sufficiently loose, the next row will be worked satisfactorily. The worker may need to make several attempts before being satisfied with the end result. Resist the urge to discard the rejects; instead, attempt as many as necessary and eliminate only when all spaces are filled.

Bring the needle over the loose foundation thread as illustrated at A in diagram 35 and work a row of detached buttonhole stitch into the in-between spaces of the previous row, enclosing the foundation thread. For the next and successive rows, attach the foundation thread as at A in diagram 38. It will be noted that two threads are located here: one is the foundation thread of the previous row; the other, the thread which came to make the first stitch on the previous row. Locating both these threads ensures a good edge to the finished shape and firm anchorage for ease of working; there will automatically be one stitch less on each successive row. Continue in this manner to the last row of one, single stitch.

Pyramids need to be attached either to a padded roll or to a foundation bar. To attach a pyramid to a padded roll when the end of the pyramid is close to it, take the needle through the padded roll, and back through it from underneath, pick up the last single stitch worked on the pyramid and then, from underneath, work into the end stitch of each row. Finally, come up between the last two stitches on the first row. The thread is now back to where it began to build the pyramid. Work one buttonhole stitch on the next bar to the right. Finish the thread and restart as in diagram 37 if adjacent pyramids are to be worked. Always use a separate thread for each pyramid which has more than eight stitches on

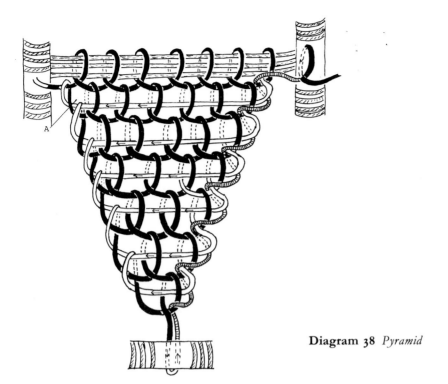

Diagram 38 *Pyramid*

the first row. If you are a beginner, always use a separate thread for each pyramid, so that any one can be eliminated independently if necessary.

Pyramids that do not reach the padded roll or foundation bar can be connected by a one-thread bar, as in diagram 32 (*see p. 39*). Finally, bring the needle up into the last, single stitch worked on the pyramid and complete as above. If the bar is to be longer than ⅛ in. (3 mm), then three threads must be laid over the distance and whipped.

Sometimes it is necessary to work a pyramid with a foundation bar running underneath it. On the first row, work a number of stitches, as required, into the first section, single buttonhole stitch on top of and parallel with the bar involved and repeat the same number of stitches as in the first section; the total will be an odd number. The pyramid is worked completely free of the bar running beneath, so the number of stitches on the first row is treated as a whole. As the last, single stitch is being worked, pick up the bar at the same time; this secures the shape to the foundation bar. Then complete as above.

It may be necessary to decrease deliberately in order to tailor a shape to fit into a specific area. To do so, work as for the third row of the petal (*see diagram 36*). On successive rows, always take the foundation thread back into the loop to the left of the first stitch. There is a stepped edge on the left which will be rectified in the final whipping up the right-hand side, as above.

Bugs

These shapes are always worked over an already whipped bar – in groups or in isolation. Bugs can be as large as the situation allows. The end result always works out larger than the initial plotting of the first row of buttonhole stitches: this is because of the buttonhole stitches worked on top of the bar to make a continuous shape and to pass from one side to the other. The minimum number of stitches in the first row is five, otherwise the end result will be nondescript.

Begin the thread as in diagram 30 (*see p. 38*), at position A in diagram 39. *Work the necessary number of buttonhole stitches over

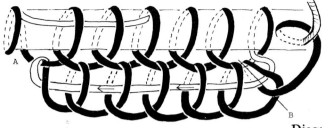

Diagram 39 *Bug*

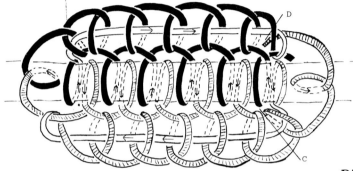

Diagram 40 *Second half of the bug*

the bar, taking in the end of the thread, and leaving sufficient space between the stitches to accommodate the first row of stitches on the second half of the shape. Take the needle back to the left and down into the loop to the left of the first stitch, as at A. Work a second row as in the diagram. Turn the work to the left so that the bar already worked is held vertically. Work another buttonhole stitch into the last in-between space; there are now two stitches in the same space, as at B. Then work one buttonhole stitch on top of the bar, parallel with it, and draw the thread out of this stitch vertically to close up the length in the stitch and give a firm outline to the end result *. Turn the work to the left again and repeat from * to *, taking up the spaces in between stitches over the bar already worked, in order to arrive at the same number of stitches as on the initial row. The last stitch will be between where the thread joins in and the very first stitch, as at C in diagram 40.

To complete the shape, bring the needle from underneath into the loop before the first stitch on the second row of the first half, as at D. To finish the thread, take the needle down to the underside through the shape and through the bar already worked, taking care not to pull the thread so tight that it upsets the shape. Take the needle back and forth through the bar immediately under the shape to finish thread, or back and forth through the bar to work to an adjacent situation, if this is reasonably close, as in pattern 1 (*see p. 54*).

Weaving

This is needle-weaving over three uprights. This shape is always worked over a whipped bar, beginning at the end nearest to the centre of the pattern or point of radiation, as the beginning is usually thicker than the finishing end.

Begin thread as in diagram 30 (*see p. 38*), at A in diagram 41, working in the end of thread with the most convenient upright. Lay three foundation threads in an anticlockwise direction to form a shallow shape, as in diagram 41. Hold the work so that the foundations are in a vertical position with the working thread on the right at the base, as at A. Take the needle under the middle upright so that the first over stitch is on the foundation threads and can be tucked close up to the foundation bar so as to

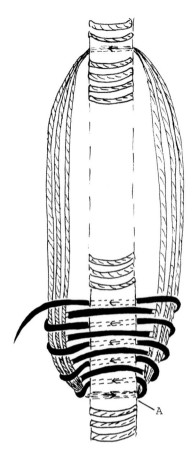

Diagram 41 *Weaving*

upright. Continue in this manner until no more stitches can be packed in. As the end approaches, the middle upright can no longer be picked up in one movement. The needle is then taken down under the middle upright and out towards the left and, in another movement, comes up between the middle upright and the left-hand upright. The rows should be close depthwise, so that no foundations are visible, with stitches wrapping the uprights without being loose but also without narrowing the shape. After the first few rows of weaving are worked, the three uprights should be parallel. If they are not, the three foundation circuits have been laid too loose.

Finish the thread as in diagram 16 (*see p. 26*), in the bar beyond the end of the weaving.

Oval buttonhole-stitched shapes

Begin the thread as for a circle, as diagram 30 (*see p. 38*). Lay the threads in an anticlockwise direction to form a shallow shape of three circuits. Begin to buttonhole stitch, continuing in an anticlockwise direction and making the first and last stitch in each half parallel with the bar already worked, as in diagram 42. Picots can be added to this shape. Take care not to draw the foundation threads through from the second half. Place one buttonhole stitch on top of the bar in order to pass from one half to the other. To complete: place one buttonhole stitch on top of the bar, bring the needle up from underneath between the first two stitches of the first half. Finish the thread as in diagram 16 (*see p. 26*).

cover the foundation threads. Take the needle over and under the left-hand upright and tuck this stitch close up to the bar. Pass over the middle upright and under the right-hand

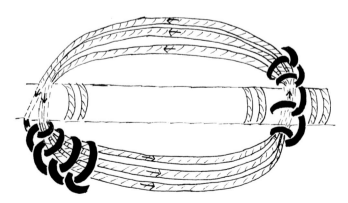

Diagram 42 *Oval buttonhole-stitched shape*

Bullion knots

Bullion knots are a typifying feature of Ruskin work. They are worked as a traditional edging; they also appear in clusters of eight in the centre of many patterns. Bullion knots can be added to give a textural effect or to eliminate a harsh junction of two crossed bars. In this case, a cluster of four can be worked or two laid obliquely over the junction. It is not good practice to work bullion knots in isolation over single whipped bars.

Bullion cluster of eight

Begin the thread by passing the needle back and forth through the underside of the centre to secure, then bring it up through the centre and draw the thread through. *Take the needle into one of the spaces between two foundation bars and up through the centre in the same place as the thread. Do not draw the needle out. Fold your work so that the needle can be held upright. Wrap the thread from the centre anticlockwise round the needle ten times as in diagram 43. Ensure the wraps are evenly twisted and come down to the base of the needle. With the thumb and first finger of the left hand, hold the ten wraps whilst withdrawing the needle and thread to its complete length. Now, hold the thread with the right hand and, with the help of the first finger nail of the left hand, curve the bullion knot to fit

into the selected space. Take the needle into the same section again and up through the centre. This completes the bullion knot and, with thread coming out of the centre it is ready for the next knot *. Repeat from * to * seven times more, but do not come up through the centre on the last repeat; instead, take the needle back and forth three times on the underside to secure the end.

Bullion knots worked obliquely

The direction of the oblique will be dictated by the pattern. Begin the thread as for the cluster. Bring the needle out at one end of the oblique, take it in at the other end and out at the same place as the thread. Wrap this thread ten times round the needle and complete as above. Make another bullion in the same manner as in diagram 44, following the same direction if the situation requires it. Finish as above.

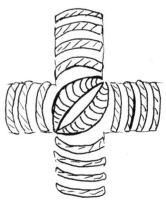

Diagram 44 *Bullion knots set obliquely on a junction*

Bullion knots as an edging

These are traditionally single, but they can be worked in pairs or trebles, when the third knot is laid over the top of a pair. Traditionally, single bullion knots are worked approximately $\frac{3}{8}$ in. (1 cm) apart, inclusive of the previous knot. Begin the thread at the far right-hand corner of the article, so as to be working from right to left as in diagram 45. Take the needle through the hem and bring it out two threads inside the outside edge of the fabric at the corner. Make a small stitch within the depth of these two threads and split the thread, bring-

Diagram 43 *Bullion knot centre*

45

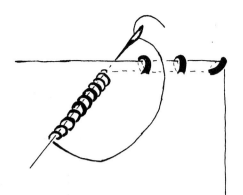

Diagram 45 *Bullion knot edging*

Diagram 46 *Woven centre*

ing the needle out at the same place again. Bring the needle up from the underside at the same depth. Before drawing the needle out wrap the thread round it twelve times in an anticlockwise direction. Hold, as for the cluster, draw the needle and thread through, curve the knot closely over the edge of the fabric and bring the needle and thread through to the right side, ensuring that the bullion knot is set diagonally over the corner. Take the needle and thread through the two layers of fabric of the hem to the next position, two threads inside the fabric edge. Bring the needle and thread out on the right side of the fabric and, from underneath, bring the needle up to take ten wraps. Complete and repeat as above. Continue towards the next corner of the article. Approximately 2 in. (5 cm) away from the corner, plot the distances so as to avoid ending with uneven spacing.

Woven centres

These are not frequently applied as they do not launder very well, but they are most useful where the article is going under glass when bullion knots would be too bulky.

Begin the thread as for the bullion knots in the previous section, and weave under and over the eight bars as in diagram 46. Because eight is an even number, the unders and overs will fall on the same bars each time. Work four circuits and finish the thread into the bar as in diagram 16 (*see p. 26*), at the outside of the completed shape.

This working is applied to a four-bar junc-tion, as in pattern 2; in this situation only three circuits are made – otherwise work as above.

To neaten cut ends

Scallop-shaped corner finishing is the traditional finish. This is worked where threads have been withdrawn for the working of the four-sided stitch border at the corners of squares, borders, or where borders are interlocked with the pattern areas. It is preferable to leave these corner workings until all handling of that particular area is completed, otherwise the finishing shape will become flattened and not so pleasing. If the long ends become a source of irritation whilst working the pattern area, they can be flicked through to the underside at any stage after the pattern area has been mounted on to the leathercloth, then returned to the right side for this stage.

Reduce the length of the cut ends to approximately $\frac{1}{16}$ in. (2 mm). Using a Sharps needle and working thread, begin at the left-hand end of the corner, as at A in diagram 47. Leave an end of thread approximately $\frac{1}{2}$ in. (1.3 cm) long and make a running stitch close to the inside edge of the corner, around to the right-hand end of the corner to B. Pick up the first thread involved in the first block of four-sided stitch, one thread deep into the fabric,

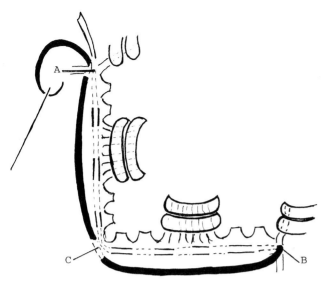

Diagram 47 *Corner neatening, stage one*

and come back to the left in order to work buttonhole stitch, leaving the thread loose on top of the fabric and picking up a small amount of fabric at the corner as at C. Then, at the left again, pick up the first thread involved with the first block away from the corner, one thread deep into the fabric, as at A in diagram 47.

Beginning with a short buttonhole stitch into the space where the two threads have been withdrawn, increase the length of each stitch until four stitches are worked. Then reduce the length of the stitch, 3–2–1, making seven stitches into the same inner space as at A in diagram 48, to form a scallop or shell shape. Make the next buttonhole stitch into the outer corner space as before and increase the length of buttonhole stitch to the fourth stitch. Maintain the same length of stitch around the corner and make the stitches as close as possible. When back to the straight of the grain, reduce the length of stitch, 3–2–1. Make the next stitch into the next space and repeat the first shape.

To complete, take the needle to the underside of the work and finish the thread off by taking the needle back and forth through the backs of the stitches. When working this finish where a hem is involved there will be no backs of stitches, so finish the thread into the hem.

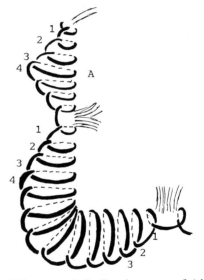

Diagram 48 *Scallop-shape corner finish*

Where a double or multiple row of four-sided stitch border has been worked there will be a seven-stitch scallop for each pair of withdrawn threads either side of the corner.

Where borders have interlocked there will be a seven-stitch scallop for each pair of threads withdrawn.

Corners can be neatened with other finishes, one being a straight buttonhole-stitched shape. Prepare the corner as for the scalloped corner and work as far as returning back to the

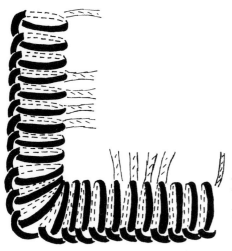

Diagram 49 *Straight-edge corner finish*

left with the loose foundation thread at A in diagram 47. Then, pick up the first thread two threads deep in the fabric, instead of one. Work a straight row of buttonhole stitch, two threads deep into the fabric, the whole way around the corner, as in diagram 49. Finish as for the scallop corner.

Removing the leathercloth

Once the worker is satisfied that the pattern is complete, it is time for the biggest thrill of all, especially on the first occasion, when it is finally proved that the pattern does not fall apart. The leathercloth is removed by cutting the back stitching on the underside of the leathercloth. This can be done quickly and without danger of cutting a wrong thread. The leathercloth will now peel away and any threads remaining in the four-sided stitch border can now be easily picked out. The same piece of leathercloth can be used many times, until it becomes too soft to maintain an area satisfactorily.

To press completed work

Ideally, this should be done before the bullion knot edging is applied. Roll the article in a damp towel, such as one that has been spun after washing. Place the whole thing in a plastic bag and leave to soak for a few hours,

or preferably overnight, by which time the article will be evenly damp, and any surface soiling will have been dislodged. Unroll and place the article right side down on to a padded ironing surface. With a hot iron, *press*, do not iron; the use of steam is preferable but not essential. Press until the whole article is hot and steaming. To rectify any distortion, take hold of it at each side within the hem (otherwise the hem will become unnecessarily stretched) on the straight of the grain, and gently stretch. Repeat regularly down the length of the article and then do the same in the opposite direction. Return to the ironing surface and, with right-side down, continue to press, using the point of the iron to persuade any part of the lace work into the desired position. Whilst still damp, turn the article right-side up and gently smooth the fabric area, avoiding the pattern area. Stop before the fabric is completely dry. Lay the article flat where it can dry out. In this way, your article will be crisp and pristine without being shiny, especially if linen has been used. The author recommends pressing before resorting to washing. If work appears to have become unduly soiled during working, it is amazing how this disappears during the above process, and it should be repeated before deciding the article really does have to be washed.

The usual order of working

Always cut fabric out by drawn thread; this begins to rectify any distortion.

Work hems
The depth of hems will be up to the worker's personal preferences. Some articles will warrant a deeper hem on one or two sides – for example, with chairback covers and samplers a deeper, lower hem is effective while a deeper hem on the ends of long runners will give a well-balanced layout. Hems need tacking and slip stitching before drawing further threads. Draw further threads for the desired number of rows of four-sided stitch. A tip here: if the worker is anxious to work the patterned areas of the article, then just allow for the depth the required number of threads will take up. In

this way the spacing of drawn-out threads does not become distorted by others being misplaced. But it must be added that this only applies to the outer border where pattern areas are not involved. When laying out a patterned area on a large article, particularly a square article, it is advisable to lay tack lines at the centre; for a runner or a lampshade a central, horizontal tack line will be sufficient.

Lay out pattern areas

There are a few don'ts in this respect, the main one being: when planning a wall hanging or sampler, do not place a pattern right in the middle of the area and avoid the sides of pattern areas being lined up by the eye to make a continuous line. Patterns set on the diagonal plane will lead the eye into and around the pattern areas. Before being committed to cutting threads on an article that has a complex layout it is advisable to make a plan. Using a plain piece of paper the overall size of the article in mind, outline the hems and depth of border stitch. Use a different-coloured or patterned-paper which will be a contrast to the background for the shapes of pattern areas, to help arrive at a pleasing and well-balanced layout. Pattern areas can be any size, so long as they are square or a multiple of a square. Many patterns can be worked over varying sizes.

Work four-sided stitch

Work this around pattern areas, as diagrams 5 and 6 (see p. 20) or diagram 7 (see p. 21). If a woven corner is to be worked, as in diagrams 8 and 9, then it must be worked now.

Plot inside areas

This only applies to independent squares as in diagram 12.

Mount pattern areas on to leathercloth

When more than one row of four-sided stitch has been worked (see diagram 12), make the back stitch through the innermost row. For patterns plotted diagonally, use one piece of leathercloth and secure the largest right angle, so avoiding distortion of the diagonal plane.

Spaced whipping

As diagram 14 (see p. 24)

Padded roll

As diagram 15 (see p. 25). Remove surplus fabric from the inside area.

Square foundation bars

These are those bars using original threads, as in diagram 18 (see p. 26); for an insertion, refer to diagram 26 (see p. 35).

Diagonal foundation bars

As in diagram 19 (see p. 27), or, for an insertion, refer to diagram 27 (see p. 36).

Diamond foundation

As in diagram 20 (see p. 27). This is not worked in many patterns but, when it is, it is worked, at this stage. It will be noted that some patterns have further foundation bars. If the pattern also has a diamond foundation bar, the working of this helps in the alignment of those extra foundation bars. The working of the extra foundation bars would follow the working of the diamond foundation bar.

Patterns

When deciding which part of the pattern needs to be worked first, try to identify the part that is recognised at first glance. If that part is worked in proportion, regardless of the pattern drawing being the same size as the actual pattern area, the other components will either fit in or be adapted. For example, if there are pyramids or other dominant shapes, it is likely that these will need to be worked first. Work bullion knots last.

Neaten corners

As in diagrams 47 and 48 (see p. 47) or diagrams 47 and 49.

Remove leathercloth

Press

Part II

PATTERNS & EDGINGS

Patterns 1–60

John Ruskin brought the original patterns from Italy where he saw a similar type of work on church linen. We are not quite sure in what form these patterns reached Marion Twelves but, because of our methods of working, it is assumed they came in the form of line drawings. If not, it is felt that the method of working would have been to produce motifs, which would then have been applied to the fabric. It is most likely that pattern 3 was one of those originals, as it is very typical of the form of needlepoint John Ruskin would have seen in Italy.

Patterns have been handed down from worker to worker over the years. This collection is used mainly as an inspiration and a guide. As no two workers proportion in the same way or work at the same tension it is necessary to adapt and, in this way, new patterns are constantly being evolved, very often without the worker being conscious of the design, resulting in an original pattern; other students will work out their own patterns using graph paper and endeavour to reproduce them exactly in their work. Whichever method is adopted, it is hoped that the worker will enjoy the working and achieve satisfaction in reflection. When referring to diagrams always refer to the written instruction as well.

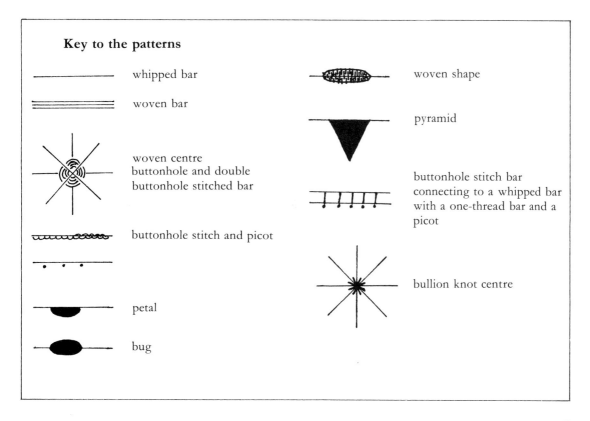

Key to the patterns

——————————— whipped bar

════════════ woven bar

woven centre
buttonhole and double
buttonhole stitched bar

buttonhole stitch and picot

petal

bug

woven shape

pyramid

buttonhole stitch bar
connecting to a whipped bar
with a one-thread bar and a
picot

bullion knot centre

Figure 10

Pattern 1

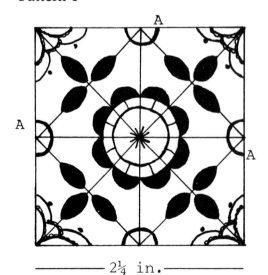

——— $2\frac{1}{4}$ in. ———

This is a good pattern for beginners as all shapes are small workings. Follow the order of working as far as and including the diamond foundation bar.

Plot the centre unit so that the petals will not touch the bugs. Begin with the centre whipped circle, approximately $\frac{1}{4}$ in. (6 mm) from the centre junction, as in diagrams 30 and 31 (*see p. 38*), working an even number of whip stitches in each section. Lay threads for the second circle less than $\frac{1}{8}$ in. (3 mm) away. Work the petal as diagram 35, with a one-thread bar from the middle stitch on the first row. Complete petal as diagram 36 (*see p. 40*).

Work the bugs: begin the thread at the end close to the four-bar junction, as in diagrams 39 and 40 (*see p. 43*). Thread permitting,

54

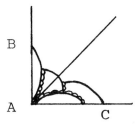

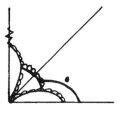

Diagram 50 *Corner working for Pattern 1, stage one*   **Diagram 51** *Corner working for Pattern 1, stage two*

instead of finishing after each shape, take the thread backwards and forwards through the bar and junction to the next position. The bug in this situation usually has six stitches on the first row. Take care not to let the bug on the diagonal bar encroach too near the corner and so restrict the corner working.

The small half circles are three threads and whip stitch beginning the thread at A in Pattern 1.

The corner working is rather complex: follow diagram 50. Begin thread at A, lay three foundation threads to form a shallow, curved shape approximately $\frac{3}{8}$ in. (1 cm) long, work in buttonhole stitch and finish off thread. Re-join the thread at B, lay three threads to correspond with the first shape and work in buttonhole stitch to halfway. Then lay three threads to connect the two shapes, passing through the

diagonal bar, and pick up the thread between two buttonhole stitches to attach. Work two buttonhole stitches, lay three threads to point C, work in buttonhole stitch with a picot, as in diagrams 33 and 34 (*see p. 39*), at halfway point. Work to the connecting bar and work a third buttonhole stitch, then one on to the diagonal bar. Work three stitches on to the second half of the connecting bar and continue to B. Follow diagram 51, pass the thread backwards and forwards through the roll to the same distance between the corresponding two points, lay three threads and repeat as in the corresponding bar, finish the thread.

Work a bullion knot centre as in diagram 43 (*see p. 45*).

Neaten the corners as in diagrams 47 and 48, or diagrams 47 and 49 (*see pp. 47 and 48*).

Remove the leathercloth.

Pattern 2

———— $2\frac{1}{4}$ in.————

This is a pattern that was worked extensively in the early days of the cottage industry.

Follow the order of working as far as and including the diamond foundation bar.

Lay a circle of three threads for the innermost circle as in diagrams 30 and 31 (*see p. 38*), no more than a $\frac{1}{4}$ in. (6 mm) from the centre junction. Whip with an even number of stitches into each section. Lay threads for the next circle to work the pyramids, with a one-thread bar to link to the inner circle as in diagram 32 (*see p. 39*), on the first row of the pyramid. Ideally, all the threads for this unit should be laid so that the finished pyramids fall short of the diamond foundation bar. Work pyramids as in diagrams 35 and 38 (*see pp. 40 and 42*).

From the single stitch at the end of the pyramid take the needle through the diamond

Figure 11

foundation bar at a point that places the end of the pyramid equidistant between the square and diagonal bars. Take the needle out through the padded roll at the corner of the pattern and back again to lay three threads between the corner and the single stitch at the bottom of the pyramid. Whip stitch back up to the bottom of the pyramid and complete as in diagram 38 (*see p. 42*).

To work woven corners, begin the thread in the corner of the square and begin to weave as in diagram 41 (*see p. 44*), maintaining the spacing of the three uprights. Finish weaving towards the left, taking the needle and thread through the left upright, through the padded roll and back to lay three threads through each upright to form an arc that will enclose the weaving. Work in buttonhole stitch with a picot in each section. It will be noted that the two outer sections require more stitches than the two inner sections.

Work the double half circles as for the full circle as in pattern 3.

Work a woven centre as in diagram 46 (*see p. 46*), with smaller weavings at the junction of the pyramid bar and the diamond bar, but only work three circuits.

Neaten the corners as in diagrams 47 and 48, or diagrams 47 and 49 (*see p. 47*).

Remove the leathercloth.

Figure 12

Pattern 3

2¼ in.

This is probably one of the patterns that John Ruskin brought back as a drawing.

Follow the order of working as far as the diagonal foundation bars.

Lay a circle of three threads halfway from the centre to the outside edge on the square bars, as in diagrams 30 and 31 (*see p. 38*), taking the thread through the other seven bars at the same distance from the centre.

Work the pyramids over these foundation threads with (here) 11 stitches on the first row, as in diagrams 35 and 38 (*see pp. 40 and 42*).

Lay a circle of three threads for the innermost circle, as in diagrams 30 and 31 (*see p. 38*), and whip with an even number of stitches in each section. Lay three threads for the second circle and work in buttonhole stitch. From the

57

centre stitch in each section work a one-thread bar and then picot as in diagrams 32, 33 and 34 (*see p. 39*), working one buttonhole stitch on top of the bar in passing to the next section. Repeat a quarter of this unit in each of the corners.

Work a whipped, inverted V-shaped bar over three foundation threads at the outer ends of the square bars.

Work a bullion knot centre as in diagram 43 (*see p. 45*).

Neaten the corners as in diagrams 47 and 48 or diagrams 47 and 49 (*see p. 47*).

Remove the leathercloth.

Pattern 4

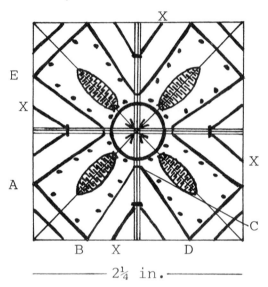

——— 2¼ in. ———

This pattern has woven square foundation bars. These can be a feature of any pattern where worked shapes are not applied to the square bars, except perhaps where a circle of eight pyramids is to be worked; this would then break the formation into four quarters.

Follow the order of working as far as the padded roll, then work woven square bars and diagonal foundation bars.

Begin the thread at A, which is halfway from the corner to the square bar and trace the thread to B; where the thread has passed over the diagonal bar, take the needle and thread through, then out through the padded roll at B. Bring the needle back through the padded roll at B so that both threads are emerging at the same point on the inside edge of the roll. Take the needle and thread through the woven square bar at C and out through the roll at D.

Repeat from A to the full circuit and lay two more circuits. Work in buttonhole stitch and picots, as in the pattern, to the inside in a clockwise direction. Place two buttonhole stitches on the woven bar, one into each column of weaving. At E, carry straight on to the next bar; linking the last buttonhole stitch and the first one on the next bar holds the buttonholing in position. Continue to the full circuit. Threads can be finished and re-started at any position into the padded roll as in diagram 37 (*see p. 41*).

Lay the inner circle of three threads; work buttonhole stitch and picot.

Work woven shapes as in diagram 41 (*see p. 44*).

Work a bullion knot centre. Because of the width of the woven bars, the bullion knot cluster will form four pairs.

Whipped straight bars are worked at the corners.

Inverted V bars at the outer ends of the square bars are whipped with a bullion knot lying over the width of the woven foundation bar. Lay three threads beginning at X, whip up to the woven bar. Take the needle and thread through the woven bar, take the needle through again but, before withdrawing, make bullion knot of ten twists, and withdraw the needle. The knot will now lie over the width of the woven bar. Bring the needle and thread through again to secure the knot and continue to whip the second half of the shape.

Neaten the corners as in diagrams 47 and 48 or diagrams 47 and 49.

Remove the leathercloth.

Figure 13

The next 12 patterns are useful for working on to place mats or to fill awkward areas on a sampler or lampshades. They can also be worked as alternatives in the centre four units on a window pattern. Some of these patterns can be worked into squares varying from 1 in. to $1\frac{3}{4}$ in. (3.5 cm to 4.5 cm).

Pattern 5

After the basic grid, the diamond bar threads are laid as in diagram 20 (*see p. 27*) and worked in buttonhole stitch and picots or double buttonhole stitch if this pattern is to be worked in a larger area or on a lampshade. Work the square next; this will be whipped. The inner circle can now be fitted into the remaining space. To work the corner units, lay three threads to form a quarter arc, buttonhole stitch, with one stitch on the bar (*see C in diagram 50, p. 55*). To complete second half arc, see diagram 51, p. 55.

Pattern 6

The centre unit of this pattern is worked as the centre unit of pattern 3, but without the picots. For the outer shape, begin the thread on the outside of the shortest square bar (if there is one) and pick up just the loop of the buttonhole stitch from which the one-thread bar was worked on the inner unit, then through the diagonal in an anticlockwise direction at the same distance from the inner unit as on the previous bar. Lay three circuits and work in buttonhole stitch – picots can be worked, if the worker so desires. At the junction of two loops, make the last buttonhole stitch close to the inner unit, turn the work and make the next stitch into the next loop.

Pattern 7

Begin the thread on a diagonal bar. Lay a square of three circuits and work the first row for the pyramids slightly spaced in order to accommodate a row of buttonhole stitch immediately inside later. The first row consists of a number of stitches in the first section, one stitch on top of the bar and the same number of stitches in the second section as in the first. The pyramid is worked free of the bar running underneath except on the last row, when the bar is picked up as the last stitch is being worked. Complete as usual. To work the corner unit, lay three threads so as to be able to work buttonhole stitch from left to right as in diagrams 52 and 53. It will be noted that the foundation threads for the third loop do not pass through the bar. Attach the third loop to the bar with a buttonhole stitch and continue straight on from the third loop to complete the second loop.

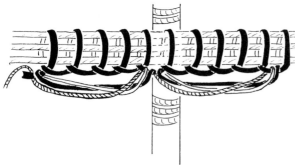

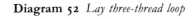

1st foundation thread
2nd foundation thread
3rd foundation thread

Diagram 52 *Lay three-thread loop*

Diagram 53 *Three-loop shape*

Pattern 8

The pyramids are worked first. Lay three threads across the corner. Where the pyramid ends determines the size of the inner circle.

Pattern 9

To work the pyramids: begin the thread for the foundation threads on a diagonal bar, so as to be at the beginning of a row on the completion of the three circuits for one of the pyramids. The picot is worked on to the left edge as the pyramid is being worked. Attach the foundation thread in the usual way. Into the same place, make a detached buttonhole stitch, then make the picot, then bring the needle up from underneath into the same place yet again and proceed to work the row and complete the pyramid. In this case, the pyramid is being worked with the square bar running underneath, to which the last stitch of the pyramid is attached. Whip up the right side and, in doing so, make the second picot to correspond with the other, making a detached buttonhole stitch into the end stitch of the same row. Complete as in diagrams 38 and 37 (*see p. 41*). It is advisable to use a new thread for each pyramid.

Pattern 10

This pattern is as for the centre unit of pattern 1 (*see p. 54*).

Pattern 11

The inner circle is worked first and is usually whipped. Work the bugs as in diagram 39 (*see p. 43*), beginning thread at the circle end.

Pattern 12

Proportion the pyramid circle as for pattern 3 (*see p. 57*).

Pattern 13

In this pattern the thread is begun on the square bars and stitches will be slightly spaced to accommodate an inner circuit, when pyramids are all complete, with a picot in each section. It may be necessary to decrease the number of stitches on this inner row, missing an in-between space when working the buttonhole stitch into which the picot will be worked.

Pattern 14

Lay three threads as in diagram 20 (*see p. 27*), work a pyramid directly on to them towards the centre of the pattern. It will be necessary to decrease on nearly every row in order to tailor the shape to fit within the square bars. To do this refer to the instruction for the working of a pyramid (*see p. 41*). In this situation, it is often necessary to work two bullion knots set obliquely over the centre.

Pattern 15

The centre circle is whipped but, on enlargement, buttonhole stitch and picot could be worked. Work the petal as in diagrams 35 and 36 (*see p. 40*), spacing the stitches on the first row to work buttonhole stitch and picot on the other side later. Begin working the petal near to the circle.

Pattern 16

Work the basic grid, including the diamond foundation bar. Begin the thread at one of the outer corners, pass through the diamond bar, then through the centre in an anticlockwise direction to form a figure of eight for the foundations only. Work in buttonhole stitch with picots, passing the thread through the centre on the first shape and placing stitches on top for the second shape.

Patterns 17 to 22 can be worked into areas varying from $1\frac{3}{4}$ in. to $2\frac{1}{4}$ in. (4.5 cm to 5.6 cm).

Pattern 17

The shapes in this pattern are explained in Patterns 1 and 9 (*see p. 54 and p. 61*).

Pattern 18

Lay three threads for the outer square, work three rows as for a pyramid and then the three loops as in diagrams 52 and 53 (*see p. 60*).

Pattern 19

The threads for the inner square need to be laid so that the pyramids finish well short of the end of the square bar. This allows the border to be laid and worked leaving a margin between it and the pyramid. This corner working is useful when there is a large area to fill. Work as for the corner unit of Pattern 3 (*see p. 57*). After working the first one-thread bar, lay threads and work as for the corner unit of Pattern 1 and diagram 51 (*see p. 54*). Continue to the next one-thread bar. Lay the threads through the diagonal bar and into the loop between the last stitch of the previous shape and the first one on the arc and work this loop, complete the arc and take the thread back and forth through the padded roll to complete the whole shape.

Pattern 20

The pyramids must be completed by halfway along the diagonal bar. Work the pyramids from the corners first: in this way the trials and errors will be independent, with the opportunity of four attempts, by which time the worker will know the size of the circle to lay. After the second pyramid has been attached to any bar and before whipping up the right side of the pyramid, make a bullion knot over the bar. The scallop loop shape is worked, basically, as in diagrams 52 and 53 (*see p. 60*). Always buttonhole stitch to the last half loop on each row, finally attaching the whole shape to the square bar as the end loop is worked. Complete by working the last half loop of each row back to the base line.

Pattern 21

Work the pyramid to attach it to the padded roll with a one-thread bar if the distance is less than $\frac{1}{8}$ in. (3 mm). Otherwise, lay three threads and whip. Lay threads for the loops to the inside of the pyramids, as in diagram 52 (*see p. 60*) but in a clockwise direction. The size of the inner circle will be determined by the remaining inner space.

Figure 14

Pattern 22

The inner unit is as Pattern 1; the scalloped buttonhole-stitched shape is laid as in diagram 52 (*see p. 60*). Begin the thread into the petal and work in an anticlockwise direction passing the threads through the bar. Lay the threads for the complete circuit before buttonhole-stitching. The corner unit is as Pattern 5 (*see p. 59*).

Patterns 23 to 28 can be worked into areas varying from 2 in. to 2½ in. (5 cm to 6.3 cm).

Pattern 23

Work the pyramids, laying the circle so that they finish to allow the shallow-arced circle to follow. The pyramids are left suspended until all eight are complete. Begin the thread and lay the threads as for Pattern 6 (*see p. 60*), passing the thread through the end stitch of each pyramid. To work the connecting bar between the pyramids, bring the thread up through the edge of the pyramid on the right, split the end of the thread and pass it through the bar to the left. Pick up the edge of the pyramid on the left to correspond, lay two more threads and work in buttonhole stitch. Finish the thread by whipping down the edge of the pyramid.

Pattern 24

Lay the threads to work the inner circle so that the next circle can be at halfway on the square bars. Whip with a number of stitches divisable by three or four and lay threads for the pyramid circle, working two or three one-thread bars on the first row. In the illustration the pyramids reach the outside edge; if this does not happen in practice, it is preferable to make a one-thread bar rather than distort the circle. For the double buttonhole-stitched snowflake centre, begin the thread at the outer end, in such a way that the thread emerges from the circle, and buttonhole stitch towards the centre, making a picot where there is most space — usually two stitches from the outer end. Make the last stitch close to the centre, * turn, work anticlockwise to the next bar and buttonhole stitch and picot to the outside. Take the needle through the circle then through the bar and back through the circle to work double buttonhole stitch — in this way the buttonhole stitch will be prevented from twisting later — return to the centre, making the last stitch beyond or to the centre of the first stitch *. Repeat from * to * completion. The linkage between pyramids is a matter of personal choice, using the method described in the previous pattern.

Figure 15 *Traycloth illustrating an independent insertion linked with a border, using Patterns 23 and 26 alternated*

Pattern 25

The main unit is made up of two four-pointed star shapes. Begin the thread on the outside end of the square bars and, in an anticlockwise direction, take the thread through the diagonal to fix a deep pointed shape. Complete three circuits and work in buttonhole stitch. Begin the thread on the outer end of the diagonal bar at the same distance from the centre as for the other shape. Take the threads through the other shape where they cross and place a buttonhole stitch on the top. The inner area will determine the size of the circle.

Pattern 26

Work the main unit as for pattern 6 (*see p. 60*). Work the inner circle; this could be nearer to the centre than illustrated. Work the oval buttonhole-stitched shape as in diagram 42 (*see p. 44*), and the corner as Pattern 5 (*see p. 59*).

Pattern 27

Work the outer circle of three-looped shapes, allowing for double buttonhole stitch later, then work the next innermost circle of shapes. The double buttonholing on both these circles can now be completed. The remaining area will determine the size of the inner unit.

Pattern 28

Buttonhole-stitching on the diamond bar makes for easier attachments later. Whip the inner square. Work the pyramids so that they attach the diamond bar. The distance between the attachment of the pyramid to the diamond bar and the diagonal bar determines the length of the loop which, in turn, determines the size of the other shape.

Patterns 29 to 34 can generally be worked into areas from 2–3 in., (5–7.5 cm) some can be worked into even larger areas.

Pattern 29

This pattern has extra foundation bars which divide up the circular grid radiating from the inner circle. Lay the inner circle and work with buttonhole stitch outermost, and with an even number of stitches slightly spaced into each section. Lay the threads for the extra bars. Beginning the thread in the padded roll at a point that divides the circumference, attach the thread to the inner circle by picking up the central loop of the buttonhole-stitching. Having laid three threads, whip stitch. Lay threads

for the outer circle beginning on a square bar. Note the distance from the centre. Register at the same distance from the centre on the other bars to complete three circuits. Buttonhole stitch to the inside on one section only using an even number of stitches. Refer to diagrams 52 and 53 (see p. 60), and work to halfway on the third loop. This is now a template to determine the position of the last circle. Allowing for a short length of one-thread bar, lay the threads for the last circle and whip stitch. Return to the template, attach it to the finished circle and complete as in the instructions for diagrams 53 (see p. 60) and 37 (see p. 41). Repeat 15 more times. Work woven shapes on to the basic foundation bars the full distance between the first and third circles, beginning the thread at the centremost end. Work double buttonhole stitch on alternate bars with a picot two stitches from the outer end. Work an inner circuit of buttonhole stitch and picot on the first circle and an outer circuit on the second circle. To work the corner shapes, begin the thread at the halfway point and lay the threads for a shallow buttonhole-stitch shape, as in diagram 42 (see p. 44), innermost. Complete, then lay threads for the second shape which will be smaller

69

Pattern 30

This pattern is not easy and should not be attempted until the worker is really familiar with her tension. The completed pyramids need to end parallel with or slightly inside the centre one-thread bars on the two adjacent shapes.

Pattern 31

Work the centre unit attaching pyramids to the padded roll with a three-thread bar. Whip stitch and complete the pyramid. Lay threads for the petal circle; the linking buttonhole-stitch bars can be worked at the same time as the petals.

Figure 16

Pattern 32

Lay threads for the pyramid circle and work the pyramids, attaching them to the padded roll with a three-thread bar – if it is to be longer than $\frac{1}{8}$ in. (3 mm) – or else a one-thread bar. Work the inner unit for Pattern 6 (*see p. 60*), minus the inner whipped circle.

Pattern 33

After the diamond foundation bar, lay and whip three threads to form the right angle to secure the pyramid foundation threads. Lay continuous threads for the undulating bar, at a distance for the pyramids that is slightly less than halfway on the right-angle bars. Work the pyramids and outermost buttonhole stitch, followed by a complete circuit inside. Work the centre unit as for pattern 10 (*see p. 61*).

Pattern 34

Again, this is a pattern best left alone by beginners. Lay threads for the outer circle and work the pyramids. Lay the next innermost circle and work a pyramid towards the centre of the pattern, placing the necessary number of one-thread bars; where the pyramid ends determines the centre circle. Work this, then attach the pyramid and proceed with the remainder.

The next 12 patterns are called window patterns; they have an extra foundation grid which divides the square grid into 16. Work to the diamond bar of the basic foundation grid; in some patterns threads only are laid at this stage. Lay the threads for the extra bars in line with the junction where the diamond bar threads pass through the diagonal. These patterns are useful for moderately large areas where the lace work is to be mounted on the bevel, as on a pincushion. The extra grid ensures regular attachment to the padded roll, thereby preventing it from being pulled out of shape. These patterns can be worked into square pattern areas from $2\frac{1}{2}$ in. to 3 in. or $3\frac{1}{2}$ in. (6.4 cm to 7.5 cm or 8.8 cm).

Pattern 35

After working the extra foundation grid, lay the circle for the pyramids as in Pattern 13 (*see p. 62*). Where the pyramids end determines the size of the circle; it is preferable not to have less than six stitches on the first row of the petals. The small circles need to be very small; as there are only four spokes it is difficult to maintain a circle unless it is small and the stitches are closely packed.

Pattern 36

The centre unit is as Pattern 35 but the circle is slightly larger. The double buttonhole-stitch shape is as Pattern 24 (*see p. 66*), but begin the thread at the centre so as to work in an anticlockwise direction. Work the bullion knot on the end as in Pattern 4 for the inverted V bar (*see p. 58*).

Pattern 37

Work the groups of pyramids as Pattern 9 (*see p. 61*), with or without the picots. The centre unit is two whipped circles laid close together, then bullion knots worked close together passing through both circles.

Pattern 38

After the window foundation grid, it will be noted that there is yet another foundation bar to complete the grid: a V that completes a diagonal cross in the two squares on each side of the pattern. Work the centre unit as in Pattern 10. When working the corner petal unit lay the threads for the right-angle bar at the same time or continuously.

Pattern 39

The foundation threads for the pyramids are laid as a rectangle along the diagonal plain. Work the pyramids as in Pattern 14 (*see p. 62*). Remaining foundation threads are whipped and form the other diagonal in the outer corner squares.

Pattern 40

The centre unit is as Pattern 9 (*see p. 61*), with a circle large enough to allow the pyramid to reach beyond the window grid junction. Lay the threads for the corner unit and whip stitch other than where picots are required. Then work as the corner unit for Pattern 2 (*see p. 55*).

Pattern 41

This is very straightforward: the units are as in pattern 13 (*see p. 62*).

Pattern 42

This pattern again is very straightforward: the centre unit is as Pattern 13 (*see p. 62*), and the petal units are three-quarters of Pattern 10 (*see p. 60*).

Pattern 43

This is one pattern where the diamond foundation threads are left unworked until after the window bars are completed. The pyramids are now worked in the direction shown in the illustration. The centre unit is as Pattern 13 (*see p. 62*), and the bugs as in Pattern 1 (*see p. 54*).

Pattern 44

The three foundation threads for the pyramids are laid in a continuous circuit. The pyramids are worked as in Pattern 14 (*see p. 62*), and the centre unit as in Pattern 13.

Pattern 45

The diamond foundation threads are dealt with as in Pattern 43 (*see p. 77*), but with the pyramids worked in the other direction. The threads for the independent pyramids are laid at the same time as working. The centre unit is as in Pattern 10 (*see p. 61*). Note the woven shapes need to begin at the outer end and fall short of the petal unit.

Pattern 46

The square immediately inside the four centre squares is worked in buttonhole stitch and one-thread bars; the corner arcs, except the last one, can be worked at the same time.

The following two patterns are suggestions to be used for insertions or right angles, as illustrated, repeating or adding units as desired into unit sizes from $\frac{7}{8}$ in. to $1\frac{1}{2}$ in. (2.2 cm to 3.8 cm). For the foundation grid procedure refer to the order of working for insertions, as in diagrams 24 and 25 (*see pp. 31 and 32*).

Pattern 47

Lay the foundation threads for the pyramids using the same method applied in diagram 27 (*see p. 36*), where pyramids are not required, the threads are whipped. The double button-hole stitch and picots are worked after the pyramids, continuously from one shape to another as much as possible.

Pattern 48

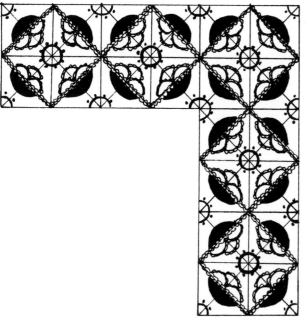

32). Work single buttonhole stitch along the entire length before beginning the double buttonhole. To work the petal shape, count a number of in-between spaces to the *right* of the diagonal bar. Begin the thread in the next outermost space by bringing the needle from underneath and splitting the end of the thread. Lay the foundation thread to the left, leaving the same number of spaces in between to the left of the bar. Work two rows as for a pyramid. On the third row, decrease as in diagram 36 (*see p. 40*). Complete as for the petal and take the needle through the double buttonhole-stitching. Lay the foundation threads for the two base line loops in the same manner as in diagram 52 (*see p. 60*), but, because it is necessary to begin at the left, when the three threads are laid the needle is at the wrong end so a fourth thread needs to be laid. Complete as in diagram 53 (*see p. 60*). The remaining inner area determines the size of the circle, which, in turn, determines whether or not a bullion knot centre is necessary.

Lay the foundation threads for the double buttonhole-stitch diamond grid, following the same method as applied in diagram 25 (*see p.*

The next two patterns are suitable for small multi-unit areas, for unit sizes ranging from $\frac{3}{4}$ in. to 1 in. (2 cm to 2.8 cm).

Pattern 49

To lay the foundation grid, which is all whip-stitched, refer to diagram 54. A and B are the original threads to which one thread is added as in the last paragraph of the instruction for 'Insertion circumjacent to the outer border' (*see p. 30*), C is as diagram 19 (*see p. 27*); D is the other diagonal but, because it extends out into the small square, follow the instruction for diagram 20 (*see p. 27*), to pass from one square to another; E is as B diagram 20. Complete the grid in this manner. Work the inner and outer arcs; work the woven shapes on to the extra grid bars to fill the distance between the two arcs.

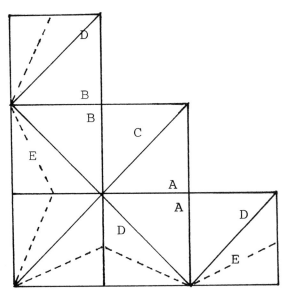

Diagram 54 *Grid for Pattern 49*

Figure 17 *Traycloth illustrating the use and siting of Pattern 49*

Pattern 50

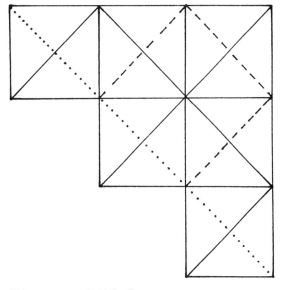

Diagram 55 *Grid for Pattern 50*

Lay and work the foundation grid as in the previous pattern as far as D. Complete as in diagram 55: work the diamond grid following the broken line; complete following the dotted line. The independent pyramids are worked as in Pattern 20 (*see p. 64*), the centre unit as in Pattern 10 (*see p. 61*).

The next two patterns are based on the window pattern foundation grid; the length can be increased by a unit repeat as for the plotting for an insertion (*see p. 29*). These patterns can be worked in sizes from 2½ in. to 3 in. (6.3 cm to 7.5 cm). All the square foundation grid is whip-stitched. Work all the short verticals before following diagram 26 (*see p. 35*) for the horizontal foundation bars. When a particular size or shape has to be repeated a number of times it is advisable to leave just one at foundation thread stage as a specimen, so enabling the worker to repeat a regular size.

Pattern 51

Work the diagonal grid as in diagram 27 (*see p. 36*); work the buttonhole-stitch circles encircling the eight-spoke junctions; the woven shapes radiate from this circle. The circles with picots are worked small and the stitches are closely packed so as to maintain a circle.

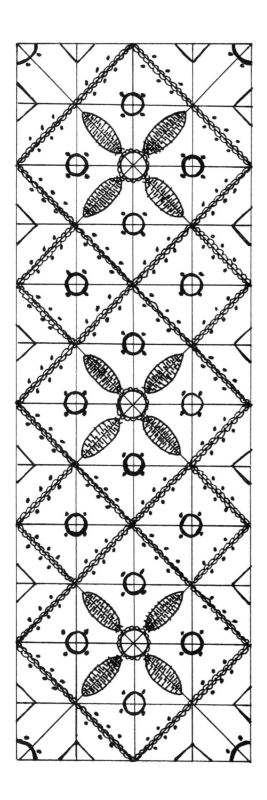

Pattern 52

When working the diagonal foundation bar observe that the pattern, as a section of this bar, is worked in double buttonhole stitch and picots. The whole of the diamond foundation bar is worked in double buttonhole stitch and picots (refer to Pattern 48 *see p. 80*).

Increasing the length of the next two patterns is not as straightforward as in the previous two patterns. It can be done but care must be taken in the planning; it is advisable to draw it in full before working on the fabric. Again, these two patterns are based on the window pattern foundation grid, but neither has a diagonal nor a diamond grid. It will also be observed that the next two patterns are not based on a multiple of the depth, so the size of the individual square will be the unit, which, in this case, could be $\frac{1}{2}$ in. or $\frac{5}{8}$ in. (1.3 cm or 1.5 cm).

Pattern 53

Work the bold shapes, such as the shaped pyramids, first. Lay as many continuous foundation threads as possible.

Pattern 54

Again, position the shaped pyramid units first. It will be noted that one of the foundation bars forming the spokes to work the buttonhole-stitch and picot circle stretches from pyramid to pyramid only. Refer to diagram 56 to work the shape with the central H. Continue to buttonhole stitch three and a half sides. Repeat the linkage as in diagram 56, and complete the H with a one-thread bar connection or a three-thread bar and whip stitch. Complete the shape.

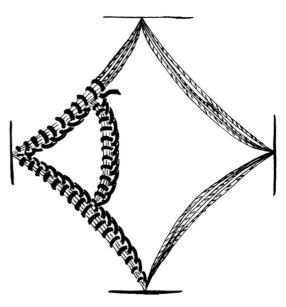

Diagram 56 *H-shape as in Pattern 54*

Figure 18 *Square mat illustrating Pattern 54 as an insertion circumjacent to the border*

The next two patterns can be repeated in units of two, and are most effective worked in unit sizes of $\frac{3}{4}$ in. or $\frac{7}{8}$ in. (2 cm or 2.2 cm). It will be noted that the basic foundation consists of one upright and one diagonal foundation bar; the latter needs care in positioning so that it passes through the corner correctly.

Figure 19 *Enlargement of Pattern 55 and figure 8, showing the buttonhole-stitched loop edging which overlaps an outside edge*

Pattern 55

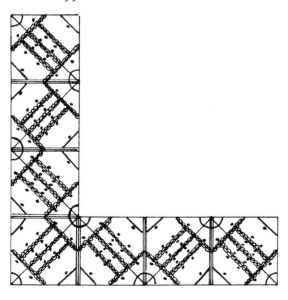

In this pattern the upright is woven as in diagram 21 (*see p. 28*). The double buttonhole-stitched inverted V on the inside circuit is worked first. As the inverted V bars are being worked from the outer circuit the double buttonhole stitch and picot bar linkages are worked. On the first and third linkage bars it is necessary to lay four foundation threads in order to continue working.

Figure 20 *Box top illustrating Pattern 56 used in conjunction with Pattern 23*

Pattern 56

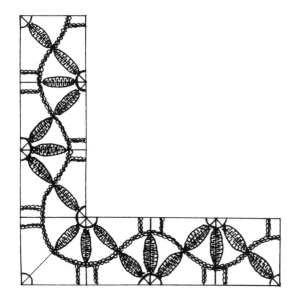

After completing the foundation grid as above, the double buttonhole-stitch undulating bar is laid, passing through the diagonal bar at halfway, and creating a gentle curve as it passes each three-spoke junction. Picots can be added here if the worker so desires. Work the small whipped arc at the three-spoke junctions, working the woven shapes to radiate from the same point.

Pattern 57

This pattern can be worked into a $3\frac{1}{2}$ in. to $4\frac{1}{2}$ in. (9 cm to 11.5 cm) pattern area. Lay the foundation threads for the outer circle and work two rows of buttonhole stitch. Work the first circuit as usual. A foundation thread must be included in the second circuit. If on completion of the first circuit the remaining thread is long enough to reach a full circuit, then join a new thread and proceed. Otherwise, begin the new thread, leave an end long enough to use as a foundation thread and incorporate as required. On completion of the second circuit cut off the foundation thread and finish the working thread as usual. On the second circuit there will be no buttonhole stitch on top of the bar.

Then work the shapes of two rows of buttonhole stitch radiating from the circle which has just been completed. Begin by plotting one shape on to a square bar. Begin the thread on the circle. At A lay three foundation threads and buttonhole stitch, * continue to the next shape, lay one foundation thread and finish off thread. Re-join at A, lay two more foundation threads and buttonhole stitch *. Repeat from * to * as necessary. With a long length of thread begin on a foundation bar, leave a sufficiently long end to be incorporated as a foundation thread to reach full circuit and work through position A as in Pattern 4 at E (*see p. 58*).

Pyramids can now be worked. The shape inside the one just explained is buttonhole stitch with a picot towards the outer end. To work the undulating circuit it will be noted that the buttonhole stitch reverses. Begin the thread at B to lay the three threads for the outer shape; buttonhole stitch and picot; take the needle through the two rows of buttonhole stitch, lay three threads, work buttonhole stitch and finish the thread. Repeat as necessary. To work the outer linkage, begin the thread at the same side as B, lay three threads, buttonhole stitch, take a foundation thread back to the left, link into the outermost stitch where the foundation threads were attached and leave fairly loose to maintain the curve. At halfway attach to the padded roll with a one-thread or whipped bar.

When working on large areas it helps the control of the foundation bars if the centre junction is couched down to the leathercloth after being whipped, but release it before working the bullion knot centre.

Figure 21 *Box top using Pattern 57 with a covered bead in the centre*

Pattern 58

This pattern is based on the window pattern foundation grid and can be worked into an area from $3\frac{1}{2}$ in. to $4\frac{1}{2}$ in. (9 cm to 11.5 cm). The foundation threads are laid to work the pyramids in the corners in a continuous manner; the double buttonhole-stitching is not worked until all pyramids are complete.

For the centre unit the circle for the pyramids is laid and the pyramids worked; the innermost circle is then laid and worked in buttonhole stitch, one-thread bars and picots. The circular units inside the pyramid corner units are worked in a similar way; the outer is worked first and then the inner. If it turns out that the inner circle is to be very small, this is quite all right as the picots will form an attractive centre.

The outer units are two rows of buttonhole stitch with picots on the second row.

Pattern 59

This pattern can be worked into an area ranging from 4 in. to 5 in. (10 cm to 12.5 cm). The inner double circle unit is worked as for Pattern 3 (*see p. 57*), with a picot on the first and third one-thread bar. Lay the foundation threads as in Pattern 29 (*see p. 69*), which are whip-stitched except where the pyramids are to be worked.

The fourth circle out from the centre is buttonhole-stitched, with the buttonhole-stitched loop worked at the same time. * Buttonhole stitch one section less one stitch, lay three threads in the same manner as in diagram 52 (*see p. 60*) in between the first two buttonhole stitches, buttonhole stitch the loop, work one stitch on the circle and one buttonhole stitch on the bar*. Repeat from * to * as necessary. The outside units are worked in the same manner.

Pattern 60

This pattern has a foundation grid that divides the window pattern grid yet again; there are no diagonal foundation bars. Lay and work the diamond foundation bar. Lay the threads for the pyramids as continuously as possible; it will be noted that all pyramids can be worked from two rectangles. The foundation threads for the inner buttonhole-stitched and picoted shapes are laid as in diagram 56 (*see p. 85*). The buttonhole-stitch and picot circle need to be laid quite small so as to stand out as fairly bold units; there are two bullion knots laid obliquely over the centre junction of these units.

Edgings

Some form of edging is essential. No matter which form is chosen or how simple it is, the end result always justifies the time and effort involved. Even the simplest edging is guaranteed to enhance the work already done and is therefore, doubly satisfying.

Bullion knots

Single

The traditional edging is a single bullion knot worked over the outer edge of the fabric two threads in from the edge. The traditional spacing is $\frac{3}{8}$ in. (1 cm), but on small items it is preferable to work the knots approximately $\frac{1}{4}$ in. (6 mm) apart. Bullion knots can also be used as means of joining two edges together as in a pincushion, cushion or needlebook. The instruction for working bullion knots will be found in the text relating to diagram 45 (*see p. 45*).

Double

Bullion knots can be worked in pairs, side by side. These are worked as above but, after making the knot, bring the needle through to the right side slightly to the left of the first knot and work the second knot. Continue as above. Double bullion knots are most suitable where extra strength is needed, such as joining the edges of cushions, or, on larger articles, when a deep hem has been laid.

Treble

Treble bullion knots can be worked, usually on to large items such as tablecloths, when double bullions would not be bold enough to give a well-balanced effect. Treble bullion knots are worked as for the double knots, with a third knot over the fold of the previous two. After completing the second knot, take the needle in at the same place as the thread last came out and bring it out at the outer edge of the hem to the left of the two knots. Take the needle in at the other side of the two knots, passing under the two and making contact with the fold of the fabric, and out where the thread came out. Make the bullion knot – this will lie across the fold of the two knots – and pass the thread through the hem to the next position, as before.

To finish a thread when making an edging, take the needle and thread through the hem (between the two layers of fabric) for approximately $\frac{1}{2}$ in. (1.3 cm) and, bringing the needle out on the wrong side, make a back stitch over one thread of fabric. Take the needle and thread through the hem as before without pulling, which would distort the fabric, and cut off the thread close to the fabric.

Buttonhole-stitched loops

These form a very versatile edging suitable to many situations. Buttonhole-stitched loops can either be worked singly or in various multiples, depending on the required effect. Multiple loops are usually applied to the edges of articles which will be surrounded by a margin of area in use, such as place mats and runners, etc. The size of this surface, will determine the space these multiple loops can occupy. Both single loops and multiple loops can be inter-spaced with bullion knots, worked as in diagram 45 (*see p. 45*). Picots can be worked on single loops or on the end loop of multiples.

An exception to the rule occurs here: it is necessary to lay four foundation threads so as to work the loops consecutively. These loops can be very shallow so that they lie very close to the edge of the fabric or they can stand off slightly, but if they are too deep there will be a tendency for them to twist and they will then not launder easily. These threads need to be laid slightly shallower than the required completed shape.

Singles

Begin the thread at the bottom left-hand cor-

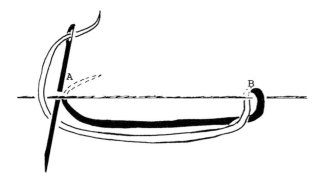

Diagram 57 *Four-thread loop, stage one*

ner of the article and work left to right, by
taking the needle through between the two
layers of fabric in the hem for approximately
½ in. (1.3 cm) and out on the outside edge of
the article, as at A in diagram 57. Make a tiny
stitch which will split the thread to secure it.
Having decided the length of the loop (nine or
ten threads distance between loops is average
on the linen we normally use), take the needle
in on the right side of the fabric at B and out
on the underside approximately, one-thread
deep into the fabric to form a loop stitch.

As the next corner of the article approaches
the shapes need to be as even in length as
possible, as with the bullion knots, so it will be
necessary to plot the last 2 in. (5 cm) or so, so
that the last repeat ends at the corner. A
bullion knot can be worked diagonally over
the corner.

Three-loop unit
A three-loop unit can either be worked as a
continuous edging or interspaced with a bullion knot over the outer edge of the fabric.

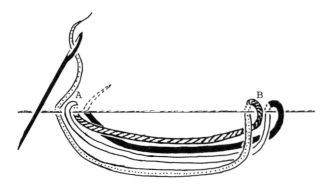

4th foundation thread ┄┄┄┄┄

Diagram 58 *Four-thread loop, stage two*

Repeat, forming a loop stitch in reverse at A,
then at B in diagram 58, then back to A, *but*
bring the needle up from the underside to
complete the fourth foundation thread. With
the thread now on the right side of the work,
work in buttonhole stitch over these four
threads; a picot can be worked at halfway if
desired.

Begin the thread as before at A in diagram
58, then to B, then to A then back to B,
bringing the needle up from underneath here.
The thread will now change direction without
upsetting the formation of the previous loop.
In the same manner, attach the thread at C in
diagram 59, then to B, then back to C. Now
lay the fourth foundation thread by bringing

94

Figure 22 *Enlargement of Pattern 54 and figure 18,
showing the buttonhole-stitched loop edging overlapping
the edge of a hem, here with a picot at halfway*

Diagram 59 *Four-thread base line loops*

the needle up from underneath at B, then from underneath at A. Work one and a half loops in buttonhole stitch and complete as in diagram 53 (*see p. 60*).

Multiple-loop unit
If a large multiple-loop unit is desired, it may be necessary to finish and restart a thread, as working the whole with one length of thread would present problems. Make sure that this happens at the stage of laying the foundation thread so that both ends of the threads can be worked in.

Loop which overlaps the outer edge of a hem
This edging gives a very pleasing result, especially when applied to a narrow hem, or where the surrounding area is going to be limited: picots can be added. It is a firm and stable edging and is useful to add to articles that will need to be laundered frequently (*see figures 19 and 22*).

This edging again is worked from left to right. Begin the thread in the same manner and in the same position as for the previous two edgings, but bring the needle out on the underside of the fabric two threads inside the edge of the fabric at A in diagram 60. Without the stitches showing through on to the right side, bring the thread closely around the outside edge of the hem and attach it at B, taking a good hold of a small amount of fabric two threads inside the edge of the fabric. Then back to A, back to B and back to A, making four foundation threads lying close to the edge of the fabric. Work in buttonhole stitch to B, making a picot at halfway if desired. Take the needle through to the underside which is the beginning of the next shape. Lay the next foundation threads between the underside of B and position C. The spacing of the loops is as before — approximately $\frac{1}{4}$ in. (6 mm) or nine or ten threads. The last repeat will complete as at A.

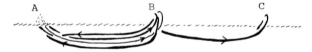

Diagram 60 *Laying threads for buttonhole-stitched loop which overlaps the outer edge of a hem*

Part III

ARTICLES

Ruskin lace will provide all those with the love of the needle with a channel for self expression and creativity, but deciding what to make can in itself present a problem. Sit down or wander around the home observing the blank spaces on the walls, the side tables, the dressing tables, particularly if they have plate glass protection; chairs that need protection to which some form of decoration can be added; the work box that has been waiting for a replacement pincushion or needlebook. Lampshades display this form of craft beautifully, although a lampshade is not recommended as a first article, and tablecloths and bedspreads can be long-term projects destined for family heirlooms.

Once the article has been chosen the decision for the depth of hem and pattern layout needs to be made. This will depend on the size of the article, its situation and, as always, personal choice. There are no laws, but it is perhaps worth stating that simplicity is the art of good design. Do your own thing. Take care to refer to the specific areas of your book for instruction.

It will be noted that most patterns can be worked over a size variation of approximately $\frac{1}{2}$ in. (1.2 cm) or more. It is advisable to work a few independent squares before venturing to the more complicated right angle of units or the multi-unit shape. The most beneficial size of square to work is approximately $2\frac{1}{4}$ in. (5.6 cm) as there is scope for practice in all stages, which will help to acquire a rhythm and regular tension.

Some of the following article sizes are designed specifically for the Glenshee Evenweave linen fabric we usually use which is 52 in. (132 cm) wide, so as to utilise the width to the best advantage with the minimum of wastage. In the main, the sizes of articles given are intended as suggestions. It is essential to remove the selvedges of the fabric; these will otherwise cause distortions in the hem after laundering. Draw a thread from the inside of

the selvedge then cut along the line of same. When purchasing linen of suitable weight for Ruskin work request that it be cut along a drawn-out thread.

Traycloth

The actual size is debatable as there are trays and trays, but a finished size of $10\frac{1}{2} \times 16\frac{1}{2}$ in. (27×42 cm) is average. The depth of the hem is also debatable; this can be $\frac{1}{4}$ in. (6 mm), $\frac{1}{2}$ in. (1.3 cm) or even deeper on the ends. The eventual size of the piece of fabric will be calculated according to the depth of hem which has been decided in 'To lay a hem' (*see p. 17*).

A single or double row of four-sided stitch can be worked immediately inside the hem.

The permutations of design layout are endless and can be as simple or as complex as the worker desires. A few suggestions follow: (1) a square set diagonally in opposite corners; (2) a square in each corner, with a different pattern in each corner. These two layouts could be joined by a border of four-sided stitch linking the outer right angles of the squares. This link-up must be considered as the first square is being plotted. (3) An insertion at one or both ends of the cloth, depending on the length in proportion to the width. Here an insertion made up of an odd number of repeats is preferable, unless the worker intends to repeat the same pattern throughout the length of the insertion. (4) One larger square or other shape with three smaller squares in the other corners; these can be independent or linked with a border of four-sided stitch as in the first suggestion. Finally, any one of the various edgings can be added, as desired.

Place mats

A $\frac{1}{2}$ yd (46 cm) piece of Glenshee Evenweave linen 52 in. (152 cm) wide will make four place mats. The size of a place mat can be determined either by the size of the dining table and

Figure 23 *Place mats*

how many place settings the owner intends it to make, or the width of the fabric and how it can be best utilised. As a Glenshee width is 52 in. (132 cm), from a $\frac{1}{2}$ yd (46 cm) piece with selvedges removed the fabric can be equally divided into four mats approximately 18 × 12$\frac{3}{4}$ in. (46 × 30.5 cm) with no wastage. With a $\frac{1}{2}$ in. (1.3 cm) hem the completed article will be approximately 16$\frac{1}{2}$ × 11$\frac{1}{4}$ in. (41.8 × 28.6 cm) which will accommodate a place setting.

When considering the pattern layout avoid lace work in the upper right-hand corner which would make the positioning of a glass precarious and would also lose the focal interest. This is an article when the proverb 'simplicity is the art of good design' should be heeded. Natural fibre, natural colour on a natural wooden surface can present a stunning combination. Independent squares could be set on the diagonal, one at the bottom right

and another at the top left. These patterns could range from 1$\frac{1}{2}$ in. to 2$\frac{1}{4}$ in. inside area. An alternative could be an insertion, at one end only and preferably to lie on the left, made up of units ranging from 1 to 1$\frac{1}{2}$ in. (2.5 to 3.8 cm).

For the slightly more experienced worker a set of place mats could be made up from a variety of shapes or layout. For instance, two with diagonal squares, two with insertions, two with a right-angle unit in the top left-hand corner and two with a small multi-shape in the top left-hand corner. If a set of six were required, then make one of each of the above and divise two more different layouts. Allow the choice of edging to link the whole together as a set. Single bullion knots are usually sufficient, spaced at $\frac{3}{8}$ in. (1 cm) intervals.

Chairback covers

A $\frac{1}{2}$ yd (46 cm) piece of Glenshee Evenweave linen 52 in. (132 cm) wide will make a pair of average chairback covers. Size is debatable as there are many sizes of chairs, but a $\frac{1}{2}$ yd (46 cm) piece cut in two widthways of the fabric will give two pieces 26 × 18 in. (66 × 46 cm), and when the selvedges have been removed will result in a finished article 23 × 16$\frac{1}{2}$ in. (58.5 × 41.8 cm) which is roughly average. To arrive at this measurement, lay a $\frac{1}{2}$ in. (1.3 cm) hem on one end and the two long sides, with a 2 in. (5 cm) hem on the front drop end, as in diagram 2 (*see p. 18*) and diagram 61. Draw threads and work double four-sided stitch as in diagram 7, along all sides.

Chairback covers are a splendid way of showing off and enjoying Ruskin lace. Various pattern layouts are possible. Strong bold patterns are here worked to the best advantage, and can be in the form of independent squares, insertions or right-angle unit shapes. A few suggested pattern layouts are illustrated in diagram 62.

Runners

Experience reveals that of the many runners made no two of the same size can be recalled.

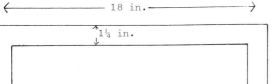

←————— 18 in. —————→ **Diagram 61** *Laying a deeper hem on one end*

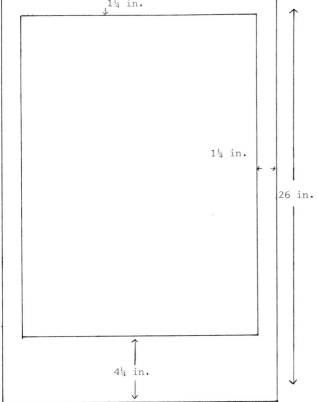

1¼ in.

1¼ in.

26 in.

4¼ in.

Diagram 62 *Suggestions for chairback pattern layout*

Figure 24 *Pincushions illustrating, from top left, Patterns 35 and 38, a variation of Pattern 24, and Pattern 32*

A runner is usually intended to enhance and not necessarily cover up, therefore it is advantageous to site it where there will be a good margin of surface all around. Think of the edging when deciding the margin; this is one situation where the three-loop unit can be worked to good advantage.

Pattern layout will be specifically determined by the siting of the objects which will also occupy the same piece of furniture.

If the runner is to be long and narrow, here is a situation where a deep hem on the ends and a narrow one on the sides will help to balance the proportions. If the runner is to be short and wide then the same depth of hem can be laid all round, from $\frac{1}{4}$ to 1 in. (6 mm to 2.5 cm). A single or double row of four-sided stitch can be worked.

Pattern areas can now be plotted avoiding areas to be otherwise occupied. In the case of a long, narrow runner, large square patterns will probably be the answer; if these are to be sited towards the ends, then it is possible to leave quite a margin at either end in order to attain a balance. It will help to cut squares of paper the size you have in mind and practise doodling before committing the scissors. Often on the short, wide runners an insertion plotted along each end is sufficient or one of the layouts suggested for the chairback cover.

Pincushion

There are pincushions of all shapes and sizes; the following measurements are just one suggestion.

Requirements
Two pieces of fabric, 5 × 5 in. (12.5 × 12.5 cm)
Two pieces of coloured lining fabric, 5 × 5 in.
(12.5 × 12.5 cm)
Sheep wool, ideally, or synthetic filling.

Lay a $\frac{1}{4}$ in. (6 mm) hem on all sides of the two pieces to be used for Ruskin work (refer to instructions for diagram 1, 2 and 3 on pp. 17–19).

For the top piece, draw threads for a double row of four-sided stitch and on the other single four-sided stitch. Work as instructions for diagrams 4, 5, 5b, 6 and 7 (*see pp. 19–21*). On the top piece work woven corners as instructions for diagrams 8 and 9 (*see p. 21*).

The remaining inner area on the top piece will be pattern. Proceed as for the order of working to completion of the pattern chosen. When choosing a pattern for an article that is to be mounted at tension, make sure that the pattern has plenty of connections with the padded roll so as to avoid fluting of the padded roll, and that a bold, strong pattern is chosen. Complete, neaten corners on both pieces and press.

Make a pad the same size as the finished fabric pieces from the lining fabric by joining three sides. Pack well with the filling. If sheep wool is used, avoid washing if possible as the lanolin content will help prevent pins and needles rusting. Having said this, some types of fleece can have too much lanolin, but if it is not distinctly sticky to the touch it should be fine. If there is no alternative but to wash, then submerge the wool and leave to soak in a mild soapy solution, not detergent, until cold. Avoid excessive agitation as this will cause milling or shrinkage. Rinse well and spread out to dry naturally, teasing out well before stuffing the pad.

Along one side of the top piece, work single bullion knots as in diagram 45 (*see p. 46*), excluding the corners, approximately $\frac{1}{4}$ in. (6 mm) apart. Secure the two pieces of fabric to either side of the pad with pins and join the two pieces of fabric together along the other three sides with bullion knots. Take care to avoid making contact with the pad so that decades later it may be renewed without upsetting the stitchery. Make bullion knots over the corners at right-angles and diagonally – three in all; this protects the corners. With a separate thread, join the fourth side with a slip stitch.

Flat, sandwich pincushion

Requirements
Two pieces of fabric, 5 × 5 in. (12.5 × 12.5 cm)
Two pieces of coloured lining fabric, 5 × 5 in.
(12.5 × 12.5 cm)
Two pieces of very thin card, $3\frac{1}{2} × 3\frac{1}{2}$ in.
(9 × 9 cm)
Two pieces latex foam or wadding, $3\frac{1}{2} × 3\frac{1}{2}$ in.
(9 × 9 cm)

Overcast the raw edges of the fabric. Plot a 2 in. (5 cm) pattern area square centrally on to one piece of fabric as in diagram 10 (*see p. 22*). Work the desired pattern to completion. Press. The other piece of fabric can be treated in the same way or work a square border of four-sided stitch only, approximately $1\frac{1}{2}$ in. (3.8 cm), as a light relief.

Secure the foam and wadding to the outer side of the pieces of thin card, a similar weight to that of good-quality greetings card. Cover the padded outer side of the card with lining fabric by lacing; do not glue. Cover the lined, padded, outer sides of the cards with the fabric, centralising the pattern, by lacing. Secure the two pieces together with bullion knots as in diagram 45 (*see p. 46*), $\frac{1}{4}$ in. (6 mm) apart, making two at right-angles and one diagonally at the corners.

The pins are then placed between the pieces of card. As there are four thicknesses of fabric between the cards the pins are quite secure.

Figure 25 *Flat pincushion*

Needle book

Requirements

Two pieces of fabric, 5 × 5 in. (12.5 × 12.5 cm)
Two pieces lining fabric, 4½ × 4½ in. (11.5 × 11.5 cm)
Two pieces Welsh flannel

Lay a ⅜ in. (1 cm) hem on all sides of both pieces, i.e. measure 1 in. (2.5 cm) from the outside edge of the fabric, pick up the next two inside threads and proceed as in the instruction for diagrams 1, 2 and 3 (see pp. 17–19).

For the top piece, draw threads for double four-sided stitch and work as instruction for diagram 7 (see p. 21). Work woven corners as in diagrams 8 and 9 (see p. 21). The whole of the inner area will be pattern. Proceed as order of working.

The under-piece can be worked as the top or just with a single border of four-sided stitch and three rows of single four-sided stitch worked vertically as on the reverse side of the pot-pourri sachet (see figure 27, p. 107), the centre row being longer than the other two. Two seven-stitch scallops will be needed to neaten the cut ends of thread. Complete both pieces and press.

To line both pieces allow single turning, overcast raw edges, fold under turning and tack into position so that the lining fabric comes to the outside edge of the hems. Secure the lining to the fabric with bullion knots on three sides of each piece.

To make up the book, ideally using Welsh Flannel, make two double pages. Cut along the grain of the fabric, fold the outer page in half and mark the fold. Secure with a running stitch the fold of the other piece slightly off centre so as to avoid excess bulk at the fold. Reduce the edges of all pages to the same overall size, ideally using pinking scissors. Secure the completed book to the under-side of the lined piece of fabric within the width of the hem of the unknotted side, so that the stitching will not show on the right side. Place the top piece of fabric so as to enclose the book and join the two pieces together with bullion knots along the fourth side.

Pot-pourri sachet

This is an article first designed by Mrs Raby which makes a popular and pleasing gift.

Requirements

A piece of fabric, 15 × 5 in. (38 × 12.5 cm)
A piece of coloured lining fabric, 12 × 4½ in. (30.5 × 12 cm)

A 1 in. (2.5 cm) hem is laid at each end and a ¼ in. (6 mm) hem on the long sides. Begin plotting at one end of the fabric, as in diagram 63 where a single line represents two drawn-out threads. Measure 2¼ in. (5.6 cm) from the outside edge at one end of the fabric and pick up the next two innermost threads on the pin. Measure ⅝ in. (1.5 cm) from the outside edge on both sides and pick up the next two threads well away from the point where the cut threads will meet at the junction of the two corners. Cut the three pairs of picked-up threads and draw back towards the end of fabric, forming two right angles.

Fold the length of fabric in half along the grain of one thread and run a marker thread in this position. Measure ¼ in. (6 mm) from the fold, pick up two threads on side A, cut these

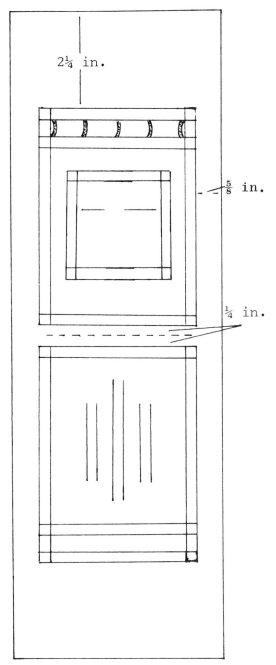

2¼ in.

$\frac{5}{8}$ in.

$\frac{1}{4}$ in.

Diagram 63 *Pot-pourri sachet layout*

angles. Measure $2\frac{1}{4}$ in. (5.6 cm) from the end, pick up two threads, cut these and draw back to complete the other rectangle.

Fold the hems as in diagram 2 (*see p. 18*), with long sides first, to form a $\frac{1}{4}$ in. (6 mm) hem. Cut away excess bulk as in diagram 2 (*see p. 18*), but in the case of a $\frac{1}{4}$ in. (6 mm) hem only the depth of the first turning is removed. Fold the ends to form a 1 in. (2.5 cm) hem. Tack and slip stitch as in diagram 3 (*see p. 19*).

Complete the thread-drawing for the four-sided stitch border on both rectangles as in diagram 4 (*see p. 19*). Leave a margin of 12 threads from each end immediately inside the four-sided stitch border, pick up the next two threads, leave four, pick up two and cut and draw back to the outside of the border on the sides, forming an isolated block of four threads as at a right angle or corner. Woven loops will be worked across this margin later to take a draw cord.

Plot a square for a pattern as suggested in diagram 10 (*see p. 22*); this can be repeated on side B if desired, or three columns of four-sided stitch as illustrated in figure 27 (*see p. 107*). Work four-sided stitch borders and pattern as per order of working.

Neaten all cut ends of threads. Where two rows of four-sided stitch borders interlock there are two pairs of threads to neaten on the straight. Work two seven-stitch shapes as in diagrams 47 and 48 (*see p. 47*). Press.

Woven bars span the 12-thread margin. Lay six threads formed by three circuits, as in diagram 41 (*see p. 44*), securing the threads into the margin threads one and 12. Work as in diagram 21 (*see p. 28*). Start and finish working threads by running through the crosses on the under-side of the four-sided stitch. Place five woven bars equally spaced on each side of the sachet, one inside each four-sided stitch border at the hems, one centrally and one in each quarter.

The lining is made of a colour and type of the worker's choice, to enclose the full width and the four-sided stitch borders at each end. Allow turnings: these will probably need to be overcast. Fold turnings to the under-side and tack into position as in diagram 64. Work bullion knots along the ends beginning and

two threads and draw back to form a rectangle with the other cut threads.

To draw threads for side B, measure $\frac{1}{4}$ in. (6 mm) from the fold, pick up two threads and trace the two pairs of threads already cut on side A through the margin at the fold; these form the sides of B. Cut these three pairs of threads and draw back to form two right-

105

Figure 26 *Pot-pourri sachet using linen spun and woven by the author*

ending a ¼ in. (6 mm) from the sides, as in diagram 64, making the knots approximately ¼ in. (6 mm) apart.

Fold in half and join the sides with bullion knots as in diagram 45 *(see p. 46)*. Begin with two bullion knots close together at the bulk of the 1 in. (2.5 cm) hem and the lining, and work towards the fold making the knots ¼ in. (6 mm) apart. Re-start at the same place on the other side and repeat. Then work bullion knots at the same spacing around each open end.

There are various methods of making twisted cords, but the method used here is as follows.

Use the same thread as that used in the needlepoint and three pencils or similar objects. Estimate three times the finished length and as many thicknesses as required, but six to

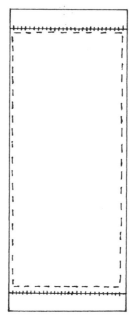

Diagram 64
Lining pot-pourri sachet

106

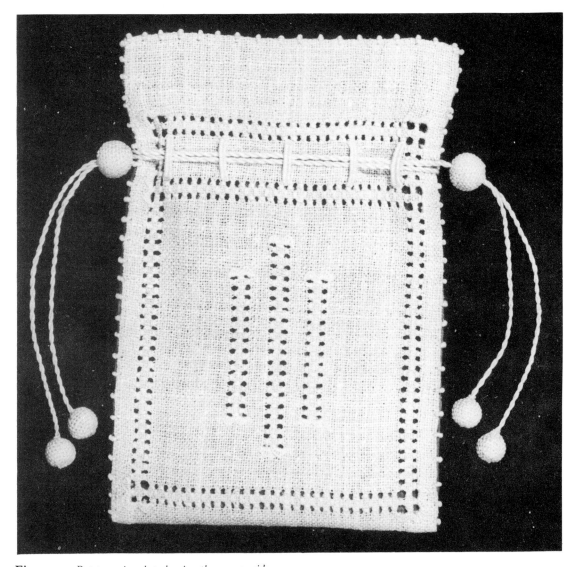

Figure 27 *Pot-pourri sachet showing the reverse side*

eight are average. Threads with a softer twist will tend to make a softer cord, so adjustments may need to be made. Make a loop at each end to take a pencil. If you can enlist the help of an assistant, take an end each and twist in the same direction. If not, you will need to secure one end and the performance takes twice as long. Twist until very hard, taking note of the direction of twisting. With care, fold in half, placing the third pencil in the fold. Proceed to twist in the opposite direction until the cord is again quite hard. Remove the third pencil. When tension is released some twist will

unwind but a good depth of twist will be maintained; it will be noticed that when cut the cord does not easily untwist as with a single twisted cord.

Cut two pieces of cord approximately 20 in. (51 cm) long. Thread each piece through the full circuit of woven bars in both directions and knot the ends together, or finish as desired. In figure 27 it will be noted that wooden beads have been threaded on to the cord enclosed in a continuous circuit of buttonhole stitch. To thread the beads on to the cord: at the third pencil end all the threads are doubled; pass a length of fine thread through

107

all the loops and then thread a needle with both ends of the same thread. Before cutting the cord thread one small bead and one large bead on to the far end of the cord (loosely knot the end of the cord to contain the beads), thread the cord through the woven loops for one full circuit, pass the cord through the large bead again and thread on another small bead. Cut the cord as required. On to the remaining length, thread one small bead and one large bead, thread the cord through the woven loops in the reverse direction to the first circuit, thread through the large bead again and add the last small bead.

To work over the beads the working thread must be long enough to complete the buttonhole stitch and provide a foundation thread. When a bead needs to be attached to the end of the cord untwist approximately 1 in. (2.5 cm) of cord, spread out the ends and fold back over the bead. Thread a Sharps needle and hold in the right hand. With the right hand make two anticlockwise circuits of the cord just above the bead to control and enclose the loose ends, as in diagram 65. Leave a long end of thread to be incorporated as a foundation thread later. Work a circuit of buttonhole stitch over the two anticlockwise threads. If these threads become loosened in so doing, draw on the free end to close. Now incorpor-

Diagram 65 *Covering a bead*

ate the free end and continue in detached buttonhole stitch. To increase, work two stitches into one in-between space as necessary; decrease by missing an in-between space. To finish the thread, pass the needle through the bead, through the cord and back through the bead, make a contact with the last circuit and repeat. Tie the needle thread and foundation thread together, thread the needle with the foundation thread and pass through the bead as above. Cut off both threads and excess cord threads.

For the larger beads that need to slide freely on the cord, work as above, but there will be no ends to enclose. To finish off threads do not pass through the bead but through the mass of buttonhole-stitching, making a back stitch over a loop without it showing. Repeat, unthread the needle and treat the foundation thread in the same way.

Bag

The base is an octagon based on a 10 in. (25 cm) diameter circle. The measurement of the sides of the octagon determines the finished width of the panels; the finished height is approximately $10\frac{1}{4}$ in. (25.6 cm). This bag could be used as a work bag as originally intended but, of course, it could have other uses.

Requirements
Fabric, 12 × 52 in. (30.5 × 132 cm)
Coloured lining fabric 27 × 45 in. (68.5 × 115 cm)
2 mm hardboard or other suitable material, 12 × 24 in. (30.5 × 61 cm)
1 mm card, 12x12 in. (30.5x30.5 cm)
4 mm latex foam, 24x24 in. (61x61 cm)

To make the panels cut eight pieces from the fabric, each measuring $4\frac{3}{4}$ × 12 in. (12 × 30.5 cm). Plot as in diagram 66, where a single line represents two drawn-out threads. Lay a $\frac{1}{4}$ in. (6 mm) hem on three sides and a 1 in. (2.5 cm) hem on the top. Tack and slip stitch. Complete the thread-drawing for single four-sided stitch border. From the top border count 12 threads immediately inside and draw

Figure 28 *Associated Country Women of the World Handicraft Competition, third prize in 1977; designed and worked by the author*

threads for another border. At the base end draw threads for the fourth side of a square. The measurements of the area between the side borders determines the size of the square. On four of the panels the whole of this area is pattern. Work all four-sided stitch *. Work the pattern area following the order of working and the pattern chosen. On the other four panels, work as above to *, then plot a smaller square inside the square already plotted by leaving a margin of eight threads on all sides. Work patterns from the $1\frac{1}{2}$ in. (3.8 cm) group. Press. Work woven bars exactly as for the pot-pourri sachet (*see p. 105*).

From the 2 mm hardboard cut the base and eight squares the width of the panels. Chamfer the inside edges of the base and three inside edges of the squares (male assistance may need to be enlisted here). From the 1 mm card cut a base lining fractionally smaller than the hardboard base. Secure 4 mm latex foam to the outside of the base and the inside of the base lining card, and both sides of the squares. Use the minimum of glue possible and avoid glue coming in to contact with edges where stitching has to be worked later.

Cover the outside of the base with fabric, secure with glue or lacing and cut away excess

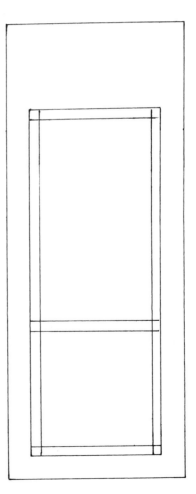

Diagram 66 *Bag panel*

109

bulk where the turned-under fabric overlaps. Cover the inside of the base lining with lining fabric in the same way. Secure base and base lining together.

If it is intended to include some pockets to the inside of the bag, they should be secured to the lining fabric pieces before the squares are covered. When cutting out the lining fabric pieces to cover the squares, allow a 1 in (2.5 cm) turning all around. Secure the lining fabric to the inside area of the square; as both sides of the square are padded, lacing would be preferable to glue. Join the squares together with ladder stitch, keeping all the unchamfered edges in the same position to become the top, unattached, edge later. Take care in positioning the pockets – they are not too functional upside down! Secure the joined squares to the base without the stitches making contact with the extreme outer edge of the base.

Join the long sides of the panels together with bullion knots, alternating the large patterned panels with the small patterned panels. Leaving the top ends open, as in the pot-pourri sachet (*see p. 106*) and work bullion knots around the open ends.

Make a twisted cord, as for the pot-pourri sachet, long enough to form two generous circuits plus 16 in. (40.5 cm) for finishes as in figure 28.

Lampshades

The traditions of Ruskin work restrict the shape of a lampshade to that of a drum. As drum-shape lampshade frames are not manufactured, a top and bottom loose ring is used with a self-adhesive card stiffening material to maintain a firm shape. The self-adhesive card has a peel-off backing which exposes a tacky surface to which a coloured lining fabric can be adhered. The lace-worked fabric is then mounted on to it, producing a very attactive way of displaying Ruskin work. Because each frame is made up by the worker, she can choose the height of the shade. The loose rings are obtainable in diameter sizes ranging from 6

Figure 29 *Lampshade illustrating a random pattern layout*

to 18 in. (15 to 46 cm), the usual being 7, 8 or 9 in. (18, 20.5 or 23 cm).

Requirements
One plain ring and one ring with a utility or gimbal fitting
Self-adhesive card of height and circumference required
Coloured lining fabric to cover the above plus sufficient to cut bias strips
Fabric, the height plus hem allowances × the circumference, plus 3 in. (7.5 cm)
$\frac{1}{4}$ in. (6 mm) straight tape to bind the rings

Lay a $\frac{1}{2}$ in. (1.3 cm) hem on both long sides and one end, as in diagram 67. Place a tack line to show the expected circumference and one centrally horizontal; this will help if any pattern unit needs to be plotted from the centre of the height.

The pattern layout can be random or very organised. As the layout can not be viewed as a whole when the lampshade is completed it is not, therefore, necessary to balance it. Avoid pattern areas being sited so that two come together when the ends are eventually joined. If patterns are plotted in the top corner at one end, then plot the last pattern in the lower corner at the other end. The layout does need to be fairly concentrated as, when mounted, the size of the unworked areas becomes exaggerated. Squares can be linked and set obliquely; these squares do not need to be all the same size. Insertions can be included, though not longer than three units. These are usually placed horizontally as odd insertions placed vertically tend to break the continuity of the layout. A layout using vertical insertions only, however, is very pleasing; the number of units high will be determined by the plotting height available which, in turn, will determine the number of insertions required to fill the circumference.

Pattern areas can be plotted from a margin of $\frac{1}{2}$ in. (1.3 cm) at the hemmed end to within $\frac{1}{2}$ in. (1.3 cm) of the tack line registering the net circumference. Complete all the lace work.

To make up the shade, paint the rings (not the fitting bar) with any type of paint – even nail varnish is adequate. Bind the rings with

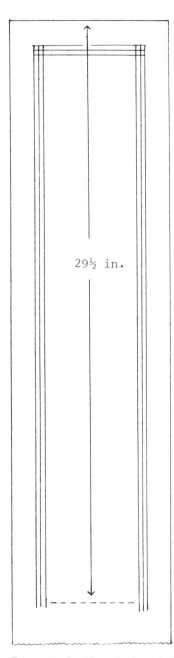

$29\frac{1}{2}$ in.

Diagram 67 *Hems for lampshade fabric*

Figure 30 *Lampshade illustrating an organised pattern layout*

the $\frac{1}{4}$ in. (6 mm) straight tape with a generous overlap. Bind the rings with $1\frac{1}{4}$ in. (3.2 cm) wide bias strips cut from the coloured lining fabric. Make any joins needed on the bias, and use a separate length for each ring. Stretch out the bias under an iron set at a heat suitable for that type of fabric – this will reduce the width

considerably – and press a narrow turning on one long side of the strips. Place the strip around the ring horizontally, tucking the raw edge under the folded one; if it is too bulky then reduce the width of the strip using thread to match that of the coloured lining, secure with over-sewing along the outer circumfer-

112

ence of the ring, so that these stitches will be covered when the stiffening is attached.

Measure the depth of the lace-worked fabric at a point where the pattern is most concentrated; this determines the depth of the self-adhesive card. Cut the self-adhesive card, depth × net circumference plus 2 in. (5 cm). Using spring-type clothes pegs, peg the self-adhesive card to the covered rings, allowing an overlap of $\frac{1}{2}$ in. (1.3 cm). Cut off the excess. Cut the lining fabric to this size, plus at least $\frac{1}{4}$ in. (6 mm) all round – more can be left then reduced later. Roll the lining fabric on to a card roller (kitchen tissue or tin foil), wrong side outer-most. The self-adhesive card tends to be slightly unwieldy. Place one end on to a table or working surface, tacky side upper-most, with the surplus hung over the edge, and control it by leaning against it. Peel off approximately 4 in. (10 cm) of the backing and place the lining fabric on to it, registering it straight with equal allowance at the end and both sides. Do not press together. Peel off and unroll to the other end, a few inches at a time. Reduce allowances to $\frac{1}{4}$ in. (6 mm) and ease the lining off the tacky surface at the edges to fold under the allowance. The lining fabric can come to the outside edge on the long sides but *not* at the ends; leave an $\frac{1}{8}$ in. (3 mm) margin of tacky surface showing here.

Secure the lined self-adhesive card to the rings, lining outermost with spring pegs. Using stab stitch attach the self-adhesive card to the rings, recessing the rings approximately $\frac{1}{8}$ in. (3 mm)–no more. Begin the thread with a knot. To work from right to left, * pass the needle on the slant through the self-adhesive card in a forward-moving direction into the ring covering, pass back through the ring covering in the same place as the needle came out and through the self-adhesive card again on a forward-moving slant. Leave approximately $\frac{3}{8}$ in. (1 cm) and repeat from * to within $2\frac{1}{2}$ in. (6.3 cm) of the end. Secure the thread. Turn the shade upside down, begin the thread $2\frac{1}{2}$ in. (6.3 cm) from the end and proceed from *. Press worked fabric. ** Whilst still damp, pin, so that the tacked circumference line is on the end of the $2\frac{1}{2}$ in. (6.3 cm) flap, into the lining fabric only. With pin heads towards the length of fabric, wrap the fabric around the shade. If the hemmed end will meet the tack line with a little stretching, then all is well; if not, note the distance by which it falls short, re-set a tack line in this position and place this in the same position as above. The four-sided stitch border may need to be extended. Remove the pins. Work bullion knots along the short hemmed end, approximately $\frac{1}{4}$ in. (6 mm) apart, leaving the corners free. If the linen has dried out or become crushed then re-press and re-attach as from **. Stab stitch the lined self-adhesive card and the worked fabric together as in diagram 68, $\frac{1}{4}$ in. (6 mm) in from the end of the self-adhesive card and $\frac{3}{8}$ in. (1 cm) apart. Because there is a $\frac{1}{2}$ in. (1.3 cm) overlap this stitching should not be visible from the inside of the completed shade. Reduce the surplus outer fabric to $\frac{1}{4}$ in. (6 mm) from the stab stitch and oversew the raw edge.

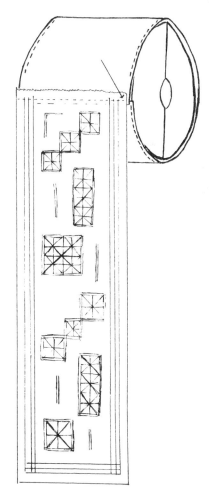

Diagram 68 *Attaching lampshade fabric to self-adhesive card*

113

Wrap the fabric around the shade and pin the hemmed end to reach the tack line. The pinning may need to be repeated a few times in order to make the end reach the desired position, so pin, then begin at one end and persuade it to reach a little further across, repeating if necessary. Remove the tack line. Using self thread, ladder stitch the two ends together.

Secure the top and bottom edges together with bullion knots, two threads deep into the fabric and over the top of the self-adhesive card, taking a good hold of the latter. The bullion knots will need quite a few more twists than usual, especially when passing over where the two ends meet. Put as many twists on the needle as is necessary to form the length the knot has to reach. When knotting the second circumference the fabric may need stretching to fit. This will ensure the fabric is evenly taut over the shade.

Wallhangings

These are a versatile use for Ruskin work. A wallhanging will be free-mounted and will, therefore, need a hem lying on all sides, probably a deeper hem on the lower end. As there will be a four-sided stitch border, some of the patterns can be linked into it. Avoid placing a central pattern shape or any borders that occur on the same parallel, otherwise the eye will 'home in' on the centre pattern or connect the borders so marring the visual pleasure. Stagger or interlock the pattern areas as much as possible, as in the Victoria and Albert Museum sampler (*see the frontispiece*) or figure 31 on p. 115 of the small wallhanging. Patterns plotted on the oblique will help the eye to travel around the article. If the article is to be long and narrow avoid insertion shapes set on the horizontal as this could interfere with the visual flow; these shapes can be equally disadvantageous set vertically as this will exaggerate the narrowness. When designing a complex layout it is perferable to make an actual size plan, using a plain paper back-

ground and cutting shapes of the lace-work area sizes from either a contrast paper or newsprint. When securing these shapes to the plan allow a $\frac{1}{4}$ in. (6 mm) all around to accommodate the four-sided stitch border. Begin the thread-drawing for the pattern areas that will be most dominant, after which it may be necessary to make amendments to the plan in order to practise the above suggestions.

The worked fabric will then need to be mounted on to a backcloth; this can be of felt, leathercloth or suede and is usually of a contrasting colour. The mount will need to be stiffened along the top and a means of hanging, probably with a cord, attached. The mount will be larger than the worked fabric, as in figure 31.

Pictures

If the picture is to be glazed, the worked fabric will be laced on to a rigid mount and will, therefore, need an all round allowance of approximately 3 in. (7.5 cm). As there will be no hems, there is no need for a continuous four-sided stitch border, which makes mounting the fabric considerably easier. (If there was a continuous border the lacing would need to be extremely accurate as any variation of tension would be very obvious.) Place a tack line at the position immediately inside the frame. The mount will eventually be this size, plus the rebate depth on the frame. A coloured lining fabric will also need to be laced on to the mount.

When planning the layout, avoid any two pattern shapes on the same side occurring at the same margin from the tack line. The planning suggestions for the wallhanging also apply here.

If the fabric is to be mounted close to the glass, bullion knot centres to any pattern are to be avoided; if a slight recess between the glass and the mount can be achieved then bullion knots can be worked to advantage, as these do add depth and texture to a pattern.

Figure 31 *Small wall hanging illustrating one of the many permutations of pattern layout. This one is mounted on to felt, as the overall linen size is only $16\frac{1}{2} \times 11\frac{1}{2}$ in. (41.8 × 29.3 cm).*

Conclusion

Heaven preserve me from a wife
with fancy run wild,
with hands which never do aught else
for husband or for child.
Our clothes are torn
our bills unpaid
our house is in disorder,
and all because my lady wife
has taken to embroider.

A verse from the 'Husband's Complaint' (slightly changed), from *A History of Needle-making*, by M. T. Morral, 1852. If this verse can be read without producing a smile then this book has not been enjoyed as intended.

Figure 32 *Book back or cover: a suggestion for pattern layout which could be used in many other ways and with many other types of backings*

List of Suppliers

UK

Lockhart Textiles Ltd
Abbotshall Road
Kirkcaldy
Fife
(*linen*)

Irish Linen Depot
39 Bond Street
Ealing
London W5 5AS
(*linen*)

Mary Allen
Wirksworth
Derbyshire
(*linen and threads*)

Mace and Nairn
89 Crane Street
Salisbury
Wiltshire
(*linen and threads*)

Christine Riley
53 Barclay Street
Stonehaven
Kincardineshire
Scotland
(*linen and threads*)

Hepatica
82A Water Lane
Wilmstow
Cheshire
(*linen and threads*)

In Stitches
48 Kings Road
Brentwood
Essex
(*linen and threads*)

Selablace
76 Main Street
Addingham
Ilkley
West Yorks LS29 0PL
(*threads*)

Dorothy Pearce
5 Fulshaw Avenue
Wimslow
Cheshire
SK9 5JA
(*threads*)

George White
Delaheys Cottage
Thistle Hill
Knaresborough
North Yorks HG5 8LS
(*threads*)

D. J. Hornsby
149 High Street
Burton Latimer
Kettering
Northants NN15 5RL
(*threads*)

Mr A. Sells
49 Pedley Lane
Clifton
Shefford
Bedfordshire
(*threads*)

de Denne Ltd
159–161 Kenton Road
Kenton
Harrow
Middlesex
(*threads*)

John Lewis Partnership
all branches with craft
department
(*self-adhesive card*)

Trefriw Woollen Mills Ltd
Trefriw
Gwynedd
North Wales LL27 0NQ
(*flannel*)

Fred Aldous
Lever Street
Manchester M60 IUX
(*lampshade rings*)

Ken & Pat Schultz
Coppins
Ixworth Road
Bury St Edmunds
Suffolk IP31 1QY

Frank Herring & Sons
27 High West Street
Dorchester
Dorset
DT1 1UP

E. Braggins & Sons
23–36 Silver Street
Bedford
Bedfordshire

Iris Martin
62 High Street
Olney
Bucks

Pat Savory
Tanglewood
4 Sanden Close
Hungerford
Berks RG17 0LB

Framecraft
83 Hampstead Road
Handsworth Wood
Birmingham B2L 1JA

Honiton Lace Shop
44 High Street
Honiton
Devon

Christopher Williams
23 St Leonards Rd
Bournemouth
Dorset BH8 8QL
(*old and new lace books*)

Brian Phillips
'Pantglas'
Cellan
Lampeter
Dyfed SA48 8JD

Christine & David Springett
21 Hillmorton Road
Rugby
Warwickshire

Jane's Pincushion
Wroxham Barns
Tunstead Road
Hoveton
Norwich NR12 2QU

Stitches
Dovehouse Shopping Parade
Warwick Road
Olton
Solihull
West Midlands

The Needlewoman
21 Needless Alley
Birmingham B2 5AE

Teazle Embroideries
35 Boothferry Road
Hull
North Humberside

Leonie Cox
The Old School
Childswickham
Near Broadway
Worcestershire WR1

Jack Piper
Silverdale
Flax Lane
Glemsford
Suffolk CO10 7RS

Mr A. R. Archer
The Poplars
Shelland
Nr. Stowmarket
Suffolk IP14 3DE

Mr R. Gravestock
The Manse
Langham
Colchester
Essex CO4 5PX

Jane Playford
North Lodge
Church Close
West Kunton
Norfolk NR27 9QY

Ann Brock
1 Ingham Close
Blake Hall Road
Mirfield
Yorkshire

John & Jennifer Ford
5 Squirrel's Hollow
Boney Hay
Walsall
WS7 8YS

Chosen Crafts Centre
46 Winchcombe Street
Cheltenham
Gloucestershire GL52 2ND

Campden Needlecraft Centre
High Street
Chipping Campden
Gloucestershire

English Lace School
Honiton Court
Rockbeare
Nr Exeter
Devon

*For information on all
aspects of lace write to:*
The Lace Guild
The Hollies
53 Audnau
Stourbridge
West Midlands
DY8 4AC

USA

International Old Lacers
P.O. Box 1029
Westminster
Colorado 80030

Berga Ullman Inc
P.O. Box 918
North Adams
Mass. 01247

Frederick J. Fawcett
129 South Street
Boston
Mass. 02030

Osma G. Tod Studio
319 Mendoza Avenue
Coral Gables
FL 33134

Robin and Russ Handweavers
533 N. Adams Street
McMinnville
OR 97128

Lacis
2990 Adeline Street
Berkeley
California 94703

Happy Hands
3007 S.W. Marshall
Pendleton
OR 97108

Arbor House
22 Arbor Lane
Roslyn Heights
NY 11577

Lace Place de Belgique
800 S.W. 17th Street
Boca Raton
FL 33432

Baltazor Inc
3262 Severn Avenue
Metairie
LA 7002

Van Sciver Bobbin Lace Supply
310 Aurora Street
Ithaca
NY 14850

The Unique and Art Lace Cleaners
5926 Delmar Boulevard
St Louis
MO 63112

The World in Stitches
82 South Street
Milford
NH 03055

Robin's Bobbins
Rte. 1 – Box 294A
Mineral Bluff
GA 30559

Bibliography

Rev. H. D. Rawnsley, *Ruskin and the English Lakes*, J. MacLehose and sons.

Frederick A. Benjamin, *The Ruskin Linen Industry of Keswick*, Micheal Moon.

H. H. Warner, *Songs of the Spindle and Legends of the Loom*, N. J. Powell and Co.

Marguerite Blake, *Revival of Spinning and Weaving in Langdale*

Patricia Baines, *Spinning Wheels, Spinners and Spinning*, B. T. Batsford Ltd.

D.M.C. Needlemade Laces, Th. de Dillmont.

Jane Lemon *Embroidered Boxes*, Faber and Faber.

Index

Edward Lear
IN THE LEVANT

Self-portrait, 21 April 1849

EDWARD LEAR IN THE LEVANT

Travels in Albania, Greece and Turkey in Europe 1848-1849

COMPILED AND EDITED BY
SUSAN HYMAN

JOHN MURRAY

For Justina, Patrick, Nora, Tobias
and Claudia Gregory

Introductory material and notes, and
selection of excerpts © Susan Hyman 1988
First published 1988
by John Murray (Publishers) Ltd
50 Albemarle Street, London W1X 4BD

British Library Cataloguing in Publication Data

Lear, Edward, *1812–1888*
Edward Lear in the Levant: travels in Albania,
Greece and European Turkey, 1848–1849.
1. English graphic arts. Lear, Edward –
Correspondence, diaries, etc.
I. Title   II. Hyman, Susan
760'.092'4

ISBN 0–7195–4614–1

Designed by Peartree Design Associates
Typeset by Butler & Tanner Ltd
Printed and bound in Great Britain
by Butler & Tanner Ltd, Frome and London

Contents

Editorial Note

In the excerpts from Lear's writings the original spelling of place names, the original punctuation and the original inconsistencies in both have been retained, except in a very few instances where confusion would otherwise arise; where modern place names differ from the Victorian ones, these are included in square brackets. Lear's footnotes to the excerpts are indicated by an asterisk. Those appended by the author are distinguished by a dagger.

The majority of the illustrations date from 1848 to 1849. The nonsense drawings, Tennyson illustrations and several of the Ionian drawings are taken from a wider span. Lear was not an artist of pronounced 'periods' and his pencilled drawings were often 'penned out' and coloured after a lapse of many years. Where the choice of illustration has not been strictly chronological, efforts have been made to avoid misrepresentation.

There are important collections of Lear's Greek drawings in the Gennadius Library in Athens and the Houghton Library at Harvard, both of which have been recently catalogued. Smaller collections are in the Ashmolean Museum in Oxford, the Graves Art Gallery in Sheffield, the Museum of the City of Athens and the Benaki Museum in Athens; the last also owns a collection of over two hundred drawings mistakenly attributed to Lear but actually by his travelling companion, Franklin Lushington. A set of signed lithographic proofs for the Albanian Journal is in the Metropolitan Museum, New York.

Apart from the published Albanian Journal, there are several primary sources for Lear's Levantine tour. The original letters to his sister Ann have vanished, but a careful typescript survives in a private collection. The journals of his tours with Charles Church and Franklin Lushington have also disappeared, but another typescript, cut and edited by Church for publication, is in the Westminster School Library. Thirty volumes of Lear's diaries for the years 1858–87 are now in the Houghton Library at Harvard; the earlier volumes have been lost or destroyed. Lear's acrimonious correspondence with Richard Bentley, the publisher of his Albanian Journal, as well as the contracts and accounts relating to that book, are preserved for posterity in the British Library.

For permission to cite or quote from unpublished material I would like to thank: Sir David Attenborough; the Bodleian Library; the Earl of Derby; Maldwin Drummond; James and Rosemary Farquharson; Donald Gallup; the Hertfordshire Record Office; the Houghton Library, Harvard

University; the Huntington Library, San Marino, California; Dr Robert Michell; the Pierpont Morgan Library, New York; the National Library of Scotland; the Robert Manning Strozier Library, Florida State University, Tallahassee; the Somerset Record Office; Somerville College, Oxford; Lord Tennyson and the Lincolnshire Library Service; Trinity College, Cambridge; the Westminster School; Malcolm Wagstaff; and Derek Wise.

For help in picture research I would like to thank the following: the Ashmolean Museum; the Blacker-Wood Library of Zoology and Ornithology, McGill University; Bradford City Art Galleries; the Trustees of the British Museum; Christie's; Davis & Long Galleries, New York; N. H. D'Oyly; the Fine Art Society; the Gennadius Library, Athens; the Government Art Collection; the Houghton Library, Harvard University; the Museum of the City of Athens; the National Portrait Gallery; the Pierpont Morgan Library, New York; William Proby; the Museum of Art, Rhode Island School of Design; and Sotheby's. I am also grateful to Thomas Agnew & Sons and Spink & Son for permission to photograph Lear's illustrations to Tennyson which were formerly in their possession.

I would also like to thank the many private collectors who have assisted me, particularly the numerous, generous descendants of Charles Church. I have been kindly helped too by many museums, galleries, auction houses, universities, libraries and record offices too numerous to mention here.

My personal thanks to James Byam Shaw, Sir Richard Brinsley Ford, Kate Fleet, Ray Gardner, Joanna Giatromanolaki, Lucy Goodison, George Hart, Kenneth Kidd, Anne Kirker, Charles Lewsen, Mercedes Lopez-Tomlinson, Lady Martin (for fascinating information about lost Lears), Stella Martin, Vanessa Martin, David Posnet, Vanessa Toll, and Stella and Stylianis Tsagarakis. For their assistance and advice I am particularly grateful to the infallible Elizabeth Garzon and to Hugo Little.

In Athens I would like to thank Karen Olsen for her help and hospitality, as well as her family and friends: Nikos Stavroulakis, Dori Kanellos, Eleni Giorgiadi and Loris Carlson. I am also grateful to Stathis Finopoulos, Basil Mostras, Evangelos Averoff-Tossizza, Eugene Vanderpool, Craig Mauzy, the British Council, the British Embassy, Cristina Varda and George Huxley at the Gennadius Library, Manos Haritatos at the Museum of the City of Athens and the American School of Classical Studies, where part of this book was prepared.

At Harvard I would like to thank Nancy Finlay at the Houghton Library for her expert help, and the Masters of Lowell House, William and Mary Lee Bossert, and their assistant Sheila Schimmel for many kindnesses during my stays there.

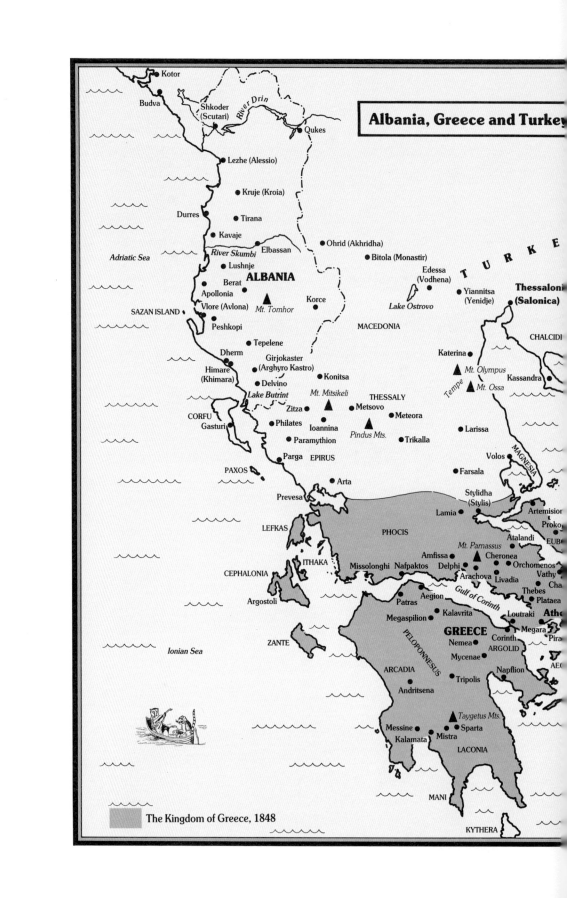

Albania, Greece and Turkey

Kotor

Budva

Shkoder (Scutari)

River Drin

Qukes

Lezhe (Alessio)

Kruje (Kroia)

Tirana

Durres

Kavaje

Ohrid (Akhridha)

Elbassan

River Skumbi

Bitola (Monastir)

Lushnje

ALBANIA

Edessa (Vodhena)

Berat

Yiannitsa (Yenidje)

Thessaloni (Salonica)

Apollonia

Vlore (Avlona)

Mt. Tomhor

Korce

Lake Ostrovo

TURKE

SAZAN ISLAND

Peshkopi

MACEDONIA

CHALCIDI

Tepelene

Katerina

Dherm

Girjokaster (Arghyro Kastro)

▲ *Mt. Olympus*

Himare (Khimara)

Konitsa

Kassandra

Delvino

Lake Butrint

Mt. Mitsikeli

THESSALY

Tempe

▲ *Mt. Ossa*

Zitza ▲

Metsovo

CORFU

Philates

Meteora

Gasturi

Ioannina

Pindus Mts.

Larissa

Paramythion

Trikalla

MAGNESIA

Parga

EPIRUS

Volos

PAXOS

Arta

Farsala

Prevesa

Stylidha (Stylis)

Lamia

Artemisio

LEFKAS

PHOCIS

Proko

Atalandi

EUB

Mt. Parnassus

Amfissa

Cheronea

ITHAKA

Missolonghi

Nafpaktos

Delphi

Orchomenos

Vathy

CEPHALONIA

Arachova

Livadia

Cha

Thebes

Aegion

Gulf of Corinth

Plataea

Argostoli

Patras

Loutraki

Ath

Megaspilion

Kalavrita

Megara

GREECE

Pira

ZANTE

Corinth

Nemea

ARGOLID

Ionian Sea

PELOPONNESUS

Mycenae

Napflion

AE

ARCADIA

Tripolis

Andritsena

▲ *Taygetus Mts.*

Messine

Sparta

Kalamata

Mistra

LACONIA

MANI

The Kingdom of Greece, 1848

KYTHERA

in Europe *c.* 1848

IN EUROPE

Black Sea

Bosphorus

**Istanbul
(Constantinople)**

Golden
Horn

Sea of Marmara

SAMOTHRACE

Ag. Oros
Mt. Athos

Sithonia

LIMNOS

Gelibolou (Gallipoli)

Troy

Aegean Sea

LESBOS
(MYTILENE)

Izmir

Kimi

Eretria

Skala Oropo

Marathon

OETIA

ATTICA

Gulf of Euboea

Sounion

SYROS

RHODES

Lear in the Levant

It is so sweet to find one's self free from the stale civilisation of Europe! Oh my dear ally, when first you spread your carpet in the midst of these Eastern scenes ... think of the people that are 'presenting their compliments', and 'requesting the honour', and 'much regretting', – of those that are pinioned at dinner-tables or stuck up in ball-rooms, or cruelly planted in pews, – ay, think of these, and so remembering how many poor devils are living in a state of utter respectability, you will glory the more in your own delightful escape.

ALEXANDER KINGLAKE, *Eothen*

They rode through the street, and they rode by the station,
They galloped away to the beautiful shore;
In silence they rode, and 'made no observation',
Save this: 'We will never go back any more!'
And still you might hear, till they rode out of hearing,
The Sugar-tongs snap, and the Crackers say 'crack!'
Till far in the distance their forms disappearing,
They faded away, – And they never came back!

EDWARD LEAR, 'The Nutcrackers and the Sugar-tongs'

The poetry of Edward Lear chronicles a number of immortal voyages, but in the pantheon of eccentric British travellers he takes pride of place not for these nonsense journeys but for his own. In an age that abounded in travel writers and travel painters, he was both, leaving a visual and verbal record of foreign lands that was unique in his own time and possibly unequalled in any other. Both in art and in literature he aspired to the profession of 'Poetical Topography', the precise, conscientious and sometimes inspired account of strange peoples and places. His single-minded devotion to the principles of the Picturesque and the aesthetics of classical landscape was retrograde even in his own day, but his appetite for the anarchic and absurd is remarkably modern. The weeping icons of Athos and the whirling dervishes of Albania would have been appreciated by the French Surrealists, who numbered the nonsense poet among their honorary ancestors.

Of the world's great travellers, Lear was among the most improbable. His health was precarious, his illnesses legion. He had no education or social position and was frequently on the verge of ruin. Gentle and pacific, he was terrified of dogs, horses and firearms, prone to severe seasickness and driven to distraction by noise and disorder. Yet he travelled incessantly for over five decades, visiting parts of Europe that were still dangerous and undiscovered, the Near East and India. In the heyday of grand hotels and fashionable resorts, he travelled on foot or on horseback, usually alone or with a solitary servant, avoiding the solicitudes of both British officials and local grandees. In old age and ill-health, he maintained his independence; abandoning the amenities of a Viceregal tour in India, he set off on an extended expedition by tonga, train and elephant. A prodigious worker, his energies and accomplishments were extraordinary even by Victorian standards: he wrote numerous travel journals, publishing four of these and three volumes of views; he painted as many as seven thousand water-colours and hundreds of oils; and in his diaries and in countless letters he recorded his experiences with the same delight in detail that informed his art. In his quest for the unspoiled and unchanged in landscape and local custom, he left a record of a world that has since been totally transformed.

Lear's Levantine tour of 1848–9 inspired some of his finest work as a travel writer and artist. His published account, the letters and journals on which it is based, and the collection of drawings that he amassed together comprise one of the most extensive records of Greece and Albania in the last century. His Greek topographies capture a countryside of great wild beauty and a landscape rich in Byzantine, Venetian and Turkish remains at a time when both were fast vanishing, as Greece returned to the western world and entered the modern age. Lear's *Journals of a Landscape Painter in Albania &c* is the most fully realised of his travel books; at the western edge of Turkey in Europe he discovered his *ultima Thule*, a land that had remained impossibly remote, geographically isolated and trapped in time.

Lear was born in Holloway in 1812, the twentieth of twenty-one children of a prosperous London stockbroker. His experience of exile dated from an early age. An awkward, ailing little boy, he suffered from bronchitis, asthma, epilepsy and strange overpowering sadnesses. After financial disasters, the family home was sold and the family itself scattered over several continents. Lear's parents seem always to have been rather remote figures in his life and now they abandoned him entirely; he was adopted by his elder sister Ann, herself old enough to be his mother, who raised and educated him as best she could. In the truest sense he was a self-made man. Edward Lear, the quintessential Victorian polymath – nonsense poet, natural historian, traveller, painter, musician and linguist, friend of royalty, statesmen, scholars, artists and men of letters – was his own most surprising creation.

He was soon travelling in widening circles. His childhood albums are full of drawings of birds and flowers, and at the age of 16, by his own account, he began contributing illustrations to volumes of natural history. Lear had no scientific training or inclinations, but he did have rare gifts as an ornithological draughtsman. His lithographs of the family of parrots, published in parts between 1830 and 1832, were compared by contemporaries to the best work of Audubon, and he went on to provide plates for many eminent naturalists. This success led to another more decisive one when in 1832 Lear was invited to draw the aviaries and menageries at Knowsley Hall near Liverpool. On his arrival he settled in the servants' hall, but he was soon diverting the Earl of Derby and his guests at dinner and enchanting the children of the house with his nonsense rhymes. During his four years there he met many future friends and patrons, and for the rest of his life he moved with innocence and apparent ease in the highest society. His adoption by the aristocracy is one of the most curious aspects of his career; possibly he was too obviously an outsider to have posed a challenge to the accepted order. From his own descriptions there is no doubt that he attended ducal dinners with the same detached delight that he brought to more exotic entertainments in the hinterlands of Albania and the Abruzzi.

Knowsley Hall shaped his artistic tastes as well, for when not drawing wattle crowned cranes and toco toucans he had the opportunity to study a gallery of Old Masters which included works by Titian, Poussin and Salvator Rosa. He visited other private collections, and at Petworth House he made a water-colour copy of a landscape with figures by Claude, an Elysian idyll inspired by an Old Testament subject. The ambitious oils which Lear hoped would secure his reputation and the carefully composed word pictures which occupy so large a place in his travel writing both derive from an outdated aesthetic and a desire to please exalted patrons. His 'Poetical Topography' belongs to a hoary humanistic tradition that sought to fuse fidelity to nature with poetic sentiment and historical allusion. Horace's famous simile, *ut pictura poesis* ('as is painting so is poetry'), might

Lear's water-colour study after Claude's Landscape with Jacob and Laban's Daughters *in the Egremont Collection at Petworth House*

have provided a motto for a lifetime's work. The marriage of the muses was consummated quite literally in Lear's illustrations to Tennyson's verse, and his long struggles with figure painting sprang less from a desire to portray people than from a wish to paint in the grand manner. Pre-Raphaelitism attracted him not only through its commitment to 'truth to nature' but also because it offered an ethical credo, a moral programme for landscape to stand in stead of neoclassical doctrine. Lear recounted with pleasure the pronouncement of a visitor to his studio that his 'father was a poet' and his 'mother a photographer'. A cross between the literal and the lyrical is typical of his best work; although his topographies were esteemed so exact that they were used to illustrate a reconstruction of the Persian

Wars,† he left as well an image of Arkady. At times the union of opposites was difficult to sustain. Some of his vast canvasses and more florid literary excursions recall the hybrid offspring of another unlikely alliance: 'Our mother was the Pussy-cat, our father was the Owl/And so we're partly little beasts and partly little fowl.'

During his Knowsley summers Lear went on sketching tours in Ireland and the Lake District. The experience was a revelation; he returned elated by his new-found freedom and invigorated by mountain walks and drawing *en plein air*. In later years he recalled this happy discovery: 'the charm of early artist life. . . The calm & brightness of the view; & the lovely sweetness of the air. . . days & years of outdoor delight'. Now he decided to leave England for Rome, and to embark on a new career as a landscape painter. His eyesight was deteriorating; the close observation needed for his natural history studies was becoming more difficult and he fretted that 'no bird under an ostrich shall I soon be able to see to do'. His health was always problematic and the English climate aggravated his chronic asthma and bronchitis. But the real attraction of 'abroad' was something wider and more undefined – independence, the possibility of a new life and the longed-for opportunity to travel.

Over the next half-century he led a peripatetic existence, creating temporary homes in Rome and Corfu and in later life a more permanent one in San Remo, returning at intervals to England, and, like the heroes of his nonsense sagas, eternally setting sail for a destination somewhere between escape and exile. When not dreaming of 'troppicle regents & specific highlands', he immersed himself in books about Arctic explorations, Borneo and the Fiji islands. Exotic place-names were intoxicating in themselves, and he was never so enraptured as when planning some new excursion. 'I strongly long to go to Egypt', he wrote. 'I am quite crazy about Memphis & On and Isis and crocodiles & ophthalmia & nubians, and simoons and sorcerers & Sphingidae'. Travel to Lear was both purpose and pretext; it fulfilled his deepest personal needs and his most pressing practical ones. Movement itself was a constitutional necessity; strenuous exercise contained his epileptic attacks and the stimulus of new settings was an effective antidote to melancholy. His paintings required a constant supply of new views, his journals required fresh incidents and adventures and he himself needed a goal to justify the long years of wandering: 'I want to topographize all the journeys of my life so that I shall have been of some use after all to my fellow critters.'

Lear's first travel book, *Views in Rome and its Environs,* published in 1841,

---

† G. B. Grundy, *The Great Persian War and its Preliminaries,* 1901.

contained twenty lithographic plates with descriptive notes and was sold by subscription. He made his début as a travel writer in 1846 with the two volumes of *Illustrated Excursions in Italy,* a record of a picturesque tour in the Abruzzi and the Papal States. It was much admired by Queen Victoria, who invited him to give her drawing lessons, and by this time Lear, whose *Book of Nonsense* appeared in the same year, had become something of a literary lion. In later years he wrote books for a more popular audience. Of his three *Journals of a Landscape Painter,* Albania and Illyria appeared in 1851, Calabria in 1852 and Corsica in 1870; and in 1863 he published another set of topographic plates, *Views in the Seven Ionian Islands.* But a list of printed works scarcely indicates the range of his endeavours. He seemed always to be writing up several journeys at once, and his diaries and letters refer to a bewildering number of journals – Nubia, Palestine, Syria, Petra and the Nile; Mount Athos, Crete, Cerigo (Kythera), 'Zagori Albania' and 'General Greek'; the Corniche and India. Most of these are now lost, although fair copies of the Cretan and Indian manuscripts survive.† The Nile Journal was completed for publication with a dedication to Holman-Hunt and advertised in 1872 on the back cover of *More Nonsense* but has disappeared without trace. Considering his other attainments, it is surprising that Lear was also one of the most prolific travel writers of his age.

'Fair Greece, sad relic'
From Christopher Wordsworth's Greece: pictorial, Descriptive and Historical, *1839*

From his letters and diaries it is clear that one of Lear's persisting dreams was to publish 'a more general Topography of Greece to be one day printed with my journals'. At various times he contemplated a series of illustrations to the scholarly and comprehensive topographical surveys of William Martin Leake,‡ in somewhat the same spirit as he later tried to adapt his collected landscapes to the poetry of Tennyson. To his friend Chichester Fortescue (later Lord Carlingford, a Liberal MP and one of Lear's closest friends) he wrote, 'I cannot but think that Greece has been most imperfectly illustrated: the detached views in Athens &c – in various towns excepted. (N.B. I don't except that vile squash of Captn Devereux's.) Wordsworth's popular vol. is all too much for effect & has not much character I think I recollect. Williams' Greece I cannot recall –.§ But the vast yet beautifully simple sweeping lines of the hills have hardly been represented I fancy – nor the primitive dry foregrounds of Elgin marble peasants &c. What do

---

† *The Cretan Journal,* based on Lear's diary rather than the surviving fragment of his journal, was edited by Rowena Fowler and published in 1984; the Indian Journal, edited by Ray Murphy, was published in 1953.

‡ Topographer of Greece, Egypt and Asia Minor, he was sent on a mission to the court of Ali Pasha in 1808.

§ W. Devereux, *Views on the Shores of the Mediterranean,* 1847; Christopher Wordsworth, *Greece: Pictorial, Descriptive and Historical,* 1839; and Hugh Williams, *Select Views in Greece,* 1829.

Aegina

you think of a large work (if I can *do* all Greece – of the Morea &
alltogether?'

As time passed, Lear came to consider himself 'a painter of Greek scenery
principally', a view that has been vindicated by time; although many of his
ambitious classical oils have long been consigned to the corners of senior
common rooms or the safekeeping of storage, his Greek drawings are now
much prized by collectors. The pencilled sketches which he later 'penned
out' and coloured in his studio were kept as blueprints for possible com-
missions and never intended for public exhibition. It was not until the
1920s, when the first large lots of these drawings were sold at auction, that
the scope of his achievement was recognised. In his lively calligraphic line
and luminous colour washes he caught the 'spirit of place' of a new kingdom
in an antique land. No artist before or since has so completely escaped from
classical or romantic conventions, or observed the landscape of Greece so
accurately or extensively.

During his decades of travel in the Mediterranean, the Near East and
India, Greece remained Lear's beau ideal. Although he lacked the conventional classical education, he was raised on the Greek myths; his early
sketchbooks contain vignettes of classical temples and Athenian owls and
he composed verses on the vanished glories of antiquity in a rousing
romantic vein. Byron was his childhood hero and as an old man Lear
remembered the cold spring evening when the news from Missolonghi
reached England and he sat alone in a garden weeping over the poet's death.

At the age of 17, inspired by the Greek War of Independence, Byron's example and Philhellenic nostalgia, he composed an ode on the Temple of Jupiter at Aegina† whose concluding stanza points a modern moral:

> Type of thy parent clime!
>   In ages past away,
> Greece was like thee sublime –
>   Like thee was bright and gay;
> And on thy mount wert thou,
>   Shrined in her orient sky, –
> A gem upon the brow
>   Of her fair liberty!
> But Greece has fallen like thee!
>   Desolate – wildly lone; –
> Her sons, the brave and free.
>   Forgotten and unknown.
> The echo of her fountains
>   Seems her lost children's sigh,
> And on her lov'liest mountains
>   Sits dark Captivity! –
> Aegina! – Greece! – the dead,
>   And ye have perished!

The notion of a lost Golden Age runs through all of Lear's writing, both public and private, informs his art, colours his travels and lends to his views of Greece a particular poetry; but it was the Golden Age of the artist rather than the antiquarian that stirred him; though studious, Lear was no historian and had no ambitions to become one. As he admitted to the Egyptian explorer, Amelia Edwards,'the details of the Egyptian Kings & Queens don't interest me a bit: – & never could, & never will ... Nor am I in the least able to bear any dates in mind, never having been up to the knowledge of numbers ... & although I am pretty clear about late history – I persist in believing that Queen Anne, Charles I, Edward 6 – Henry the 3rd & Egbert & Arthur all lived in one simultaneous sublime society & drank tea together in the New Forest or Tunbridge Wells.' The end of Lear's journey lay in a personal past – not in the classical records of the scholar or the sublime ruins of the romantic, but in some half-imagined, half-remembered image of innocence. In the clear colours of the Aegean, in the certainty of southern light, he pursued and sometimes glimpsed in the distance his longed-for Elysium: 'a bright blue & green landscape with purple hills &

The Owl of Minerva
From an early sketchbook

---

† The Doric temple at Aegina was successively identified with Zeus, Athena and Aphaia.

winding rivers & unexplored forests, and airy downs & trees . . . & all sorts of calm repose.' The inspired accuracy of Lear's Greek views reveals 'The Professor of Poetical Topography' and 'Bosh Producing Luminary' at the height of his descriptive powers.

Artistic inclinations apart, the idea of a monumental Grecian *magnum opus* made sound practical sense. Greece had long been a destination for classical scholars and aristocrats perfecting their education, but in the early nineteenth century a particular combination of circumstances popularised the country among a wider travelling public. When the Continent was blockaded during the Napoleonic Wars, the British maintained control of the Mediterranean and ensured a safe passage to Greece and eastern countries farther afield. On their cession to the British in 1815, the Ionian islands quickly became a familiar haven for English visitors. Philhellenic literature and the death of Byron fighting in the War of Independence inspired a new band of pilgrims, and by the second decade of the century Athens had become a fashionable resort of the new wealthy middle classes, as well as of scientists, diplomats, military men, intelligence officers, traders, missionaries, artists and writers. The *Quarterly Review* acknowledged the contemporary vogue: 'No man is now accounted a traveller who has not bathed in the Eurotas and tasted the olives of Attica, while, on the other hand, it is an introduction to the best company and a passport to literary distinction to be a member of the "Athenian Club" and to have scratched one's name upon a fragment of the Parthenon.'

Among travelling artists and writers, Lear was well qualified to record the country, for he had made a serious study of its language and literature, travelled widely in its ancient and modern realms and during almost every winter from 1856 to 1863 made Corfu his winter home and studio. It was a time of extreme anti-British sentiment, shortly before the Ionian islands were ceded to Greece, and in the claustrophobic English community 'things are *not* going on very pleasantly', Lear noted. 'I expect it is not the Happy Valley just now.' He had always followed Greek politics with avid interest, from the establishment of the new kingdom by the Great Powers in 1832, to the choice of the young Bavarian Prince Otho as its first monarch in 1833, the bloodless revolution of 1843 which resulted in the institution of a constitutional monarchy, and Otho's eventual deposition and deportation in 1862. Otho was subsequently replaced by an 18-year-old Danish prince who became King George I of the Hellenes, but in the interregnum speculation about his eventual successor was rife. Prince Alfred (Αλφρεδος), Victoria's second son, was the local favourite; and William Ewart Gladstone, who had once served as High Commissioner Extraordinary in the Ionian islands was one among a throng of unlikely contenders. ('Fancy Mrs

Crossing the Pindus
The top-hatted artist Louis Dupré
(centre) *carries his portfolio*
From Dupré, Voyage à
Athènes . . .

The Temple of Poseidon at Sounion

Gladstone Queen of Greece', Lear wrote in delight to Fortescue.) Lear himself considered this enticing opportunity, but was forced by a series of unexpected events to relinquish his claim: 'You may not have heard (it is not generally known,) that I refused the throne of Greece, King Lear the first – on account of the conduct of Goneril & Regan my daughters, wh. had disturbed me too much to allow of my attention to governing.'

Since Lear declined the crown, the boundaries of Greece and Turkey have been redrawn many times and the geographical distinctions cited by Victorian writers are not notable for their precision. Lear's plans for a work on 'all Greece' would certainly have included regions which were commonly identified with the Levant: Greece itself, as well as Albania, Thessaly, Macedonia, Epirus and other districts of Turkey in Europe. The Levant has always been a romantic and ill-defined term, but for the Western traveller it generally began where the Grand Tour ended, extended throughout the Ottoman Empire and was distinguished by an extreme exotic appeal. Greece was also a portmanteau province; in Murray's guide of 1854 it was generously defined as 'Classical and Historical Greece, that is to say, The Ionian Islands, The Kingdom of Greece, The Islands of the Aegean Sea, and the provinces of Macedonia, Thessaly and Albania, not yet reunited to Christendom.' Charles Church, a close friend and travelling companion, edited an anthology† of Lear's travels 'in Hellenic lands' in which Constantinople and the Troad were included. Lear's ambitions for a 'General

† Now in the Westminster School Library and apparently intended for publication, it is entitled, 'With Edward Lear in Greece: being recollections of travel in Hellenic lands two generations ago; with extracts from his letters and journals, and illustrated by his sketches. Edited by his fellow traveller, Charles M. Church, Canon and Sub-Dean of Wells'.

Greek' topography were never achieved, but the scope of his great and geographically inexact design survives in the letters and journals which document his Levantine tour of 1848–9.

In the spring of 1848 Lear was preparing to leave Rome. It was the year of revolution in Europe and the political situation in Italy was precarious. There were uprisings throughout the country, the roads were filled with troops and as the English colony in Rome dispersed and headed home, Lear considered whether he should follow. It was at this time that he met Charles Church, a classical scholar just down from Cambridge and on his way to visit his uncle in Athens. The two men became friends and Church spent pleasant evenings in Lear's rooms chatting, smoking and leafing through portfolios, while his host entertained him with ludicrous stories about visitors to his studio, quoted Ruskin, recited at length from Tennyson and (like the owl) 'sang to a small guitar – with voice pathetic & plaintive but not melodious'. Lear was tempted to accompany Church to Athens. Greece had always been his goal, but the state of the country was unsettled; there were rumours of revolution and frequent reports of travellers attacked by bandits and in the end Church left without him.

Then a letter arrived from George Ferguson Bowen,† President of the University of Corfu, inviting Lear to visit him and tour the Ionian islands. These had recently come under British protection and were a convenient starting point for tours of Greece, Albania and Ottoman domains. Lear must have been intrigued by well-known accounts of the early history of the University, an eccentric institution founded by Frederick North, later Earl of Guilford. The original professors wore gorgeous tunics of violet and orange with red leather buskins, and North himself caused a sensation by parading about London dressed as Plato. By April Lear was in Corfu, enchanted by the beauty of the place, but already planning further excursions. Having fled political upheavals in Italy he found nationalist uprisings in the Ionian islands as well and he was ready to move on.

'Greece is at present, like almost all places, a good deal excited & disturbed', he wrote to his sister Ann. 'I rather incline to a tour in Albania which is perfectly tranquil.' From Corfu the Albanian coast is preternaturally lovely; Lear noted the luminous purple mountains of Epirus 'wonderfully fine' and in the town 'here and there... an Albanian all red & white – with a full white petticoat like a doll's – & a sheepskin over his shoulder'. The English residents regularly sailed across the straits for the excellent hunting and fishing, and had he prolonged his stay Lear no doubt

† Later Chief Secretary in the Ionian islands and Governor of New South Wales. During Lear's residence in Corfu, Bowen became one of the few men Lear sincerely hated. In letters between Lear and Fortescue, Bowen is invariably referred to as 'brute', 'beast' or 'Sir Gorgeous Figginson Blowing'.

would have made this conventional passage. Sudden invitations, illness and epidemics were to alter all his plans; shaken by the 'dice-box of small events', he arrived in Albania in September, but his route was an arduous and exotic one through Turkey in Europe, and the course of his travels took him to regions where no Englishman had yet been.

Lear was not long in Corfu before meeting a friend from Rome, Sir Stratford Canning, the British Ambassador to Turkey. He was returning to Constantinople with his family and invited Lear to join their party. To Lear, who had not yet visited the Levant, the invitation was the greatest good luck and a temporary solution to uncertainties. What 'astonishing fortune to travel', he wrote to his sister. 'Don't you long to have a letter from me full of Turks & crescents & minarets?' He departed on a 'private steamer conveying His Excellency to the Grand Sultan!!!' There were naval salutes and champagne and after dinner Canning rose and declaimed Byron's 'Siege of Corinth'.

Arriving in Athens at the beginning of June, Lear rediscovered Charles Church. His uncle, Sir Richard Church, who led the Greek troops to victory in the War of Independence, was now an unofficial elder statesman of the new nation; at his house in Adrianou Street at the base of the Acropolis he entertained a polyglot company of politicians, senators, old warriors, journalists, university professors and diplomats. Charles Church remembered his uncle's aide-de-camp, who had been present at the deaths both of Byron and the Albanian chieftain Ali Pasha, as a 'tall, grey handsome old Suliot, blind in one eye, in blue and silver embroidered vest and leggings'. There were other 'men of the war in the Albanian dress, embroidered vest and *fustanella*, for the most part not talking much but smoking solemnly the long cherry-stick chiboques, or playing with their amber beads.' 'Everything around told of the new Greek life working itself out under strange conditions beneath the shadow of the Acropolis. In 1848 the times were interesting.'

With letters of introduction from the general, Lear and Church set off to explore Attica and Boetia, planning to continue to the Cannings in Constantinople and then return by way of Mount Athos, 'the Holy Land of the Greek'. It was Lear's first experience of Levantine travel in the rough, and he responded in extremes of desperation and delight. Most of mainland Greece had been devastated in the War of Independence, and the peace of the countryside was still imperilled by marauding soldiers, bands of organised brigands and the occasional, enterprising, independent bandit. The landscape often lived up to expectation, but the horses were poor, the roads non-existent, inns unheard of and the food meagre. The stringency of travelling conditions can be guessed from those passages in Murray's guide

General Sir Richard Church

which exhort the visitor to an ennobling stoicism: 'no small portion of the pleasures of travel in Greece arises from sheer hardship, which increases so much of our real enjoyment by endowing us with a frame of mind and of body at once to enjoy and endure.' The guide continues with encouragement to the antiquarian: 'If there is little physical, there is much moral entertainment . . . Even the ferocious attacks of vermin, which soon find out an Englishman, are exactly described in the graphic accounts given by Aristophanes of similar sufferings in the Greek houses of old, a reflection with which the classical scholar may endeavour to console himself in the watches of the night.' Despite the classical parallels, there was disappointment in store for the student who tried to draw too close an equation between the ancient and modern Greeks. Alexander Kinglake sadly reported the 'almost universal and unbroken testimony against the character of the people whose ancestors invented virtue.'

Despite an inauspicious beginning and some daunting discomforts, the tour was a success. Lear and Church travelled up the coast of Attica, spent a week on the verdant island of Euboea and then crossed over to mainland Boetia; but in July Lear fell ill of a fever, probably malaria, which left him weak, bald and looking 'very venerable'. When he was strong enough to make the passage to Constantinople, Lady Canning nursed him back to health at the summer embassy on the banks of the Bosphorus in Therapia and eventually he recovered sufficiently to lionise the city and attend a foot-kissing ceremony in the Seraglio, which gave him 'a wonderful idea of the Barbaric despot sort of thing one has read of as a child'. In a cemetery opposite the Adrianople gate he noted the results of a recent rebellion against the Porte: '7 stones raised round –; these are over the heads of all the great Ali Pasha's family – whom Sultan Mahommet decapitated.'

When Lear finally sailed to Salonica in September to rejoin his friend, he found that Church had been delayed and he himself was stranded. A cholera epidemic was devastating Europe, Salonica was shut up and deserted, the population camped in the environs 'living in tents' and 'eating melons', and most roads from the city were sealed. There was no possibility of reaching Church in Athos and by lingering he ran the risk of infection or quarantine, famously defined in Murray's guides as 'imprisonment with a chance of catching the plague'. He had his dragoman as well as himself to consider, for in the corrupt and class-ridden lazarettos travellers with means could purchase comforts, but servants were kept in conditions that might have been designed to effect a speedy demise.

'In this predicament', he wrote, 'I really could not bear to go back to Constantinople . . . So I struck out a new path, – & resolved to come right through Macedonia to Scutari – & so down and to Ioannina & Athens.'

It was a wild, unfrequented route across mountainous terrain, but its unfamiliarity was itself enticement: 'if I am able to execute this plan – I shall see all Albania & have a new and interesting set of drawings on quite new ground.' Within a few weeks of setting out he had hatched an ambition not only to increase his portfolio but 'to publish an entirely new book'.

Lear travelled through Macedonia and Epirus until the onset of cold weather in November, before breaking his journey to spend the winter in Egypt. On his return to Greece the following spring he made a tour of the Morea with a new friend, Franklin Lushington,† a man to whom he formed a lifelong, passionate attachment. Lear's sexual inclinations were always obscure, even to himself. He was devoted to several younger men who were conservative, conventional and – in later years – securely married; he formed firm, platonic friendships with men who were homosexual and for several decades seriously considered a proposal of marriage to a woman with whom he was never in love. Possibly his true penchant, and one encouraged from an early age, was for unrequited love, regardless of gender. He was later to remember the six-week tour he made with Lushington as the most idyllic time of his life and his image of classical Greece was always heightened by the happiness of early affections.

Lushington returned to England in April and Lear continued alone to complete his travels in Epirus and Thessaly, before crossing to Corfu in June. In the fourteen months of his Levantine tour he had visited Constantinople, classical Greece, the Ionian islands, large regions of Turkey in Europe, Egypt and Albania. In 1863 he published a set of lithographs of the Ionian islands, but of his various other projects for Greek topographies, only his Albanian Journal was printed during his lifetime. This journal and the collection of drawings he made during his tour form one of the most vivid accounts of Levantine travel in the last century and the most extensive artistic survey ever attempted of Albania.

Then as now it was the strangest corner of Europe. The narrow strait separating Corfu and Epirus offered the swiftest passage in the world between East and West, Turkey and Europe, the Middle Ages and the modern world, for the blue Chimariot mountains had formed an immemorial and impenetrable barrier against the intrusion of foreign cultures. Isolated by geography, inbreeding and eternal tribal vendettas, the country was roamed by bands of robbers, the coasts patrolled by pirates. It was not a popular destination for travellers. Gibbon placed Albania 'within sight of Italy but less known than the interior of America' and a contemporary

---

† Franklin Lushington, a barrister and magistrate, served as a judge in the Ionian islands. Lear's closest friend and one of the executors of his will, he appears to have been responsible for the destruction of some of Lear's personal papers after his death.

guide-book called it, 'one of those ill-fated portions of the earth which though placed in immediate contact with civilisation, have remained perpetually barbarian'. Apart from memorials of the patriot hero Scanderbeg, who led a long resistance against the Turks, there are practically no accounts of the country before the early nineteenth century, when the French and British established consuls at the court of Ali Pasha in Ioannina. The first travellers followed – classicists who identified Albania with ancient Illyria and hoped to discover antique sites, and others concerned with Christian

George Gordon, Lord Byron, in Suliot costume
Portrait by Thomas Phillips, 1814

history and the fate of the Eastern Church under Turkish dominion. Byron's visit in 1809, immortalised in 'Childe Harold's Pilgrimage', fixed Albania on the Romantic route. 'The wild Albanian kirtled to his knee/With shawl-girt head and ornamented gun' became a symbol of savage independence, and Ali Pasha, ruthless, luxurious and supremely cunning, the Oriental despot *par excellence*. Shortly before the Greeks rose against the Porte, Ali also rebelled, though not from the same motives. In 1822 he was defeated by loyal Turkish troops just as the Turks themselves were evicted from Greece, but the intransigent Albanians were never entirely subdued. Their heroism captured the popular imagination. The Suliot costume (in which Byron had his portrait painted) became the national dress of Greece. In England the Albanians – or Skipetars – were frequently compared to the warlike and independent Scottish Highlanders and during the Greek War of Independence, the *Athenaeum* noted, 'Tepeleni, Arghyro Kastro, Suli were names ... perpetually in the mouths of English lovers of liberty.' The Albanians were also noted for their fierce and abiding loyalty. For many years Lear employed a devoted Albanian servant, Giorgio Kokali, a 'semi-civilised Suliot, much like wild Rob Roy'.

Lear's decision to publish his Albanian Journal was more pragmatic than it may appear, for by the middle of the century there was widespread interest in this remote, archaic country. Byron's vision of the Albanian as a noble savage and of the wild brooding landscape passed into Romantic myth. 'Childe Harold's Pilgrimage' became the definitive guide for later

'The House Where Byron Stayed in Ioannina'
Engraving after a drawing by C. R.
Cockerell
From Hughes, Travels in
Greece and Albania

travellers, and even today outside the ruins of Ali Pasha's palace in Tepelene, it is available to visitors in Albanian translation. Ali himself was a splendidly evil figure, more Jacobean than Romantic in the dimensions of his misdeeds, the ruler of large areas of Greece and the Balkans and in his day one of the most famous and powerful men in Europe. Variously dubbed the 'Mohamedan Bonaparte' and the 'Ogre of Epirus', hailed by Victor Hugo as a man of genius, Ali was widely respected for his military and diplomatic acumen, skilfully playing off a succession of British and French envoys seeking to extend their influence in the Adriatic. The splendour of his court, the refinements of his cruelty and the voracity of his sexual appetites were well documented. There were reports of brides torn from the altar and beautiful boys and girls stolen from their parents to stock his harem. One horrified English visitor categorically concluded that 'of all known modern sensualists the most sensual, he exceeded whatever the most *impure imagination can conceive.'*

At the time of Lear's tour there already existed a fair body of literature on Albania, including accounts of travellers and biographies of Ali Pasha in French and English, popular novels like David Morier's *Photo the Suliot* and romantic ballads like Galley Knight's *Phrosyne*. A taste for classic vistas crowned by minarets, a predilection for what Lear calls the 'Moslem – Macedonian Picturesque', fitted easily into the orientalist vogue then current in England: the most curious product of this mood was Disraeli's early novel, *Alroy, or The Rise of Iskander,* which transforms the military hero Scanderbeg into an effete Albanian Aesthete, 'gorgeous but not classic', swathed in sables and velvet, *le tout ensemble* tellingly touched off by 'a trembling aigrette of diamonds'. Of his generation Disraeli was unusual in his support of the Ottoman Empire and his disdain for the nationalist movements of its subject peoples; during his grand tour in 1830 he volunteered to join a Turkish campaign to crush a revolt in Albania, and after his audience with the Grand Vizier in Ioannina he recorded 'the delight of being made much of by a man who was daily decapitating half the province'. Many years later the Levantine tendencies of his early travels found fuller flower in his imperial policies.

As Lear set out for Albania in September 1848, the state of the country was uncertain. Ali Pasha had controlled – and often employed – the gangs of bandits who preyed on travellers; security under the local pashas was bound to be more precarious. Lear tried to reassure Ann: 'There is no danger now in any part of Albania – & since the last insurrection the spirit of the people seems too much broken even to rob', adding sagely, 'when a man has walked all over the wildest parts of Italy, he does not prognosticate danger'. Before leaving Constantinople, he engaged a Bulgarian servant,

Disraeli with souvenirs of his Levantine tour

Giorgio Coggachio, a man of some attainments who spoke, 'Turkish, Greek, Bulgarian, Arabic & Illyric fluently, Italian and French extremely well, Albanian & English a little, & dialects of all of these without number'. He was a passable cook as well, serving Lear daily with 'a bowl of hot coffee & dry toast before sunrise – rice, fowls & a sweet omelette at 12 & tea & toast at sunset, so I live like a prince.' A Boyourdi, or letter of introduction to pashas, and a Teskere, or provincial passport were also obtained, although Lear soon discovered that various other official-looking documents, including a 'bill from Mrs Dunsford's Hotel at Malta' were equally acceptable to the Albanian gendarmerie.† Most effective of all was a quiet allusion to 'Milordos Ingliz'; the station of English travellers in the Levant was often exaggerated, partly because so many of the early ones actually had been noblemen. As ambassador extraordinary Lear was occasionally called upon to settle local disputes or convey messages to his ruler. The purchase of some gilt-covered stirrups further enhanced his mystique; in one village he heard an old Greek woman proclaim: 'this milordos is the son of a king: even his stirrups are of gold.'

The introduction to *Journals of a Landscape Painter in Albania &c* sets out in detail the arrangements and provisions necessary for a voyage into remote regions of Turkey in Europe. Some of this wisdom was no doubt bought dear, for Lear's letters and the notes on his drawings convey more candidly than his published work his virtually constant discomfort and exasperation. Across a drawing of Parga he scrawled, 'O fleas of Splantza! Did I not catch 43 just before dinner and yet now 4 more!' To his sister he complained, 'there are neither chairs nor tables here, & I cannot do anything on the ground long … living perpetually on the floor as if I had no arms or legs … breaks my back and makes my head ache.' In the Albanian khans bed was a mat on the floor and bath a portable wooden tub. A mosquito net to keep off mice and spiders was 'my most invaluable possession'. Travelling eight hours a day on a Turkish saddle, a small wooden platform on which the rider sat precariously, was agony. When drawing he was attacked by crowds of true believers who seem the very embodiment of the righteous and intolerant 'They' of the limericks; he was forced to employ a guard with a whip and soon affected a fez, as 'a hat is a signal for stones and sticks'. To some extent Lear could easily have mitigated the rigours of his journey. Had he been less independent and less jealous of his time he might have

'Ali Tebelen, Pacha de Janina'
From Dupré, Voyage à Athènes

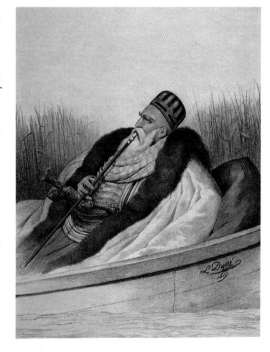

---

† Compare a recent account: 'At the barbed-wire fence we were accosted by an old shepherd with strict instructions to let nobody pass … I interpreted his "you can't get in here without a telegram from the Ministry", upon which a redoubtable lady from Kensington presented her bearer's pass to the Chelsea Flower Show. "Will this do?" she asked, as someone else hopefully produced an international driving licence, and a third showed his reader's card to Newcastle University Library' (Philip Ward, *Albania: A Travel Guide*, 1983).

Albanian Palikars
Engraving after a drawing by C. R.
Cockerell
From Hughes, Travels in
Greece and Albania

The Castle and Turkish Cemetery at Berat
Engraving after a drawing by C. R. Cockerell

enjoyed the hospitality of local beys and British representatives. Despite his complaints, he was always aware, and perhaps rather proud, that the pattern of his travels was a personal one. His explanation of the 'two alternatives' open to a landscape painter might serve as a credo for a lifetime: 'luxury and inconvenience on the one hand, liberty, hard living and filth on the other; and of these two I chose the latter as the most professionally useful, though not the most agreeable.'

Lear's observations on the countryside and people are equally idiosyncratic and always most interesting when most revealing of his own sensibilities. His 'blood boils' at the Albanian treatment of women, yoked and loaded down like beasts of burden. When he protests, abandoning his 'wonted philosophy, which ought not to exclaim at anything', he is politely reassured that 'although certainly far inferior to mules ... [women] are really better than asses or even horses.' Though he loves Greece, his attitude toward the Turks is free from Philhellenic prejudice; he appreciates their courtesy to strangers and their kindness to animals and later maintains in the face of opposition that 'the mass of Turkish people – not their governors – is honest and noble.' 'I vow if it were not for the necessity of circumcision', he wrote years later, 'I would become a Moslem even now'. He is an attentive observer of pretty women and their costumes and records plants, animals and birds with the trained eye of a naturalist. Nature and nonsense often merge in his descriptions of 'Jewesses, their hair tied up in long caterpillar-like green silk bags', a guard 'glittering like a South American beetle in purple and gold' or 'a Mohamedan sitting on a raised platform ... in his blue-green robes very like an encaged macaw'. Landscape he prefers 'savage', 'melancholy' and 'sublime'. And everywhere he remembers Byron. In Tepelene he lingers in the ruined palace 'where Ali gave audience to his Frank guests in 1809 when Childe Harold was but 24 years old† and the Vizier in the zenith of his power.' 'All was now desolation where once, and so recently, was all the rude magnificence of Oriental despotism.' Lear is seldom so stirred by antique associations as he is by the dying dreams of the modern world. Surveying the battlements at sunset, he writes, 'of all days passed in Albania, this has most keenly interested me.'

In the spring of 1849 Lear was back in England, studying for the entrance examination to the Royal Academy Schools; one of his first exhibited paintings was 'Street Scene in Akhridha, a town in Northern Albania', a work now lost. He was also planning the publication of the Albanian book and reading widely; his preparations for travelling and writing tended to be exhaustively academic. As time passed, he wore his learning increasingly

---

†Byron was 21 not 24 in 1809.

lightly, but his mind, as he himself noted, was 'concrete and fastidious', his tastes and temper scholarly. A friend recorded that before visiting a country 'he studied every book he could lay hands on that would give him the best information as to its physical characteristics and history'. In preparing his Albanian journals, he made use of several recent studies, though he particularly cites the work of William Martin Leake, the topographer and erstwhile British Consul at Ioannina. Leake's *Travels in Northern Greece* is a model of monumental nineteenth-century scholarship, erudite, dispassionate, and a rich source of information on ancient and modern history, geography, ethnography and language. Lear found his work inspiring and indispensable: 'One *must* do without comfort & one *may* do without some things one always held as necessary. But "Leake's Works" are half one's life ... the immense value of your books here ... to those who really care for the beauty and interest of Greece, is not to be told.' The discursive diary which Leake recommended as 'the most useful and faithful if not always the form of narrative most agreeable to the reader' provided the model for Lear's travel writing.

William Martin Leake
Portrait by Christian Albrecht Jensen, 1838

Lear mentions other sources: John Cam Hobhouse's *Journey through Albania* describes his travels with Byron and their splendid, seductive reception by Ali Pasha. Henry Holland's *Travels in the Ionian Isles, Albania, Thessaly and Macedonia* is a sympathetic record of the court of Ali Pasha; as his sometime medical man, Holland was once asked to recommend a good undetectable poison. The Revd T. S. Hughes published a shocked and censorious account of the Albanian ruler in *Travels in Greece and Albania*. *The Spirit of the East* by David Urquhart, an intelligent and original apologia for Islam, no doubt contributed to Lear's liberal attitudes on the 'Eastern Question'. He also studied Robert Walpole's *Memoirs Relating to European and Asiatic Turkey* and Robert Curzon's *Visits to Monasteries of the Levant* with its critical account of the Orthodox Church and the then sadly degraded Christian communities of Albania, Meteora and Mount Athos, noting characteristically Curzon's 'bad taste of ridiculing miracles'.

Many of these authorities were friends as well. The range of Lear's acquaintance was so extensive that he once predicted, 'I believe if I were the last man – someone would be created to invite me to dinner.' In his travels and at times in his nonsense and letters, he appears in the quasi-comic role of the solitary eccentric, but from contemporary accounts he was a curiously charismatic figure, eagerly adopted by fashionable and intellectual society alike. The diaries for this period of Lear's life have disappeared, but from later records it is clear that he knew a surprising number of other 'Levant Lunatics'.

Colonel Leake was a friend and mentor whom Lear consulted on points of detail. David Urquhart married the sister of a close friend; an ardent Turcophile who lived in a Moorish palace in Watford and entertained his guests naked in a Turkish bath, he was thought by Lear 'very sufficiently mad'. Sir Henry Holland, now a physician to the Queen, was a regular visitor to his studio, as were Robert Curzon, the orientalist painters John Frederick Lewis and David Roberts, the elderly diplomat Robert Morier, and the writers Richard Monckton Milnes (later Lord Houghton) and Aubrey de Vere. Lear corresponded with Byron's travelling companion, John Cam Hobhouse (later Lord Broughton), and dined with the Cretan explorer T. A. B. Spratt, the great Greek historian George Finlay and the archaeologist Charles Newton, Keeper of Antiquities at the British Museum. At the country house of friends he frequently met Austen Henry Layard, the excavator of Nineveh, who, like Byron, had been painted in Suliot costume. In later years he befriended two other authors of Albanian tours, the Oxford scholar Henry Fanshawe Tozer and Lady Strangford, wife of the Oriental Secretary to Turkey during the Crimean War. And one memorable evening he and Trelawny strolled through London after a party. They remembered Byron and the Albanian chieftain Odysseus, and like others before and since Lear noted a discrepancy between man and myth: 'He is undoubtedly a remarkable man, but the fact of his being *the* Trelawny is unsettling and puzzling.'

On 24 February 1861 Lear sat beside William Ewart Gladstone at a dinner, noting in his diary, 'Gladstone was really charming – talked of Corfu – Athens', but whether they recalled their respective candidacies for the Greek kingship is unrecorded. Lear's relationship with Alexander Kinglake, the celebrated author of *Eothen,* is uncertain and intriguing. They had many mutual friends and interests, and as inveterate diners-out in London must frequently have met. Lear must have been influenced by the self-deprecating wit of Kinglake's Eastern account as well as by the elegant egocentrism of his approach. 'I believe', Kinglake maintained in the preface to his book, 'I may truly acknowledge that from all details of geographical discovery or antiquarian research – from all display of "sound learning and religious knowledge" – from all historical and scientific illustrations – from all political disquisitions – and from all good moral reflections, the volume is thoroughly free.' The mock humility of this manifesto is often echoed by Lear, and as travel writers they have much in common. It is known that they corresponded, but neither left a record of the other; in Kinglake's case, as in that of another contemporary rival, Lewis Carroll, Lear's silence is suggestive.

Journals of a Landscape Painter in Albania &c† was published by Richard

---

†The title on the spine was *Journal of a Landscape Painter in Albania & Illyria.*

Bentley in 1851, the first of Lear's travel books in a small format, and the first to be sold commercially rather than by private subscription. The twenty lithographic plates are both atmospheric and topographically accurate, an advance on the moonlit minarets and celebrations in the seraglio which graced earlier accounts of these regions. Lear's illustrations convey the bleakness of the country as well as its beauty, its classic vistas and its desolation. Like a latter-day Dr Syntax in Search of the Picturesque, Lear assembled a series of views; the finely drawn word pictures portray the countryside seen through the eye of the artist, while the plates are both literal illustrations and evocations of the vast dramatic scene which inspired the traveller. Presenting the 'memoranda of an artist's mere tour of search among the riches of far-away landscape', Lear wisely abandons the conscientious tracts on history and geography, the learned allusions, tables and charts which burdened *Illustrated Excursions in Italy*. The Albanian Journal is modest, humorous and impressionistic, and the informality of a daily journal evidently suited him well, since he followed the form in his later travel books. Despite the elaborate comic set pieces and lengthy discussions on landscape, the published account is remarkably close to the record he left in his letters.

Map from Charles Church's copy of the Albanian Journal, Lear's routes traced in ink

It was in this book as well that Lear discovered his voice as a traveller. Humour was an effective way of approaching the exotic and he had the rare ability to appreciate the absurd without analysing it. His early training as a naturalist established scientific habits of mind which proved of use in his other pursuits; in later life he depicted strange countries and people with the same sharp eye and quizzical detachment he had earlier brought to the observation of parrots, owls and moles. Behind the professional persona of the Poetical Topographer there are occasional glimpses of another quite different man, sensitive, alienated and moody. In Lear's other travels, in the many nonsense songs which describe voyages, and in his diaries, the imagery of journeys is associated with exile, beauty in nature with paradise lost. He often recalled the engravings of landscape in a childhood copy of Robinson Crusoe, a novel about isolation and self-reliance, and in the last years of his life he was absorbed in the painting of a monumental illustration to Tennyson, an enormous oil of 'Enoch Arden's Island', the lonely paradise of another shipwrecked sailor. The private meaning of Lear's long years of wandering may be guessed at, but the enduring voice of the traveller is the public one of the Englishman abroad, with its characteristic counterpoint of the picaresque and the picturesque, the earnestly aesthetic and the absurd.

Lear's dealings with the publishers of his many books of nonsense, travel and natural history tended to be disastrous and Richard Bentley was no exception; the Bentley Papers, now in the British Library, preserve a heated correspondence. The two men quarrelled over production expenses and the terms of the contract, and when Bentley's firm foundered in 1855, Lear noted bitterly, 'as I got nothing before I can't get less now, so that makes no difference.' But though failing financially, the book was a critical success. *Journals of a Landscape Painter in Albania &c* went into a second edition in 1852 and was appreciatively reviewed in the literary periodicals as a useful practical manual, 'a perfect handbook and guide into this classical region'. Lear's host in Corfu, George Ferguson Bowen, the editor of Murray's 1854 *Handbook for Travellers in Greece* commended 'the excellent advice of Mr Lear'. Later editions continued to rely on Lear's scrupulous descriptions of the country and his sensible recommendations for travellers; for the Master of Nonsense it was a small and singular celebrity.

The tribute that most touched Lear came from Tennyson. Lear had met the poet in 1849 and two years later had sent him copies of his Abruzzi and Albania books as a wedding present. Emily Tennyson wrote back warmly: 'very often shall we delight ourselves by looking upon those beautiful drawings, which give one, as Alfred said of one in particular, something in the glory of nature herself looking upon them.' Tennyson himself responded with an encomium, 'To E.L. on his Travels in Greece'.

> Illyrian woodlands, echoing falls
>   Of water, sheets of summer glass,
>   The long divine Peneian pass,
> The vast Akrokeraunian walls,
>
> Tomohrit, Athos, all things fair,
>   With such a pencil, such a pen,
>   You shadow forth to distant men,
> I read and felt that I was there:

Subsequent images of 'naiads', 'classic ground' and 'golden age' are redolent rather of Arcadia than Albania, but the compliment was a kind one, and strengthened Lear's conviction that he was the painter best suited to illustrate Tennyson's verse. Characteristically, he later lampooned both Tennyson's lofty praise and his own most elevated aspirations.

> Delerious Bulldogs; echoing calls
> My daughter – green as summer grass:–
> The long supine Plebeian ass,
> The nasty crockery boring falls;
>
> *Tom – Moory* Pathos; – all things bare, –
> With such a turkey! Such a hen!
> And scrambling forms of distant men,
> O! – ain't you glad you were not there!

1

Ulysses'
Kingdom

In September 1847 Lear was travelling in Calabria, then part of the Kingdom of Naples, and witnessed the first signs of an insurrection that led to a full-scale revolt the following winter. As gunshots rang out one evening, his host abruptly announced, 'the Revolution has already begun'. That January the people of Palermo came out in open rebellion against the Bourbon King and within months there were uprisings against Austrian domination in Lombardy, Milan and Venice. In the year of European revolution, nationalist and democratic fervour swept France, Germany, Austria and Hungary in a succession of events as swift as they were extraordinary. As Lear's friends and patrons fled Rome, he considered his future, an unexpected offer from Corfu and the prospect of a long awaited tour in Greece.

Letters to Ann Lear

Rome. 16 October 1847

I will not lose any time here in sending off ever so short a letter, for you may possibly (in spite of my begging you never to be so,) be alarmed at the accounts the English papers contain about revolutions in Calabria & Naples – people being skinned alive & murdered etc. etc. etc. – all of which great nonsense – may have reached your ears, & have frightened you. So I hasten to add that I am neither skinned nor robbed, but quite well.

Rome. 15 November 1847

I have had a most advantageous invitation from Corfu – to come to stay there free of expense in April, & to see the Greek islands with all kind of agreeable facilities. A friend – (not a very old one,) has a Govt. situation there, & would do anything to make me enjoy such a tour, & possibly would accompany me to some of the islands. I cannot but confess I should like to see Turks & turbans & Greeks extremely.

Rome. 25 January 1848

I do not know if you read the papers – perhaps better not. But I can tell you, we are in a queer state. Sicily is utterly revolted & gone; & we wait daily for certain news ... Every day brings ugly tidings from Naples, & the English are fast leaving it & flooding here. The foolish King will not take warning, & worse events must follow. Do not be alarmed, even if you hear of any disturbances – this place is quite safe for a good time to come. At Naples all the shops are shut, & there are reports that the K. will bombard the city; others say his army has refused to fire on the people. Nobody knows the truth but everybody is running away.

Saint Peter's, Rome

*L*ife in the Papal States was becoming daily more problematic; the Pope himself was known to hold liberal views and in March Lear noted in letters to his sister 'the late wondrous change in France' and 'unexpected events in Vienna'; it was time to leave Rome. Travelling to Ancona, he found the port closed and all communications in the north broken by the revolution in Lombardy. At the end of the month as he turned south towards Naples, troops were gathering along the road.

The Villa Albani, Rome

Letter to Chichester Fortescue

Rome. 12 February 1848

It is a propitious season, the rumours of distraction prevented a many nasty, vulgar people from coming, and there is really room to move ... The variety of foreign society is delightful, particularly with long names: e.g. Madame *Pul-its-neck-off* – and Count Bigenouff; – Baron Polysuky, & Mons. Pig: – I never heard such a list. I am afraid to stand near a door, lest the announced names should make me grin. – Then there is a Lady Mary Ross, and a most gigantic daughter – whom Italians wittily call 'the great Ross-child' ... Somehow the 6 & 30-ness of my sentiments and constitution make me rather graver than of old: – also, the uncertainty of matters here and everywhere, and my own unfixedness of plans, conspire to make me more unstable & ass-like than usual ...

I have a plan of going to Bowen at Corfu, and then Archipelago or Greeceward (Greece however is in a very untravellable state just now) should the state of Italy prevent my remaining in it for the summer. But whether I stop here to draw figure, or whether I go to Apulia & Calabria, or whether I Archipela go (V. A. Archipelago, P. Archipelawent, P. P.

Archipelagone) or whatever I do. I strongly long to go to Egypt for the next winter as ever is . . .

I have a strong wish also to see Syria, & Asia Minor and all sorts of grisgorious places, but, but, who can tell? You see therefore in how noxious a state of knownothingatallness – aboutwhatoneisgoingtodo – ness I am in. Yet this is clear: – the days of possible Lotus-eating are diminishing, & by the time I am 40 I would fain be in England once more . . .

Letter to Ann Lear

Malta. 9 April 1848

My journey down to Naples by diligence was most extremely pleasant, – though naturally most unlike any previous one I had ever made. It would be quite impossible to make you understand how a few short months have changed all things & persons in Italy – for indeed I can hardly believe what passes before my own eyes. Restraint & espionage has given universal place to open speaking & triumphant liberal opinions. One of my fellow passengers was a Neapolitan noble, exiled for 16 years; – when he saw Vesuvius first, he sobbed so that I thought he would break his heart. Naples, I found yet more unsettled & excited than I had left Rome. Noone could tell what would happen from one hour to the next. The King still reigns, but I cannot think he will long do so. All the English were running away & the resident bankers etc. etc. frightfully harrassed & uneasy as to the future. As usual, I found numbers of friends at Naples & had dinner invitations for the 6 days I was to stay. The English fleet being there made a deal of gaiety . . . We left the harbour at noon on the 6th & truly glad was I to be out of Italy – I assure you – not from any fear of danger, but because the whole tone of the place is worry, worry, worry – & I am sick of it.

The steamer stopped at Malta, Byron's 'little military hothouse', where Lear found many of his friends from Rome. Malta itself, deplorably lacking in drawable landscape, never captured his imagination despite 'every variety of luxury, animal, mineral and vegetable – a Bishop and daughter, pease and artichokes, works in marble and filigree, red mullet, an Archdeacon, Mandarin oranges, Admirals and Generals, Marsala wine 10d a bottle – religious processions, poodles, geraniums, balls, bacon, baboons . . .' After a week of dinners and parties he endured a squally crossing to the Ionian Sea, taking to his bed immediately and remaining there in great misery. Never a robust traveller, Lear detested boats almost as much as he loathed and feared horses. His description of seasickness – 'bowels, stomach, toes, mind, liver – all mixed together. It does not seem to me that actual death can be more horrible' – shows a certain sense of fatality. On the evening of the third day out the wind suddenly dropped, the sea subsided, a full moon rose over Cephalonia, and Edward Lear was in Greece.

Not yet the Kingdom of Greece, for the Ionian islands did not gain their independence until 1864 and their recent history was complex. In the contest for control of the Adriatic, they passed from Venetian to French rule in 1797, were subsequently seized by the Russian fleet, returned to the French and finally ceded to the British under the terms of the Congress of Vienna in 1815. The town of Corfu swelled with the families of British military men and civil servants, and the splendid Italianate palace of the British High Commissioner served as the centre of a Lilliputian colonial court. The islands quickly became a popular retreat for English travellers who could enjoy the idyllic scenery and picturesque natives, good sport and elevating expeditions to supposedly Homeric sites with all the comforts of the Home Counties.

Letter to Ann Lear

University of Corfu. 19 April 1848

Monday evening it became still all at once among the Ionian Isles & a lovely evening we had – full moon. Cephalonia & Zante are charming. Next morning, we were at Patras, (a round about voyage, but the mails are so taken,) & then, passing Missolonghi, where Lord Byron died, we came to Ithaca, Ulysses's island – & later to Leucadia whence Sappho leaped into the sea.† About 3 this morning – we anchored in the beautiful Paradise of Corfu bay, & here I am, in the most perfect library possible, with a bedroom to match, looking out on the calmest of seas, with long lines of wooded hill fringed with cypresses & dotted with villas running down into the water. These rooms are in the University & belong to my very kind friend Mr. Bowen – whom I dare say you never heard of before – nor have I known him long – but he, being an intimate of Fortescue, & others of my old friends, & hearing that I was coming to Corfu – wrote to me in the kindest manner & put these rooms & his servant at my disposal – be he here no not. Unfortunately, he is not here, having left 4 days ago only; but, as he is gone to Cephalonia, I am going off next Saturday in the Ionian steamer to catch him, & shall then have the opportunity of seeing Zante etc. in his company – a great advantage as he is Rector of the college here,

There was an old man of Corfu. Who never knew what he should do . . .

---

† 'Sappho's Leap' on the island of Lefkas was a favourite subject of travelling artists and poets. In antiquity leaps from this rock were performed as a trial or cure for unrequited love, sometimes with rescue boats handy.

The Citadel at Corfu

& has office over all the Ionian islands. So you see I fall on my legs again don't I? I ought really to be most thankful for the number of friends I find. No sooner am I here than the Lord High Commissioner asks me to dinner, so there I dined today – & here come 2 more invitations! Gracious! I had need have as many heads as a hydra to eat all . . .

Corfu – the island, is very long & narrow & close to the coast of Albania. The city was Venetian until 1780† – but it has little to recommend it – narrow streets & poky houses. But nearest the sea, there is the most beautiful esplanade in the world – (on one corner of which I now look). On the farther side is the magnificent palace of the Viceroy, (now Lord Seaton –)‡ & beyond is the double crowned Citadel . . . This afternoon I have been wandering all about & nothing can be more lovely than the views . . . The extreme gardeny verdure – the fine olives, cypresses, almonds, & oranges, make the landscape so rich – & the Albanian mountains are wonderfully fine. All the villages seem clean & white, with here & there a palm tree overtopping them. The women wear duck, black or blue, with a red handkerchief about the head; the men – the lower orders that is, mostly

---

†Actually until 1797.
‡ Sir John Colborne, Baron Seaton. After a long military career he served as Lord High Commissioner of the Ionian islands from 1843 to 1849.

red caps – & duck full Turkish trousers. Here & there you see an Albanian all red & white – with a full white petticoat like a doll's & a sheepskin over his shoulder. Then you meet some of the priests – who wear flowing black robes & beards. Mixed with them are the English soldiers & naval officers, & the upper class of Corfiotes who dress as we do; so that the mixture is very picturesque.

Letter to Ann Lear

Corfu. 14 May 1848

Not finding my friend Bowen here ... off I set again in an Ionian steamer – starting very early, & arriving at Argostoli (the capital of Cephalonia) at midnight – where we took up Mr. Bowen, & at dawn we were at Zante, the southernmost of the larger islands ... & more like one large garden than anything I can compare it to. The town stands by the side of a beautiful bay – & is little more than one or two long streets, while behind, there rises a long, high hill, crowned by the castle. This hill is all split & cracked in a very ugly way – by continual earthquakes, which perpetually occur: & every 20 years the result is very serious; but the intermediate shocks are harmless & nobody minds them a bit – though I must say I should not like to live always in such a neighbourhood. We went to a quiet little inn – not too clean, but just decent. All the towns in the Ionian Isles are badly off for lodgings – so few people go there ... The strange feature of the place is that there are no women visible – the old Turko-Venetian custom still prevailing so far as that none of the better class of females go out a bit. Bowen having letters to all the first people, I saw a good deal of the families – & they are very courteous nice people; – all speak Italian, except the peasants ...

One day I went up Mt. Skopo, a high hill at the end of the bay – looking from the top of which a great part of this pretty isle is at your feet like a map. Nothing but a bright green carpet is like it. The carpet is all short grape vine, which produces what we call red currants in England, such as you put into 'currant dumplings', & 'currant buns'. I declare I always thought those little black 'currants' were currants. But they are real grapes, & are part of immense bunches from the little vines, miscalled also currant trees. They came originally from 'Corinth' – whence 'currant' in course of time ... that part of the island which is not all currants is olive ground. Some views of the castle hill from the gardens are very pleasing but not striking or grand. Neat little villas, neat little churches, all the roads trim & cut, – everything is pretty & nice in Zante.

On May 1st, I steamed away to Ithaca ... Ulysses's kingdom is a little island – & charmingly quiet. I delight in it. The chief town – formed of

Niphes, Corfu

Potamos, Corfu

houses entirely modern, is called Vathi – & it stands at the end of the harbour, so shut in by hills that you would think you were by a lake ... In the afternoon we went to the fountain of Arethusa, – & all along the views are quite lovely – of the opposite Greek shore, & of the Ionian Isles, Santa Maura [Lefkas] & Cephalonia. On the 3rd May I proposed going over to Cephalonia, so early I went up to the ancient ruins of Ulysses's city & castle†; vast walls of Cyclopean work – (like those in the first plate of my Roman book,) & sufficient left to attest the truth of the renown of old Ithaca ... 7 hours of a dead calm hardly sufficed to take my ferry boat over to Samos bay – but I wasn't sick, so I can't complain. Samos‡ was the greatest of all the cities here about, & that from which the suitors of Penelope came. At present there are not 10 houses – a mere fishery. In one I got a bed & ordered some supper – going forthwith up to the Citadel – the walls of which are magnificent & astonishing, & I am very glad I got there in time to draw them. Next day I walked over 14 miles to Argostoli – the capital of the Island ... fronting the grand 'Black Mountain'; here is a very decent inn ... I found the chaplain very kind, as well as the officers to whom I had letters of introduction; – an odd change in my summer life is it not? – that whereas I used to be living scantily in Italian cottages – I am now drinking champagne etc. every day at splendid tables – rather more good living than I like to tell the truth.

Argostoli, Cephalonia

*O*n 10 May Lear was back in Corfu and two days later he celebrated his birthday at a dinner given by Bowen. 'I am sure', he wrote to Ann, 'you never could have guessed 36 years ago that I should ever carve a loin of mutton for 10 Greek Professors in this University.' Waiting for the arrival of friends, he considered his next destination. The radical winds of 1848 had fanned nationalist sentiment in the Ionian islands and uprisings on the mainland; by contrast Albania and Epirus seemed a 'perfectly peaceful' prospect. Meanwhile he bought a grammar, started to study modern Greek and made his first efforts at writing and speaking a language in which he later attained some fluency. He began a walking tour of the island, exploring the coastal paths, the whitewashed villages and monasteries, making rapid sketches and detailed notes on costumes, birds and flowers. His drawings from this period evoke his delighted discovery of the Greek countryside in springtime with their pencilled memoranda: 'myrtle & cistus in flower', 'walnut', 'fig', 'ivy', 'wilderness of gray olives', 'abyss of cypress', 'sea deep deep nearly black'. Then, six weeks after his arrival, he found himself suddenly by some sublime caprice swept up by an ambassadorial suite and on his way to Constantinople.*

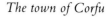

The town of Corfu

---

† These ruins on Ithaca were mistakenly identified as the Homeric citadel.
‡ The ancient capital of Cephalonia.

Athenian costume study

Letter to Ann Lear

Athens. 3 June 1848

You will be immensely pleased, particularly at the manner in which I have
the astonishing good fortune to travel. You must know that Lady Canning,
the wife of Sir Stratford Canning, our ambassador to Turkey – has often
asked me to go & see her at Constantinople, which I was obliged to her so
doing, but thought I had as much chance of visiting the moon . . .

Now since I wrote I had resolved to make a little tour to the south end
of Corfu . . . [At Gasturi] I sate down to sketch, & lo! who should come by
with a great train but all Lord Seaton's people – & Sir S. & Lady Canning
to my infinite surprise. They were on their way from England straight to
Constantinople & were to remain a week at Athens besides. – Nothing
would serve kind Lady Canning but my coming with the Embassy – so
Lady Seaton whirled me off to dinner – the next day I packed up – & on
the 30th I was actually bag & baggage in the private steamer conveying
His Excellency to the Grand Sultan!!! Did you ever hear such a funny
affair, so evidently without my own will almost? – Of course everybody
congratulated me very much. Just think: – I am always with this most
delightful family – or the secretary Lord Augustus Loftus† – I am at no
expense – to see the finest scenery in the agreeablest way, & shall have
advantages at Constantinople none but the Ambassador's friends or family
could ever hope for. You know Sir Stratford Canning is considered as one
of the very first living diplomats & has been for ages in Turkey managing
Eastern affairs; he is besides a most cultivated & amiable person, & thus this
journey is in all respects very desirable for 'your son'. Lady Canning is
goodness itself & so are the 3 daughters . . . We are not to live in Constantinople, but in a palace at Therapia on the Bosphorus. Don't you long
to have a letter from me full of Turks & crescents & minarets?

Journal

1 June 1848

Off Patras at 8–9. Drew. Consul and Vice-Consul came on board (both
'Wood'. Bosco Vecchio et Verde). Beautiful weather. Lunch at 12. At
3 p.m. Vostitza [Aegion]. Went on shore with Sir Stratford C. and Lord
A.L. Wonderful dresses! House. Greek women. I have never seen anything
so new and beautiful qua costumes for many years, since first I saw the
Rocca San Stefano and Civitella dresses in 1838.

† Augustus William Frederick Spencer Loftus, later Marquess of Ely, Ambassador to Berlin and
Governor of New South Wales.

Shall I remember these lovelinesses, these pure grey-blue seas, these clear skies, cut chiselled hills, and bright white sails, and glittering costumes, and deep shadows, when I am far away from them; if indeed I live?

The mountains grew finer as we steamed onward, opposite Parnassus, whose vast and snowy form seemed to me more grand than beautiful, and the gorges and individual characters of each hill were really sublime.

Good dinner at 6, the two Consulars of the party. On deck by sunset – gorgeous! Long talk, Sir Stratford and Lady C. Sir S. quotes Byron's 'Siege of Corinth'. Tea, very pleasant. Then in growing darkness we reached Loutraki, before 10 p.m. Acro-Corinth dimly visible . . . Perhaps indeed to-day may have been the most completely happy social day I have passed for a long time.

Head of a Greek woman

*T*he ambassador's man-of-war continued along the Gulf of Corinth and wherever it stopped the Greeks crowded the shore to see 'O Kýrios Sir Canning', as famous for his Philhellenic sympathies as for his long years of service at the court of the Sultan. The difference between the peaceful and verdant Ionian islands and the mainland ravaged by recent war was striking. The great Graeco-Roman city of Corinth was 'a scattered dirty place', its Acropolis 'a mere heap of desolation . . . so continually destroyed by Turks that only the walls are standing'. The party rode across the isthmus, boarded another steamer and arrived in Piraeus that evening to military salutes and fireworks, 'an honour', Lear confessed, 'I should always like to dispense with'.

2

Turks, Turbans and Greeks

*T*he Athens which Lear saw in 1848 was the fulfilment of a northern European dream. The village clustered at the base of the Acropolis had been chosen as the capital of the new kingdom for symbolic reasons. Bavarian and Danish court architects laid out a modern city with wide boulevards and neoclassical buildings, and soon after independence completed the Royal Palace† and the University, that curious essay in the polychrome antique which still bemuses visitors to the city. Turkish and Venetian survivals were more interesting to the

† Now the Parliament building.

The Temple of Olympian Zeus, Athens

The Temple of Apteros Nike, Athens

artist, and the great classical sites an inspiration beside which 'poor old scrubby Rome sinks into nothing'. For two weeks Lear rose before dawn, 'working like mad' in the summer heat, 'seeing nothing else and no-one', drawing until sunset.

Letter to Ann Lear

Athens. 3 June 1848

I have risen as early as I could this morning, & surely never was anything so magnificent as Athens! Far more than I could have any idea of. The beauty of the temples I well knew from countless drawings – but the immense sweep of the plains with exquisitely formed mountains down to the sea – & the manner in which that huge mass of rock – the Acropolis – stands above the modern town with its glittering white marble ruins against the deep blue sky is quite beyond my expectations. The town is all new – but the poorer part of it, what with awning & bazaars & figures of all possible kinds is most picturesque ... The hotels here are tolerably good – very clean – but *extremely* dear – & all the little comforts of dear old Italy – the ice, fruit, etc. etc. are quite unknown though the climate is infinitely hotter ... The King's Palace is a very ugly affair – though built of white marble also ... The King wears the full Greek dress and rides about often with the Queen. I wish you could see the temple of the Parthenon or the

The Parthenon

Acropolis by sunset – I really never saw anything so wonderful. Most of the columns being rusty with age the whole mass becomes like gold & ivory – & the polished white marble pavement is literally blue from the reflection of the sky. You walk about in a wilderness of broken columns, friezes, etc. Owls, the bird of Minerva, are extremely common, & come & sit very near me while I draw.

Charles Church, now living in Athens with his uncle, General Sir Richard Church, was delighted to rediscover his friend from Rome, introducing Lear to the house in Adrianou Street which had become a gathering place for ageing Philhellenes, veterans of the War of Independence and leaders of the new nation. Lear also dined frequently with the Cannings at the British Ministry. Most English travellers were liberally provided with letters to the local lions, but for a beginner in Greece Lear was moving in interesting circles in interesting times, for there were uprisings throughout the country and constant rumours of a coup d'état *in the capital.*

When the Cannings decided to prolong their stay in Athens, Lear and Church saw the chance of a tour in Attica and Boetia, hoping to reach Delphi before returning for the voyage to Constantinople. On 13 June they set off for Marathon equipped with numerous letters of introduction from General Church, a servant named Janni, a cook, three baggage horses, two iron bedsteads and two of Mr Levinge's patented muslin bell tent-cum-sleeping bags. Lear described the trip in a letter to his sister; the entries from his journal provide a less polished but more candid record of a tour that began with misadventure and ended in catastrophe. In the corner of an Euboean drawing, he summarised his sentiments in a paraphrase from Tennyson's 'Temple Art': 'I hear the roar of an unknown sea/and a new land – but I die'.

Letter to Ann Lear

Athens. 19 July 1848

I must tell you something of my last tour, – which I took with a friend, Church, – a most kind and agreeable as well as learned companion. He is besides, a good Greek linguist, and nephew of General Sir Richard Church, who was & is one of the great Athenian senators, & movers of the new country. We went first to Marathon, which as you know, is one of the famous places in the world, as that where the Athenians defeated the Persians under Xerxes. The place like all such in Greece is quite unchanged by time, & the exact points of the battle are as exactly to be followed as those of Waterloo. A vast tumulus still marks the site of the buried Persians.† All Greece, you must know, is *most thinly* inhabited, & for a whole day you may meet only a few peasants. This is the way of travelling. We hire a man who undertakes to do *everything* for a certain sum a day; he finds us horses & has others for our baggage, & for his cooking utensils & for provisions & for beds: we were in all 7 horses. We start at sunrise after a good breakfast of coffee and eggs – & we then travel till 10. Then we halt in some village or near a fountain & a tent is pitched, & in about 2 hours a most capital dinner – soup & 3 courses is set forth! So you see there is not much hardship. Then we go on till at dusk we reach some village where any house does for our night's dwelling – for little iron bedsteads with mattresses are put up directly, & on these a large muslin bag tied to the ceiling, into which I creep by a hole which is tied up directly, so that no creature gets in and one sleeps soundly in a room full of vermin. I thought I should have laughed all night long the first time I crept into this strange bag, but soon got used to it. In the morning all is packed – and off we go again. We went from the ruins of Rhamnus, all along the coast to Oropo & so to Chalchis, that famous old city in the island of Euboea or Negropont . . . Chalchis delighted me, as being full of old Turkish houses and minarets, the first I had seen –; you have no idea of the picturesqueness of the people. Every group makes one stare and wonder. The houses are very full of bow windows and lattices, but the town is very wretched. All the great towns – except 3 or 4 – are

X was King Xerxes,

---

†Lear was mistaken. It was Athenians not Persians who were buried at the site.

Storks, Larissa

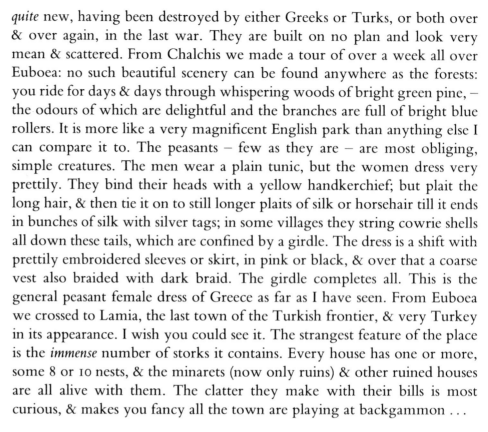

quite new, having been destroyed by either Greeks or Turks, or both over & over again, in the last war. They are built on no plan and look very mean & scattered. From Chalchis we made a tour of over a week all over Euboea: no such beautiful scenery can be found anywhere as the forests: you ride for days & days through whispering woods of bright green pine, – the odours of which are delightful and the branches are full of bright blue rollers. It is more like a very magnificent English park than anything else I can compare it to. The peasants – few as they are – are most obliging, simple creatures. The men wear a plain tunic, but the women dress very prettily. They bind their heads with a yellow handkerchief; but plait the long hair, & then tie it on to still longer plaits of silk or horsehair till it ends in bunches of silk with silver tags; in some villages they string cowrie shells all down these tails, which are confined by a girdle. The dress is a shift with prettily embroidered sleeves or skirt, in pink or black, & over that a coarse vest also braided with dark braid. The girdle completes all. This is the general peasant female dress of Greece as far as I have seen. From Euboea we crossed to Lamia, the last town of the Turkish frontier, & very Turkey in its appearance. I wish you could see it. The strangest feature of the place is the *immense* number of storks it contains. Every house has one or more, some 8 or 10 nests, & the minarets (now only ruins) & other ruined houses are all alive with them. The clatter they make with their bills is most curious, & makes you fancy all the town are playing at backgammon . . .

Journal

15 June 1848

It was 6 a.m. before we got under way. Church and I in saddle, also Janni in flare-up red Turkish dress. Cook and 3 baggage horses followed. Soon after we had left the city, perhaps an hour, we were galloping, when my horse came down like a shot. I fell over his head and was much hurt in the shoulder and side. We pass behind Lycabettus and go straight towards Pentelicus, leaving Hymettus right. Vast lines, wide plain; two little villages, Marousi, Kephissia. My arm getting worse, walked . . . very ill and in great pain. Church advised going back, but resolved to go on. Janni gave us an excellent dinner in the tent under almond trees . . . Came in sight of Bay and Plain of Marathon, descent among fine pines. Church gallopeth. Herds of goats and cattle. Sunset. Arm very bad, rubbed by Church. Mosquito.

16 June 1848

Thank God. I slept a good deal, from having been so tired, but woke in great pain. Difficult task to wash and dress. No perceptible power as yet of moving my arm, though I suffer less pain. Good breakfast. Janni not ready till 5.30, when we left. Walked, for I could not mount my horse, on account of my arm. Shady side of hill above plain of Marathon. Edge of marsh where Persians was drownded. Fine black, but savage, dogs. Superb scattered oak trees. Struck inland – a monotonous, hilly plain; oaks here and there. Sun hot; arm very bad; tired and ill.

9 a.m. came in sight of Port of Rhamnus. Drew, while C.M.C. bathed. Tremendous heat. Then, at last with great pain, mounted and rode up to the foundations of Temple.† On by ravines, with wood and grey rocks. By 1 p.m. at Varnava, a pretty village, with noble views. Dinner in tent – excellent. Directly afterwards drew – great heat. Arm a thought better. At 3 p.m. start again. Beautiful ravines – climb hills – Oleanders, blooming Acanthus (narrow leaved). Turn towards Euboea – exquisite views!

Down, down, down to Kalamos. After a long, long road, arrived at the Scala di Oropo. Khan. Mice! fleas! Tea – eggs with a fish-like flavour. Much laughter and impromptu verses:

The Hens of Oripò

The aged hens of Oripò
   They tempt the stormy sea;
Black, white and brown, they spread their wings,
   and o'er the waters flee.
And when a little fish they clutch
Athwart the wave so blue,
They utter forth a joyful note –
   'A cock a doodle doo!' (oo).

     O! Oo! Oripò-oo!
     The Hens of Oripò!

The crafty hens of Oripò
   They wander on the shore,
Where shrimps and winkles pick they up
   And carry home a store.
For barley, oats and golden corn
   To eat they never wish;
All vegetable food they scorn,
   And only seek for fish.

     O! Oh! Oripò-oo!
     The Hens of Oripò!

---

† The ancient Temple of Nemesis.

★   ★   ★

The nasty hens of Oripò.
　　With ill-conditioned zeal
All fish defunct they gobble up
　　At morn or evening meal,
Whereby their eggs, as now we find,
A fishlike, ancient smell and taste
　　Unpleasant doth pervade.

O! Oo! Oripò-oo!
The Hens of Oripò!

In better spirits they continued up the coast through fine country, Lear sketching and Church reading from Herodotus' history of the Persian Wars, breaking their journey morning and evening to bathe in the true-blue gulf or the changing currents of the Euripos. As they travelled, Church remembered, Lear 'would sing out some Italian air or chant with deep feeling some Tennysonian verse, as "The Lotos-Eaters", sitting on the yellow shore of the little bay of Aulis, or throw off some nonsense ditty.'

Journal

17 June 1848

An encampment of Gypsies amused us till starting; turbaned creatures and trowsered women, rolling about with sieves, naked children, pipes and pipkins. Off by 5 a.m. Flat ground, by the seaside. Site of the Battle of Delium. Hope Socrates did not find so many thistles to walk through!†
After this followed undulating hills by the seaside – clear and blue sea. Sometimes we walked our horses in it, sometimes up or down red, sandy roads (like drives in home-parks), between beautiful round, green sofas of Lentisk and tufts of airy, transparent Sea-pine. The opposite coast pure and cloudless – altogether a very lovely tract of scenery, and with the delightfullest of breezes, though the sun was very hot. One should make a landscape of these scenes all pale yellow, pale lilac and pale blue ... The villages hereabout are very low-roofed, low-walled, rattly-tiled, shaky, irregular, plastery, sticky, furzy, scattery places, all ochre and pale brown, tiles pale ochre-red ...

We dined, very enjoyable, quiet, not to speak of soup, fish, curried fowl, boiled fowl, and a surprising composition of plum pudding and apricots; coffee and a pipe. Exquisite air – but that one is too old, one might suppose Lotos-eating days were returned!

---

† Socrates fought in the Battle of Delium in 424 BC.

*A*t Vathy they crossed to the island of Euboea, and while Lear drew in the old Venetian city of Chalchis, Church collected a letter from his uncle. The news from Athens was alarming; insurgents had been gathering in force all along the northern frontier of the country where their route lay. They were happy to change course and continue into Euboea, stopping at the ancient sites of Eretria and Cumi, visiting the Noel† property at Achmet Aga [Prokopion] and then turning north towards Artemision. The new towns, as everywhere in Greece, were disappointing, but the island's beautiful forests had escaped the ravages of Greeks and Turks in the years of war. 'Finer than three times multiplied Dovedale or Derbyshire', Lear noted. 'The greeness – oh!'

Journal

19 June 1848

Just before sunset we got to the plain of Eretria . . . Little is left of the ancient [city] and the modern village is a queer dishevelled place of small square houses – like boxes or dominoes – many roofless and falling. We found things partly ready in one of these empty stalls – a strange land is this Greece! And after half an hour they gave us as good a tea as one could have in Grosvenor or Belgrave Square.

25 June 1848

Perfectly picturesque huttiness of Kokkinomelia. Groups of sleeping children – puppies licking them. Off by 5 a.m. having first drawn some peasants. Astonishing Swiss-like pine-woods! Magnificent view of Gulf of Volo, which we stopped to draw. Pines! Pines! Pines! and a few cattle and goats by Oleander-stream. One of our men steals little boy's jug of wine. About 10 a.m., village of Agra – mulberry tree. Women pretty; they wear dark striped chocolate and red aprons. Two storks lumberingly fly by.

    Arm bad all day. Flea bites additional . . . At 5 p.m. we send Janni to see about a boat for crossing to the mainland. General Church writes 'rebels out at Liadoriki – danger, etc.' Drew near the village Church . . . Little children played with me. Return to house. Janni came back – dreadful stories of affairs in general and about Zeituni [Lamia] in particular. We, however, decide on going to Stylidha. Tea – played and sung.

*I*n the strange days of 1848 visitors to Greece were uncommonly free from the threat of brigands. The bands of robbers who roamed the country and preyed on travellers had attached themselves either to the insurgents or to the King's

---

† Now the Noel-Baker estate.

There was an old man of
Thermopylae,
Who never did anything
properly …

irregulars, and were otherwise engaged. Sailing from Euboea to the mainland, Lear and Church encountered refugees from a local skirmish and a delightfully raffish regiment. Lear made 'sketches of one or another, much to their satisfaction and vanity.'

Journal

27 June 1848

Tacking and still tacking, we were at length off Stylidha by 9 a.m. Difficulty of landing – Caiques full of people and goods – flying – others returning. Some people calling out that all the reports about the rebels were false; others that Vellenzi, the Rebel General,† was poisoned and dead, etc., etc. At last we landed, and I instantly went to the shore to sketch the opposite mountains of Thermopylae, which are wondrous fine – all thronged with wood, channelled and furrowed – so purple, blue and green, and with such infinity of cracks and chasms of lilac and white snow on Oeta behind, and with the clearest little line of land along the shore of the Gulf. ('A great he goat' nearly destroyed me as I sate unsuspectingly on the ground). After trying in vain for a place to bathe in – water looking too shallow – and after making another sketch in sunshine, someone fetched me to breakfast in a Khan full of people. It seems that there has been some skirmishing with the Rebels, and that the Government have the best of it – so, at least, think the people of Stylidha, for the panic is over for the present, and they are returning to their homes as fast as may be. After breakfast we found a private room, washed and rested – though my arm is still very weak and painful, and a thump I got on the head last night has not improved my general condition. Bright white Gulls, in great flights, skim over the dark blue and green water. We now think of Lamia, Thermopylae, Talanti [Atalandi] and Thebes as our tour ahead. Janni says he has got fresh horses … At 2 p.m. we got away – I walking, by choice; Janni from having no horse; and Church's was a slow one … Half way on I drew. Then we began to meet the baggage of General Mamouri's army,‡ which was passing from Lamia, and very wonderful picturesquenesses did they abound in – some no-shirted, others with shirts dipped in oil; all with long guns, most with swords; many carrying mandolines, and many very ruffianly to see! All more or less fine fellows and very active. In reply to our asking about Lamia, they said all was quiet there, but otherwise took no notice of

† Ioannis Vellenzis fought in the War of Independence and later led several rebellions against the monarchy. After a national amnesty, he served as a member of parliament.
‡ Ioannis Mamouris, a revolutionary hero and a faithful supporter of Otho, he commanded the King's forces along the northern border.

us at all. We met in all some 250 or 300. Among the note-worthy objects of the baggage train was one female, one bird in a cage, and one man carrying a parasol.

Lamia is very ugly from the side by which we approached it. The khan we went to was nearly full of soldiers, as is all the town. After getting some water, I walked hastily to the other side of the place, whence, seen between minarets and cypresses, the Castle and plain show finely. All the old buildings are frequented by lots of storks – on one alone I counted 18 – which clatter and clutter with their bills incessantly. Many sit quietly on the minarets. A plentiful supply of blackguard boys surrounded Church and me while sketching . . . Returning, we soon dined, and afterwards went out on to the wooden Balcony-gallery, where some 20 soldiers were sleeping. All the air was full of stork-clatter. The bugle of sentinels calling the hour also was very curious and moody dreamy.

29 June 1848

[Hypata] No particular signs of 'Rebellion' . . . Many 'Palikari' about. Sending Janni on before, to some house with a garden attached. We went first to call on General Mamouri – but he was asleep. Then to the bit of ancient or Cyclopean wall below the village, where I drew. Very hot. We returned at 11 a.m., and called again on ὁ ςτρατηγός [the general], who was now awake. The great man, clothed in a dress of white muslin, sate smoking on a sofa. He only spoke Greek, but told C.C. that everything was now quite quiet, and that we might go anywhere. C. and I came up and found our dinner under a tent in a garden of herbs . . .

[Later] we met the fat General with Mdme. Mamouris and about 250 Cavalry and Infantry, all of whom stopped at the fountain to drink – a more wild and extraordinary procession never did anyone see – dress, attitude and their manner of skipping on or skipping, with occasional jumps, over the open plain. It was nearly sunset when we recrossed the Spercheius – a glorious scene – and dark before we reached Lamia. Shrilly sang the grass-hoppers – barked the dogs – clattered the storks. Tea, bed.

For a man of a delicate disposition, Lear was a tireless and single-minded traveller. He had the energy to push on regardless of discomfort and danger, and in every new place to start sketching the moment he arrived. Church recalled him drawing at Thermopylae 'in great heat and with much fatigue – he was at work all the time, from three o'clock in the morning, only resting during the midheat – among the crowds in the market place, among the soldiers, only intent upon his work, with infinite patience and unflagging good humour and *coolness.' Several days on from Thermopylae, he collapsed. A drawing made at Plataea includes a note, 'Ah, mi sento male!', and by the time he reached Thebes he was delirious with fever, probably malaria. In great alarm General Church dispatched doctors from Athens, and after a few days Lear was strong enough to be carried back to Athens.*

Letter to Chichester Fortescue

Hotel d'Orient, Athens. 19 July 1848

Here I am having made somewhat of a dash into Greece, but most unluckily, obliged to haul up and lay by for the present. You may perhaps see my handwriting is queerish, the fact is I am recovering rapidly thank God, from a severe touch of fever, caught at Plataea & perfected in ten days at Thebes. I do not think I should ever have got over it, nor should I, but for the skill of two doctors & the kindness of my companion Church. I was brought here by 4 horses on an Indiarubber bed, am wonderfully better, & in that state of hunger which is frightful to bystanders. I could eat an ox. Many matters contributed to this disaster, first a bad fall from my horse, and a sprained shoulder, which for three weeks irritated one's blood, besides that I could not ride. 2nd. A bite from a Centipede or some horror, which swelled up all my leg & produced a swelling like Philoctetes' toe,† and lastly, I was such a fool as go to Plataea forgetting my umbrella, where the sun finished me. However, I don't mean to give up . . .

*L**ear was too weak to travel to Constantinople with the Cannings. Prostrate in Athens during the dog days of summer, he was fussed over by the British Minister and the English residents, who arrived with daily offerings of books, jelly and porter. Towards the end of the month he rallied in strength and spirits, walking to the Acropolis 'slowly, & with a stick', visiting the Thesion in the cool quiet of an evening. On 28 July he sailed to Turkey with Church, and as they rounded the promontory of Sounion, he made a last sketch of Greece.*

Letter to Chichester Fortescue

Therapia. 25 August 1848

I continued to recover after I wrote to you . . . Then I speedily fell ill again, but differently: – yet when I got to Constantinople I was obliged to be taken up to the Hotel in a sedan chair. Well, after two days I went up to

---

† Philoctetes was stung by a serpent on his way to the Trojan Wars and had to be left behind.

the Embassy & was instantly put to bed with erysipelas & fever, and did not emerge on the banks of the Bosphorus till about August 13; and then very feebly. Since then I went a-head but had bad fever fits from not minding diet: to-day as 2 days have gone and the enemy comes not again, I have hope an am an hungered. Hunger! did you ever have a fever? No consideration of morality or sentiment or fear of punishment would prevent my devouring any small child who entered this room now. I have eaten everything in it but a wax-candle and a bad lemon.

This house is detached from the big Embassy Palace & is inhabited by attachés, and though Lady Canning is as kind as 70 mothers to me, yet I see little of them. Could I look out on any scene of beauty, my lot would be luminous; bless you! the Bosphorus hereabouts at least, is the ghastliest humbug going! Compare the Straits of Menai or Southampton Waters or

Cape Colonna (Sounion)

the Thames to it! It has neither form of hill nor character of any possible kind in its detail. A vile towing path is the only walk here or a great pull up a bare down, – of course, – sun and climate make any place lovely, & thus all the praises of this far-famed place I believe savour of picnics.

Weary and irritable, Lear recuperated at the summer embassy, dining on toast and broth, giving drawing lessons to the three Canning daughters and strolling along the Bosphorus, which he invariably and invidiously compared to Woolwich or Rotherhithe. It was the month of Ramadan, and the small villages along the shore were dull and deserted, the colourful river life curiously muted. Diplomatic dinners were 'potius aper' (Lear's Latin pun for 'rather a boar') and to the intricacies and intrigues of court life, both English and Ottoman, he was singularly immune. 'Though not in the strongest sense of the word Bohemian', he complained years later during a visit to the Viceroy of India, 'there is something antagonistic to my nature to travelling as part of a suite . . . accustomed from a boy to go my own ways uncontrolled, I cannot help feeling I should run rusty and sulky by reason of retinues and routines.'

Bebek

In his letters home Lear included occasional asides on the diminishing splendours of the Porte, but showed little interest in the high political drama being played out around him. By 1848 the Sick Man of Europe was pronounced a hopeless invalid, shattered by internal rivalries and nationalist revolts; the Great Powers kept vigil, marking time in a calculated, complex series of military campaigns, naval engagements, treaties, claims, alliances and counter-alliances. 'The Turkish moon is on the wane, and must, ere long, set forever', noted one traveller in what became a universal contemporary cliché. Among the English Sir Stratford Canning, the 'Great Elchi', was one of the authorities on the Eastern Question; when he left Constantinople for the last time in 1858, he had seen half a century of intermittent service at the British Embassy and was to enter history – possibly unjustly – in the company of the statesmen responsible for the calamities of the Crimean War. Canning was admired and respected by the Turks and established a strong personal friendship with the young Sultan, Abdul Mejid, whom he encouraged on a campaign of progressive reforms. On Lear's first outing after his illness, he accompanied the Ambassador's party to one of the great ceremonies of the Ottoman Empire.

Letter to Ann Lear

Therapia. 27 August 1848

On Monday evening Lady Canning told me that we were all going to Constantinople to see the Sultan go in procession to and from the mosque of St Sophia – & also that they were permitted (I believe the first Christians ever allowed to do so) to see the great ceremony of 'Foot Kissing' in the second court of the Seraglio … The enormous pile of buildings called 'Seraglio' is the work of hundreds of years – & many Caliphs – it stands where the old Byzantine emperors had their palace … We had only time to rush into a room close to the gate the Sultan returns by, when the procession began; I was close to the window and saw everything capitally. First came scores & scores & scores of officers of state – generals etc. on superb horses – whose hangings of velvet and gold beat anything I ever saw. The generals themselves are in modern uniform, but with many jewels. Pages & grooms (who spoil the effect of the procession by not keeping in line as the horses prance about) walk by each horse, and at intervals walk Masters of Ceremonies in scarlet and gold. After this lasted a long time … came all the Pashas (there is a great silence in all this & it is very much like a funeral for solemnity.) The Pashas have a magnificent bunch of diamonds in their scarlet caps, and their blue uniform is most richly embroidered in gold … A long space followed & a dead silence … & lastly – surrounded by scarlet and gold dressed guards with halberts or pikes, & carrying most wonderful crescent-like plumes of green and white feathers – rode the Grand Seignor himself as if he were in a grove of beautiful birds. I can't say much for His Sublimity's appearance. He is about 25 – of a mild – but worn out look – as if he cared for nothing or nobody. Wrapped in a long blue cloak, he looked positively shabby. A great shout from the troops announced his passage, and then all was still again, and he himself notices nobody; it is not etiquette. We then descended and followed a procession with a vast crowd ... & so on to the 2nd court ... on the threshold was a throne of gold tissue and all around were the infinity of Pashas, generals, etc. We got an elevated place and saw it all distinctly. The chief Emir – next in blood to the Sultan's family – clad in green from top to toe – came before the throne and offered incense (after we had waited an hour or more though) and then stood there like a statue ... Presently the music struck up, & the sultan dashed out of the dark kiosk, & sat on the throne ... After that for a mortal hour or more filed the Pashas and colonels and generals – in a most endless circle. The first kissed his foot while he stood; the second rank he sat down to & the last only threw some dust on their heads. When this was all over (and I was glad it was) the Islema or Priesthood passed in review ... You know I dislike these shows generally – but this I would not have lost – as it gave one a wonderful idea of the Barbaric despot sort of thing one has read of as a child. Sir Stratford Canning however, tells me there is no splendour now compared to former days. We were all glad to get back to the boat & the steamer & lunch ... I can't tell when I have passed so delightful & novel a day – & after a long illness, one is thankful for a change.

Officers of the Ottoman Court
From Mouradgea d'Ohsson, Tableau général de l'empire Ottoman, 1788–1824

On 1 September, immensely improved in health and suddenly excited by the beauties of the place, Lear left Therapia and established himself in the Hotel d'Angleterre in Pera, the European quarter of the capital. Misseri, the hotel's proprietor, extolled by Alexander Kinglake in Eothen, *had become something of an institution among British travellers. Making up for lost time, Lear hired a cicerone and set out to explore the city, buying silks in the Stamboul bazaars, sampling the pastries and sweetmeats of the street vendors, and visiting the mosques and the Seraglio, the great walls and the vast champs de morts with their forests of cypresses and turbaned headstones. Sailing up the Bosphorus and the Golden Horn, he drew the minareted skyline, sometimes fixing with an impressionistic speed the evanescent beauties of this world on water.*

Constantinople

Letter to Ann Lear

Salonica. 9 September 1848

A most enjoyable day on the Bosphorus, which I now like as much as I was indifferent to it at the first. In fact – a slight visit to it is very unsatisfactory, as its interest & beauty are nothing startling, like those of Constantinople, but consisting of delicate prettinesses & details not to be discovered but by frequent observation. We all set out ... at 9 o'clock – in [a] large Caique. I don't know if I have described a Caique yet; they are otherwise *canoes*; very long & narrow & pointed at each end. You sit (generally there is room for 2 only – but in the Embassy's big boat with 8 rowers – 8 or 10 can be put,) at the botttom on cushions – & it is very droll to see nothing but heads when you pass other Caiques on the water. You cannot move about much, & you must be very careful to step in the *middle* of the boat when you enter – which is nervous to think of. However –

Constantinople

once in, it is all very pleasant. Caiques are of walnut wood generally beautifully carved or gilt, according to the rank of the owner.

Well – first we went across the Bosphorus – to Unkias Skelesia – where Mahommet Ali of Egypt† is building a palace like a town – never to be finished in his day. The view is very pretty both up & down the strait, pretty woods, & pretty morgues & minarets, reflected in the clear water & pines & cypresses on the edge of the little hills. Behind is a valley of fine trees – but I did not see it, – anxious to get a good drawing. Many Turkish Caiques landed their freights of families (while we sat under the trees) – going to dine & pass the day below the trees – (Friday is their Sunday) – the women look like a bed of tulips afar off – clothed in all colours; but near, that dreadful 'tooth ache' wrapper makes them look like ghosts. They all wear yellow boots, (Armenians only are not allowed to do so) & they walk miserably, & as if crippled, & in fact, I should recommend them all to go to bed directly. Some of the great ladies – (for instance we passed some going to visit the Sultan's sister the other day –) when in their Caiques, you may perceive are covered with jewels – even through their muslin wrappers. That lady I drew was loaded all over her head with diamonds.

After Unkias Skelesia – we went to Chibuklee – another valley – with a fountain & trees – greatly frequented by the picknickers of Constantinople. Next we stopped at a kiosk hanging over the water which Lady C. (who delighted in showing the lions of the Bosphorus –) wished me to see. The inhabitants were changed since she was last there, but they politely asked us in. The whole of the room was surrounded with a high divan – sofa – a fountain in the centre – & a recess & bow window – (the Bosphorus houses look all glass –) & every part ornamented with gold & black arabesques & ivory inlay. Opposite the Castle of Europe – (Rumeli Hissar) – the view is most exquisite. First they brought pipes – the rich Turks keep a servant to each pipe – so that if there are many guests – a cloud of pipes & pipe smokers burst on your astonished sight; – next came coffee – handed in porcelain cups ... fitted with filigree stands; the Turkish coffee is all grounds apparently at first – till it stands $\frac{1}{4}$ of an hour – when it is *good* but *cool* – a disadvantage to those who can't eat this coffee. Then they handed a sweet meat very common here but the name escapes me; it is in square pieces, & made of gum, sugar & attar of roses, & is really excellent. After this we made bows & came away. The master of the house (in a rose coloured gown & blue under dress – scarlet belt, & red turban) sat smoking opposite saying never a word. – I suppose if we had laughed or talked loud, it would have been as bad behaviour as spitting or taking one's coat off at an English dinner! Well, now we all got into the Caique again, & were

---

† Mehemet Ali, Pasha of Egypt and rival to the Sultan for control of the Empire.

rowed to what is called the sweet waters of Asia, the most famous place for English picknicks near the city … We made a good lunch on the meadow – & all together I was greatly delighted with the spot.

Letter to Ann Lear

Salonica. 10 September 1848

The views from [Galata] cemetery have made it quite my second best favourite, – there are innumerable turtle doves in all these cypress groves – which are quite unmolested, for you know the Mahommedans don't hurt animals. For the same reason dogs reign triumphantly (you could not possibly bear stepping carefully over some 20 sleeping beasts!) & noone moves or pats them; towards sunset they wake up & are vicious – but harm nobody by day in the town. But if a stray dog came into their bounds – (they have particular quarters –) woe to him! Such vile beasts they are, like old, mangy wolves; if I were Sultan for but one day wouldn't I send for 10 boat loads of dogs' heads!! –

Barkia Howlaloudia

*T*he journey up the Bosphorus was an object lesson in Ottoman decadence, for one of the first sights on the European shore was the vast new palace of Dolma Bahche, built to replace the old Seraglio. The young Sultan had begun to lose interest in his bold political reforms and was increasingly seduced by the life of the harem and absorbed in grandiose building schemes. Despite warnings of impending bankruptcy, he emptied the treasuries to complete the new palace, its marble halls tricked out with gold leaf, alabaster and porphyry, its bedchamber graced by a massive imperial bed of solid silver. Completed in 1838, the Dolma Bahche crowned an endlessly expanding collection of regal residences.

Letter to Ann Lear

Salonica. 10 September 1848

On the Bosphorus; we went up as far as Baltalina, & I drew & lunched there. Much of the day went in the beautiful cemetery – a grand picture composed of rock & cypress, with tombs studding the ground like daisies on turf – & topped by the milk white towers of Rumeli Hissar, the Castle of Europe … Lastly we went to Beebek – a Kiosk of the Sultan, & very pretty – & so home by dusk. The Grand Seigneur has about 300 of these palaces on the Bosphorus & Golden Horn; sometimes he passes a night at one – sometimes a month or 2 in the bigger palaces. Some he gives to Pashas – some he bestows on aunts & sisters. But he never seems content.

A Greek (rich) family has just made a magnificent residence near Therapia – a dangerous way of amusing one's self by way of future hopes; the Sultan saw it – (passing by) & sends 5 times the value, & he wants it; so out go the family. Probably he will never go in to it himself – but he pays well & thinks it no hardship to the subject. As for the days of Bastinado & headchopping, they are utterly gone; & the Turk is gradually puffing out the last spark of his imperial existence in all matters.

I must now devote a word to conflagration general & especial. You know that nearly all the houses in Constantinople are of wood – & you may have heard of the frequency of the fires, & their extent, but you will yet be surprised to hear that since I came – (Aug. 1st) there have been 8 dreadful burnings – the least of which destroyed 60, & the largest 5,000 houses – & reduced hundreds & thousands to wretchedness. If I had not seen these things, I could not have believed them; & yet if we suppose 8 fires in 6 weeks – Islington, Camberwell, Stoke Newington, Bethnal Green, Wapping, St. John's Wood, Kensington, & Cheapside – dreadful as it would be – London would work nevertheless; & so it is with Constantinople; its immense size prevents these horrible fires from injuring the appearance of the toute ensemble ... [Since] I came – all the suburb of Ch—[word illegible] was destroyed in a line by the river. That of Besiktsche followed next week. The week after that was signalised by a frightful devastation beginning at the water's edge; – 3,000 houses in Stamboul were burned, & the Mosque of Suleiman nearly so. Sabatia, a suburb near the wall, blazed away for 8 hours on the 3rd. Another fire at Pera, & one more at Stamboul had happened just before. And now I come to the night of Wed. the 6th, – when about 12 everybody was awakened by the waiters (throughout the hotel) with the news that a tremendous fire was raging in Pera, & advancing to the inn. But Misseri said there was no danger – as there was a stone house, & a church (Greek) between him and them, where the flames would stop, & as I guessed by his coolness – he was in the right. However, I packed up, & then joined everybody else on the house top – where wet carpets, & water were all the fashion. A most horrible sight it was. I cannot conceive how anyone can like looking at a fire; to me the picturesque is quite swamped by the sight of such suffering on a wholesale scale. The flames were tremendous – & all the city light as day. The houses fell crash, crash, crash, as the fire swept on nearer & nearer – & by 4 o'clock after midnight, it reached within 2 houses of the hotel – but there it stopped ... As it was, *only* 300 houses were burnt! – no lives lost; they very seldom are – & all the property is carried through the streets by innumerable porters to the cemeteries etc. – & there the poor people live till another wooden suburb arises in less than a year's time. Such is life in Constantinople.!!

*The Sultan's new palace
at Dolma Bahche*

3

The Wilds of Albania

*A*s *the summer passed and his health steadied, Lear resolved to embark on an ambitious and long-anticipated tour of northern Greece and Albania with Charles Church. 'To see the classic Vale of Tempe, the sacred mountain of Athos and the romantic Ioannina have always been among my wishes', he noted in the Albanian Journal, 'and I had long ago determined on making, previously to returning to England, a large collection of sketches illustrative of the landscape of Greece.' Church, who was travelling in the Troad, planned to rejoin him for the sailing to Salonica, and during his last days in Constantinople Lear busied himself buying colours and drawing materials, selecting keepsakes for the Cannings and engaging a Bulgarian travelling companion named Giorgio Cogga-chio. On 9 September he boarded the steamer for Salonica carrying 'no end of letters' from Sir Stratford Canning, only to find that Church had been detained. He sailed alone in exotic company, his artist's eye engaged by 'what seemed to be a load of linen drapery & haberdashery – [but on] looking more steadfastly you see it is 15 or 16 Turkish ladies.'*

Albanian Journal

9 September 1848

3 p.m. – Came on board the Ferdinando, an Austrian steamer running between Constantinople and Salonica; and a pretty place does it seem to pass two or three days in. Every point of the lower deck – all of it – is crammed with Turks, Jews, Greeks, Bulgarians, wedged together with a

On board the Salonica steamer 'Ferdinando'

density compared to which a crowded Gravesend steamer is emptiness: a section of a fig-drum, or a herring-barrel is the only apt simile for this extraordinary crowd of recumbent human beings, who are all going to Salonica, as a starting-point for Thessaly, Bosnia, Wallachia, or any part of Northern Turkey. This motley cargo is not of ordinary occurrence; but the second Salonica steamer, which should have started today, has fallen indisposed in its wheels or boiler; so we have a double load for our share.

Walking carefully over my fellow passengers, I reached the first-class part of the deck – a small, raised triangle, railed off from the throng below, half of which is allotted to Christians (the Austrian Consul at Salonica and his family being the only Christians besides myself), and the other half tabooed for the use of a harem of Turkish females, who entirely cover the floor with a diversity of robes, pink, blue, chocolate, and amber; pea, sea, olive, bottle, pale, and dark green; above which parterre of colours are numerous heads, all wrapped in white muslin, excepting as many pairs of eyes undistinguishably similar. There is a good cabin below; but owing to a row of obstructive Mussulmen who choose to cover up the grated opening with shutters, that they may sit quietly upon them to smoke, it is quite dark, so I remain on deck. We are a silent community: the smoking Turks are silent, and so is the strange harem. The Consul and his wife, and their two pretty daughters, are silent because they fear cholera at Salonica – which the young ladies declare is *un pessimo esilio*† – and because they are regretting northern friends. I am silent, from much thought and some weakness consequent on long illness: and the extra cargo in the lower deck are silent also – perhaps because they have not room to talk. At four, the anchor is weighed and we begin to paddle away from the many domed mosques and bright minarets of Constantinople and the gay sides of the Golden Horn, with its caiques and its cypresses towering against the deepening blue sky, when lo! we do not turn towards the sea, but proceed ignominiously to tow a great coal-ship all the way to Buyukdere, so there is a moving panorama of all the Bosporus bestowed on us gratis – Kandili, Baltaliman, Bebek, Yenikoi, Therapia, with its well-known walks and pines and planes, and lastly Buyukdere, where we leave our dingy charge and return, evening darkening over the Giant's Hill, Unkias Skelesia, and Anatoli Hissar, till we sail forth into the broad Sea of Marmara, leaving Scutari and the towers of wonderful Stamboul first pale and distinct in the light of the rising moon, and then glittering and lessening on the calm horizon, till they, and the memory that I have been among them for seven weeks, seem alike a part of the world of dreams.

---

† An odious banishment.

10 September 1848

Half the morning we lie off Gallipoli, taking in merchandise and indulging in eccentric casualties – demolishing the bowsprit of one vessel and injuring divers others, for which we are condemned to three hours of clamour and arrangement of compensation. In the afternoon we wait off the Dardanelles, not an inviting town as beheld from the sea; C.M.C. [Charles Church] (says the Consul's son) sets off for Athos in two days to meet me. Again we move, and day wears away amid perplexing twinges foreshadowing fever (for your Greek fever when once he has fairly secured you is your Old Man of the Sea for a weary while; you tremble – and fly to quinine as your only chance of escape). Towards four or five the mountains of the Troad fade away in the distance; later we pass near the isles of Imbros and Samothrace; and later yet, when the unclouded sun has sunk down, a

Gallipoli

Gallipoli: 10. Sept. 1848.
Salonica Steamer.

mountain pile of awful form looms sublimely in the west – rising from the glassy calm waters against the clear amber western sky: it is Mount Athos.

11 September 1848

At sunrise the highest peaks of Athos were still visible above the long, low line of Cape Drepano, and at noon we were making way up the Gulf of Salonica, Ossa and Olympus on our left – lines of noble mountain grandeur, but becoming rapidly indistinct as a thick sirocco-like vapour gradually shrouded over all the features of the western shore of the gulf. *N'importe* – the Vale of Tempe, so long a dim expectation, is now a near reality; and Olympus is indubitably at hand, though invisible for the present. There were wearily long flat points of land to pass (all, however, full of interest as parts of the once flourishing Chalcidice) ere Salonica was visible, a triangle enclosed in a border of white walls on the hill at the head of the gulf; and it was nearly 6 p.m. before we reached the harbour and anchored.

Instantly the wildest confusion seized all the passive human freight. The polychromatic harem arose and moved like a bed of tulips in a breeze; the packed Wallachians and Bosniacs and Jews started crampfully from the deck and disentangled themselves into numerous boats; the Consular Esiliati departed; and lastly, I and my dragoman prepared to go, and were soon at shore, though it was not so easy to be upon it. Salonica is inhabited by a very great proportion of Jews; nearly all the porters in the city are of that nation, and now that the cholera had rendered employment scarce there were literally crowds of black-turbaned Hebrews at the water's edge, speculating on the possible share of each in the conveyance of luggage from the steamer. The enthusiastic Israelites rushed into the water and, seizing my arms and legs, tore me out of the boat and up a narrow board with the most unsatisfactory zeal; immediately after which they fell upon my enraged dragoman in the same mode, and finally throwing themselves on my luggage each portion of it was claimed by ten or twelve frenzied agitators who pulled this way and that way till I who stood apart, resigned to whatever might happen confidently awaited the total destruction of my *roba*. From yells and pullings to and fro, the scene changed in a few minutes to a real fight, and the whole community fell to the most furious hair-pulling, turban-clenching, and robe-tearing, till the luggage was forgotten and all the party was involved in one terrific combat. How this exhibition would have ended I cannot tell, for in the heat of the conflict my man came running with a half-score of Government Kawasi, or police; and the way in which they fell to belabouring the enraged Hebrews was a thing never to be forgotten. These took a deal of severe beating from sticks and whips before they gave way, and eventually some six or eight were selected to carry the packages of the Ingliz, which I followed into the city, not unvexed at being the indirect cause of so much strife.†

In Salonica there is a Locanda – a kind of hotel – the last dim shadow of European 'accommodation' between Stamboul and Cattaro [Kotor]: it is kept by the politest of Tuscans, and the hostess is the most corpulent and blackest of negresses. Thither we went, but I observed, with pain, that the state of the city was far more melancholy than I had had reason to suppose: all the bazaars (long lines of shops) were closed and tenantless: the gloom and deserted air of the streets was most sad, and I needed not to be told that the cholera, or whatever were the complaint so generally raging, had broken out with fresh virulence since the last accounts received at Constantinople, and nearly three-fourths of the living population had fled from their houses into the adjacent country. And no sooner was I settled in a room at the inn than, sending Giorgio to the British Consulate, I awaited his return and report with some anxiety.

Presently in came Giorgio with the dreariest of faces, and the bearer of what to me were, in truth, seriously vexatious news.

The cholera, contrary to the intelligence received in Stamboul, which represented the disease as on the decline, had indeed broken out afresh and was spreading or – what is the same thing as to results, if a panic be once rife – was supposed to be spreading on all sides. The surrounding villages had taken alarm and had drawn a strict *cordon sanitaire* between themselves and the enemy; and, worse than all, the monks of Mount Athos had utterly prohibited all communications between their peninsula and the infected city; so that any attempt on my part to join C.M.C. would be useless, no person being allowed to proceed beyond a few miles outside the eastern gate of Salonica. No one could tell how long this state of things would last; for, although the epidemic was perhaps actually decreasing in violence, yet the fear of contagion was by no means so. Multitudes of the inhabitants of the suburbs and adjacent villages had fled to the plains, and to pass them would be an impossibility. On the south-western road to Greece or Epirus, the difficulty was the same: even at Katerina, or Platamona, the peasants would allow no one to land.

Here was a dilemma! – a pleasant fix! – yet it was one that required the remedy of resolve, rather than of patience. To remain in a city full of epidemic disease (and those only who have seen an Oriental provincial town under such circumstances can estimate their horror), myself but convalescent, was literally to court the risk of renewed illness, or at best compulsory detention by quarantine. Therefore, after weighing the matter

† The Jews in Salonica are descended from those expelled from Spain in the fifteenth century: they are said to amount in number to four thousand.

well, I decided that my first step must be to leave Salonica at the very
earliest opportunity. But whither to go? Mount Athos was shut; the west
coast of the gulf was tabooed. There were but two plans open: the first was
to return by the next steamer to Constantinople; but this involved a
fortnight's waiting, at least, in the place of pestilence, with the chance of
being disabled before the time of departure came; and even could I adopt
such means of escape, the expense and mortification of going back was, if
possible, to be shunned.

The second *modus operandi* was to set off directly, by the north-west road,
through Macedonia to Illyrian Albania, by the ancient Via Egnatia, and so
rejoin C.M.C. at Ioannina. This plan, though not without weighty objec-
tion – of which the being compelled to go alone and the great distance of
the journey were prominent – appeared to me the only safe and feasible
one; and after much reflection I finally determined to adopt it. After all,
looking at things on their brightest side, when once they were discovered
to be inevitable – though I was unable to meet my friend I had a good
servant accustomed to travel with Englishmen: health would certainly
improve in the air of the mountain country, and professional objects, long
in view, would not be sacrificed. As for the risk run by thus rushing into
strange places and among unknown people, when a man has walked all
over the wildest parts of Italy he does not prognosticate danger. Possibly
one may get only as far as Monastir – the capital of Macedonia – and then
make southward, having seen Yenidje and Edessa – places all full of beauty
and interest; or, beyond Monastir, lies Akhridha and its lake, and farther
yet Elbassan, or even Skodra – highest in the wilds of Gheghe Albania.
Make, thought I to myself, no definite arrangement beyond that of escape
from Salonica; put yourself, as a predestinarian might say, calmly into the
dice-box of small events, and be shaken out whenever circumstances may
ordain: only go, and as soon as you can. So, Giorgio, have horses and all
minor matters in complete readiness at sunrise the day after tomorrow.

12 September 1848

This intervening day before my start 'somewhere or other' tomorrow I set
apart for lionising Salonica with a cicerone.

Whatever the past of Salonica, its present seems gloomy enough. The
woe, the dolefulness of this city! – its narrow, ill-paved streets (evil awaits
the man who tries to walk with nailed boots on the rounded, slippery stones
of a Turkish pavement!); the very few people I met in them carefully
avoiding contact; the closed houses; the ominous silence; the sultry, oppressive heat of the day; all contributed to impress the mind with a feeling of
heavy melancholy. A few Jews in dark dresses and turbans; Jewesses, their

hair tied up in long, caterpillar-like green silk bags, three feet in length; Greek porters, aged blacks, of whom – freed slaves from Stamboul – there are many in Salonica; these were the only human beings I encountered in threading a labyrinth of lanes in the lower town, ascending towards the upper part of this formerly extensive city. Once, a bier with a corpse on it, borne by some six or eight of the most wretched creatures, crossed my path; and when I arrived at the beautiful ruin called the Incantada two women, I was told, had just expired within the courtyard, and, said the ghastly-looking Greek on the threshold, 'You may come in and examine what you please, and welcome; but once in you are in quarantine, and may not go out', an invitation I declined as politely as I could and passed onward. From the convent at the summit of the town, just within its white walls, the view should be most glorious, as one ought to see the whole of the gulf and all the range of Olympus, but, alas! beyond the silvery minarets relieving the monotonous surface of roofs below and the delicately indented shore and the blue gulf, all else was blotted out, as it were, by a curtain of hot purple haze, telling tales to my fancy of miasma and cholera, fever and death.

The artist who twelve years earlier had escaped south for the sake of his health now began a journey across the wildest and least frequented realms of Turkey in Europe. Part of his route ran through the provinces of Macedonia, Thessaly and Epirus, then within the bounds of the Ottoman Empire, but in both ancient and modern times a part of Greece and rich in remembrance of history and myth. Albania, equally of interest to the antiquarian, was an almost uncharted territory, 'though abounding', according to Byron, 'in more natural beauties than the classical regions of Greece.' For the painter in search of the picturesque Albania offered a wealth of Oriental architecture, exquisite costume and Elysian landscape, though – Lear issues a caveat – not uniformly suitable to sensibilities inspired by Claude and Cumberland.

Albanian Journal

Introduction

The general and most striking character of Albanian landscape is its display of objects, in themselves beautiful and interesting – rarely to be met with in combination. You have the simple and exquisite mountain forms of Greece, so perfect in outline and proportion – the lake, the river, and the wide plain; and withal you have the charm of architecture, the picturesque mosque, the minaret, the fort, and the serai – which you have not in modern Greece, for war and change have deprived her of them; you have that

which is found neither in Greece nor in Italy, a profusion everywhere of the most magnificent foliage recalling the greenness of our own island – clustering plane and chestnut, growth abundant of forest oak and beech, and dark tracts of pine. You have majestic cliff-girt shores; castle-crowned heights, and gloomy fortresses; palaces glittering with gilding and paint; mountain passes such as you encounter in the snowy regions of Switzerland; deep bays and blue seas with bright, calm isles resting on the horizon; meadows and grassy knolls; convents and villages; olive-clothed slopes and snow-capped mountain peaks – and with all this a crowded variety of costume and pictorial incident such as bewilders and delights an artist at each step he takes.

Let us add besides that Olympus, Pindus, Pharsalia, Actium, etc., are no common names and that every scene has its own link with some historic or poetic association, and we cannot but perceive that these parts of Turkey in Europe are singularly rich in a combination of qualities hardly to be found in any other land.

These remarks apply more strictly to the southern parts of Albania than to the extreme north (or Ghegheria); for nearer the confines of Bosnia the mountains are on too gigantic a scale and the features of the landscape too extensive and diffuse to be easily represented by the pencil. There is, however, abundance of grandeur and sublimity through the whole country; though the farther you wander north of Epirus the less you find of that grace and detail which is so attractive in southern Greece, and more especially in Attica and the Peloponnesus.

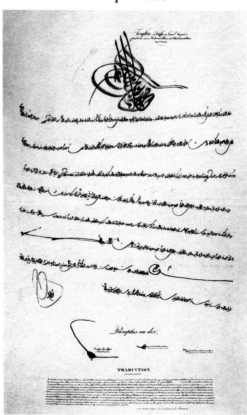

'Pass-port Turc'

*L*ear's introduction to Journals of a Landscape Painter in Albania &c became a standard source for guidebooks to Albania and northern Greece, quoted widely and at length well into the twentieth century. The economy of Lear's travelling arrangements was an innovation for English travellers in the Levant, a drastic simplification of the suite that had accompanied his recent tour with Church. It was not so long ago that Byron and Hobhouse, accompanied by two Albanian guards and Byron's xenophobic servant Fletcher, had landed at Prevesa with eight heavy trunks, three wooden bedsteads and bedding, a quantity of English saddles and bridles, a commodious canteen and eight baggage horses to carry the lot.

Albanian Journal

Introduction

To the unlearned tourist, indeed, Albania is a puzzle of the highest order. Whatever he may already know of ancient nomenclature – Epirus, Molossia,

Thresprotia, etc. – is thwarted and confused by Turkish divisions and Pashaliks; beyond these, wheel within wheel, a third set of names distract him in the shape of native tribes and districts – Tjamouria, Dibra, etc. And no sooner does he begin to understand the motley crowd which inhabits these provinces – Greeks, Slavonians, Albanians, Bulgarians, or Vlachi – than he is anew bewildered by a fresh list of distinctive sub-splittings, Liape, Mereditti, Khimariotes, and Teskidhes. Races, religions, and national denominations seem so ill defined, or so entangled, that he would give up the perplexing study in despair were it not for the assistance of many excellent books already published on the subject. Of these, the works of Colonel Leake stand highest, as conveying by far the greatest mass of minutely accurate information regarding these magnificent and interesting countries . . .

Regarding the best mode of travelling, it is almost superfluous to write, as Murray's Hand-Book† for travellers in the Ionian Islands, Greece, Turkey etc., supplies excellent information on that head; yet the leading points of a traveller's personal experience are frequently worth knowing. A good dragoman, or interpreter, is absolutely necessary, however many languages you may be acquainted with: French, German, and Italian are useless, and modern Greek nearly as much if you travel higher than Macedonia: Bulgarian, Albanian, Turkish, and Slavonic are your requisites in this Babel. Those who dislike account-books and the minutiae thereof, may find it a good plan to pay their dragoman a certain sum per diem – as C.M.C. and I did last year in Greece, where for one pound five, including their own pay, the guides are accustomed to provide for all your daily wants – food, lodging, and conveyance, that is, if you travel singly – or for one pound from each person, if your party be two or more. In the present case I gave the man who accompanied me one dollar daily, and settled for all the expenses of food, horses, etc., at fixed times; the result of which plan, at the end of the journey, was about the same, namely, that one pound five a day covered the whole of my expenditure.

Previously to starting a certain supply of cooking utensils, tin plates, knives and forks, a basin, etc., must absolutely be purchased, the stronger and plainer the better; for you go into lands where pots and pans are unknown, and all culinary processes are to be performed in strange localities, innocent of artificial means. A light mattress, some sheets and blankets, and a good supply of capotes and plaids should not be neglected; two or three books; some rice, curry powder, and cayenne; a world of drawing materials – if you be a hard sketcher; as little dress as possible, though you

Kroia
Lithograph from Journals of a Landscape Painter in Albania &c

---

† *A Handbook for Travellers in the Ionian Islands, Greece, Turkey, Asia Minor & Constantinople*, John Murray, second edition 1845.

must have two sets of outer clothing – one for visiting consuls, pashas, and dignitaries, the other for rough, everyday work; some quinine made into pills (rather leave all behind than this); a Boyourdi, or general order of introduction to governors or pashas; and your Teskere, or provincial passport for yourself and guide. All these are absolutely indispensable, and beyond these, the less you augment your impedimenta by luxuries the better; though a long strap with a pair of ordinary stirrups, to throw over the Turkish saddles, may be recommended to save you the cramp caused by the awkward shovel stirrups of the country. Arms and ammunition, fine raiment, presents for natives, are all nonsense; simplicity should be your aim. When all these things, so generically termed *Roba* by Italians, are in order, stow them into two Brobdignagian saddle-bags, united by a cord (if you can get leather bags so much the better, if not, goats'-hair sacks); and by these hanging on each side of the baggage-horse's saddle, no trouble will ever be given from seceding bits of luggage escaping at unexpected intervals. Until you adopt this plan (the simplest of any) you will lose much time daily by the constant necessity of putting the baggage in order.

Journeys in Albania vary in length according to your will, for there are usually roadside khans at from two to four hours' distance. Ten hours' riding is as much as you can manage, if any sketching is to be secured; but I generally found eight sufficient.

A khan is a species of public-house rented by the keeper or Khanji from the Government, and is open to all comers. You find food in it sometimes – sometimes not, when you fall back on your own rice and curry powder. In large towns, the khan is a three-sided building enclosed in a courtyard, and consisting of two floors, the lower a stable, the upper divided into chambers, opening into a wooden gallery which runs all round the building, and to which you ascend outside by stairs. In unfrequented districts the khan is a single room, or barn, with a raised floor at one end for humanity, and all the rest devoted to cattle – sometimes quadrupeds and bipeds are all mixed up together. First come, first served, is the rule in these establishments; and as any person who can pay the trifle required by the Khanji for lodging may sleep in them, your company is oftentimes not select; but of this, as of the kind of khan you stop at, you must take your chance.

The best way of taking money is by procuring letters on consular agents, or merchants from town to town, so as to carry as little coin as possible with you; and your bag of piastres you pack in your carpet bag by day, and use as a pillow by night.

In the more accessible regions of Turkey in Europe, travelling was considerably easier than in the new Kingdom of Greece. Throughout the empire the government had established khans at intervals of a two- or three-hour ride (in Greece these had either been abandoned or taken over by the villagers) and travellers could also rely upon the hospitality of Christian families in the larger towns. On the Menzil or post road a rider could cover sixty miles in a day by changing horses at frequent stages. Lear set off from Salonica in the company of his servant Giorgio, a Tatar (a Turkish courier) and an unpredictable driver, 'a wild gypsy Soorudji'. Following the path of the Via Egnatia, the great military road which had once connected the Adriatic with Byzantium, he passed near Yenidje the remains of Pella, birthplace of Alexander the Great, stopping at Vodhena (ancient Edessa), the sanctuary and burial place of Macedonian kings.

Albanian Journal

14 September 1848

While taking a parting cup of coffee with the postmaster I unluckily set my foot on a handsome pipe-bowl (pipe-bowls are always snares to near-sighted people moving over Turkish floors, as they are scattered in places quite remote from the smokers, who live at the farther end of prodigiously long pipe-sticks) – crash; but nobody moved; only on apologising through Giorgio, the polite Mohammedan said: 'The breaking such a pipe-bowl would indeed, under ordinary circumstances, be disagreeable; but in a friend every action has its charm!' – a speech which recalled the injunction of the Italian to his son on leaving home, 'Whenever anybody treads upon your foot in company, and says, "*Scusatemi*", only reply: "*Anzi – mi ha fatto un piacere!*" '† . . .

   Of Giorgio, dragoman, cook valet, interpreter, and guide, I have had as yet nothing to complain; he is at home in all kinds of tongues, speaking ten fluently, an accomplishment common to many of the travelling Oriental Greeks, for he is a Smyrniote by birth. In countenance my attendant is some-what like one of those strange faces, lion or griffin, which we see on door-knockers or urn-handles, and a grim twist of his under-jaw gives an idea that it would not be safe to try his temper too much. In the morning he is diffuse and dilates on past journeys; after noon his remarks become short and sen-tentious – not to say surly. Any appearance of indecision evidently moves him to anger speedily. It is necessary to watch the disposition of a ser-vant on whom so much of one's personal comfort depends, and it is equally necessary to give as little trouble as possible, for a good dragoman has always enough to do without extra whims or worryings from his employer.

---

† I beg pardon. On the contrary, you have done me a pleasure.

15 September 1848

By five I was out on the road to Yenidge, at a dervish's tomb, not far from the town, a spot which I had remarked yesterday as promising, if weather permitted, a good view eastward. All the plain below is bright yellow as the sun rises gloriously, and Olympus is for once in perfect splendour, with all its snowy peaks; but the daily perplexity of mist and cloud rapidly soars upward and hardly leaves time for a sketch ere all is once more shrouded away.

The dervish's or saint's tomb is such as you remark frequently on the outskirts of Mohammedan towns in the midst of wide cemeteries of humble sepulchres – a quadrangular structure three or four feet high, with pillars at the corners supporting a dome of varying height; beneath its centre is usually the carved emblem of the saint's rank, his turban, or high-crowned hat. As these tombs are often shaded by trees, their effect is very pleasing, the more so that the cemeteries are mostly frequented by the contemplative faithful. Often, in their vicinity, especially if the position of the tombs commands a fine view or is near a running stream, you may notice one of those raised platforms with a cage-like palisade and supporting a roof in the shade of which the Mohammedan delights to squat and smoke. There is one close by me now in which a solitary elder sits, in the enjoyment of tobacco and serenity, and looking in his blue and yellow robes very like an encaged macaw.

A quick run down the rocky pass of last evening brought me to the great plane trees and the bright stream whence Vodhena [Edessa], on its hill, is so lovely – a scene difficult to match in beauty. I met many peasants and long strings of laden mules, but no one took the faintest notice of me – a negative civility highly gratifying after all one hears of the ferocity of the aborigines of these regions. That the road as far as Vodhena is considered carriageable was proved to me by the strange spectacle which passed me on my way up to the town – eight horses pulling up the steep ascent with a carriage full of masked ladies, the beloved of some Mohammedan dignitary. Eight armed outriders preceded this apparition and a troop of guards followed the precious charge . . .

Broiled and boiled salmon trout, rice soup, and onions awaited me in the Mivart's of Ostrovo – and, let me say, that is by no means a bad supper to find in a Macedonian khan. The evening passed in the intellectual diversion of drying one's wet clothes by little bits of firewood and in packing one's self so as to sleep tolerably, spite of there being no bolt to the door. But, in truth, in so forlorn a spot as this no precautions could ensure safety against force, were robbery intended. Never, in the wildest

Monastir

of countries, have I met with any robber adventure, and not being troubled by suspicions of danger I have come to believe that carelessness as to attack is the best safeguard against any. Mats hung to the roof and window keep out some of the air (for an unglazed hole in the wall, and a series of apertures in the roof add to the charms of this hotel), but the wood smoke is the worst enemy and I am glad to seek refuge from it in slumber.

Lear's disclaimers on the dangers of travel were not mere bravado. For a man whom Holman-Hunt described as 'as uncombatative as a tender girl' innocence was the best and possibly the only protection. Near Petra, on the one occasion during his journeys where Lear came close to being murdered, his coolness and self-control undoubtedly saved his life. Travelling through northern Greece and Albania not long before, Robert Curzon encountered horrific atrocities, steadying his nerves with the stoic consolation that 'the natives do not shoot so much at Franks because they usually have little worth taking and are not good to eat.'

On 17 September Lear reached Monastir, the metropolis of Macedonia, a military centre and a prosperous market town. 'The scenery [is] most lovely', he wrote to Church, 'and the costumes chrongongerous to observe.'

Albanian Journal

17 September 1848

Descending about half past nine to the great plain of Bitola, or Monastir (the military centre and capital of modern Macedonia and Northern Albania), white minarets, extensive buildings, and gardens were a pleasant sight, as the city seemed to expand on our approaching the high mountains at the foot of which it is built . . .

Anticipating – as in every previous case during this journey – that the glitter and beauty of outward appearance would be exchanged on entering the city for squalor and dreariness, I was agreeably surprised at the great

Monastir

Monastir

extent of public buildings, barracks, and offices at the entrance of the town, and, within it, at the width and good pavement of the streets, the cleanliness and neatness of the houses. The bazaars are exceedingly handsome, some entirely roofed over and lighted from above with windows, others only partially sheltered or semi-roofed with matting on poles. Great numbers of vendors and buyers throng these resorts, the principal part of the former being merchants – Greek or Bulgarian Christians – and of the latter Christian peasantry from the neighbouring villages and country. The Turks resident in Monastir are for the most part either military or officials: Greeks and Bulgarians form the majority of the inhabitants. Albanians there are few, excepting guards or exiles (Monastir is a frequent place of banishment for rebel Beys): of Jews a vast number. Being the central situation for all military operations relating to North and South Albania, Thessaly, Macedonia, and Bosnia, the bustle and brilliancy of Monastir is remarkable, and its effect appeared particularly striking coming to it, as I did, after passing through a wild and thinly peopled region. You are bewildered by the sudden reappearance of a civilisation which you had apparently left for ever: reviews, guards, bands of music, pashas, palaces, and sentry-boxes, bustling scenes and heaps of merchandise await you at every turn.

The natural beauties of Monastir are abundant. The city is built at the western edge of a noble plain, surrounded by the most exquisitely shaped hills, in a recess or bay formed by two very high mountains, between which magnificent snow-capped barriers is the pass to Akhridha [Ohrid]. A river runs through the town, a broad and shifting torrent crossed by numerous bridges, mostly of wood, on some of which two rows of shops stand, forming a broad covered bazaar. At present three of these bridges are in ruins, or under repair after the winter's floods. The stream, deep and narrow throughout the quarter of private houses and palaces, is spanned by two good stone bridges and confined by strong walls; but in the lower or Jew's quarter, where the torrent is much wider and shallower, the houses cluster down to the water's edge with surprising picturesqueness. Either looking up or down the river, the intermixture of minarets and mosques with cypress and willow foliage, forms subjects of the most admirable beauty.

19 September 1848

It is no easy matter to pursue the fine arts in Monastir, and I cannot but think – will matters grow worse as I advance into Albania? For all the

Monastir

passers-by, having inspected my sketching, frown or look ugly, and many say, '*Shaitan*', which means, Devil; at length one quietly wrenches my book away and shutting it up returns it to me, saying, '*Yok, Yok!*'† – so as numbers are against me, I bow and retire. Next, I essay to draw on one of the bridges, but a gloomy sentinel comes and bullies me off directly, indicating by signs that my profane occupation is by no manner of means to be tolerated, and farther on, when I thought I had escaped all observation behind a friendly buttress, out rush legions of odious hounds (all bare-hided and very like jackals), and raise such a din that, although by means of a pocket full of stones I keep them at bay, yet they fairly beat me at last, and gave me chase open-mouthed, augmenting their detestable pack by fresh recruits at each street corner. So I gave up this pursuit of knowledge under difficulties and returned to the khan.

Giorgio was waiting to take me to the Pasha; so dressing in my 'best', thither I went, to pay my first visit to an Oriental dignitary. All one's gathered and hoarded memories, from books or personal relations, came so clearly to my mind as I was shown into the great palace or serai of the Governor that I seemed somehow to have seen it all before; the anteroom full of attendants, the second state-room with secretaries and officers, and, finally, the large square hall, where – in a corner and smoking the longest nargilleh, the serpentine foldings of which formed all the furniture of the chamber save the carpets and sofas – sat the Seraskier Pasha himself – one of the highest grandees of the Ottoman empire. Emim Seraskier Pasha was educated at Cambridge, and speaks English fluently. He conversed for some time agreeably and intelligently, and after having promised me a Kawas, the interview was over, and I returned to the khan, impatient to attack the street scenery of Monastir forthwith under the auspices of my guard. These availed me much, and I sketched in the dry part of the river-bed with impunity – aye, and even in the Jews' quarter, though immense crowds collected to witness the strange Frank and his doings; and the word, '*Scroo, Scroo*', resounded from hundreds of voices above and around. But a clear space was kept around me by the formidable baton of the Kawas, and I contrived thus to carry off some of the best views of the town ere it grew dark. How picturesque are those parts of the crowded city in the Jews' quarter, where the elaborately detailed wooden houses overhang the torrent, shaded by grand plane, cypress, and poplar! How the sunset lights up the fire-tinged clouds – floating over the snow-capped eastern hills! How striking are the stately groups of armed guards clearing the road through the thronged streets of the bazaars for some glittering Bey or mounted

---

† No, No!

Pasha! Interest and beauty in profusion, O ye artists! are to be found in the city of Monastir.

The Seraskier's letter to the principal Bey of Akhridha awaits my return to the khan, together with a large basket of pears for which a deal of backsheesh is required. Tea and packing for a start tomorrow fill up the evening. Giorgio seems by no means to like the idea of committing himself to Albanians, Gheghes, and Mereditti, and avoids all speech about Albanians in general or particularly. Three of these men occupy part of the gallery near me, and seem to pass life in strutting up and down, in grinding and drinking coffee, or in making a diminutive sort of humming to the twanging of an immensely long guitar. Sitting on their crossed legs, they bend backwards and forwards and from side to side, shaking their long hay-coloured hair or screwing their enormous moustaches; now and then they rise, whirl their vast capotes about them, flounce out their full skirts, and then bounce up and down the gallery like so many Richard the Thirds in search of Richmonds. But Giorgio by no art can be induced to say more of them than '*Sono tutti disperati*',† and by all, this race seems disliked and mistrusted most markedly.

*A*s he left Macedonia and turned towards northern Albania, Lear noted 'a wilder and more savage race' of men, surpassing 'all their neighbours in gorgeousness of raiment by adding to their ordinary vestments a long surtout of purple crimson or scarlet, trimmed with fur or bordered with gold thread.' The Albanian costume, which Byron held 'the most magnificent in the world' was certainly one of the most extravagant, for the fierce Skipetars were devoted to display, finishing off their finery with an incongruous assortment of precious objects: silver chains, amulets and snuff boxes worn around the neck, pistols, daggers and silver inkstands fastened to their girdles. The surrealistic touches of snuff box and inkstand must have delighted Lear; in Akhridha (Ohrid) he celebrated his arrival in the realms of Childe Harold in a series of vivid, exquisite drawings.

Albanian Journal

23 September 1848

In the afternoon, with my guide, I was able to laugh at my enemies while I drew a fine old Greek church, now turned into a mosque, and obtained lastly an extensive view from the clock tower on the castle hill, whence the town tranquilly lying among tufted planes and tall cypresses recalls the lines of Childe Harold —

---

† They are all miserable creatures.

Akhridha

And the pale crescent sparkles in the glen
Through many a cypress grove within each city's ken.

Certainly Akhridha is a beautiful place. All the hillside below the fortress is thickly studded with Mohammedan tombs – little wedges of rough stone growing out of the soil, as it were, like natural geological excrescences – by thousands. From the streets below parties of women clad in dark blue and masked in white wrappers wander forth to take the air, and near me several crimson-and-purple-coated Gheghes smoke abstractedly on scattered bits of rock; when the sun throws his last red rays from the high western mountains up the side of the castle hill long trains of black buffaloes poke hither and thither, grunting and creaking forth their strange semi-bark, which sounds like the cracking of old furniture. On the whole, the zoological living world of Akhridha is very oppressive; what with dogs, geese, buffali, asses, mules, and horses, jackdaws, goats, and sheep, the streets are a great deal too full of animated nature to be comfortable, however confiding and amiable the several species may be. As for the white-eyed buffali, they are lazy and serene brutes, very opposite in character to their relatives in the marshes of Terracina and Pesto. You may bully them, either by pushing their noses or tugging at their horns as much as you please when they are in your way, and they never resent the indignity.

The khan was swarming with magnificence when I returned to it, the Bey of Tirana and all his train having arrived. Simplicity is the rule of life with Albanian grandees; they sat silently on a mat and smoke, but their retinue bounce and tear about with a perfectly fearful energy, and after supper indulge in music according to their fashion until a late hour, then throwing themselves down to sleep in their capotes, and at early morning going through the slightest possible form of facial ablution – for cleanliness is not the most shining national virtue. These at Akhridha seem a wild and savage set and are not easy to catch by drawing. Yet tomorrow I enter the wildest parts of Ghegheria and must expect to see 'a rugged set of men' indeed. In preparation, the Frangistan 'wide-awakes' are packed up, as having a peculiar attraction for missiles, on account of their typically infidel appearance. Henceforth I adopt the fez, for with that Mohammedan sign on the head it matters not how you adorn the rest of your person.

25 September 1848

After three hours of winding along frightful paths at the edge of clay precipices and chasms, and through scenery of the same character, but gloomier under a clouded sun, we began to descend towards the seaward plains, and were soon effecting a steep and difficult passage between trunks

Akhridha

of oak trees to the purple vale of the Skumbi, which wound through the plain below till it was lost in a gola or chasm through which is the pass to Elbassan. We crossed the Skumbi, here a very formidable stream, by one of those lofty one-arched bridges so common in Turkey, and as the baggage-horse descended the last step down came the luggage once more, so that my sketches would have been lost, *senza rimedio*†, had the accident occurred two seconds sooner. Two hours were occupied in passing the opening between the rocks, which admitted only a narrow pathway besides the stream, and after another hour's ride through widening uncultivated valleys, and Elbassan is in sight, lying among rich groves of olives on a beautiful plain, through which the Skumbi, an unobstructed broad torrent, flows to the Adriatic. The same deceptive beauty throws its halo over Elbassan as over other Albanian towns; and, like its fellow *paesi*‡ this was as wretched

† Without remedy.
‡ Towns.

and forlorn within as without it was picturesque and graceful. It was 6 p.m. ere we reached its scattered and dirty suburbs and threaded its dark narrow streets, all roofed over with mats and dry leaves and so low that one had to sit doubled over the horse to avoid coming into sharp contact with the hanging sticks, dried boughs, loose mats, and rafters. The gloomy shade cast by these awnings did not enliven the aspect of the town, nor was its dirty and comfortless appearance lightened by a morose and wild look – a settled, sullen, despairing expression which the faces of the inhabitants wore. At length, thought I, these are fairly the wilds of Albania!

The wilds of Albania had always been primitive, but their recent history was unfortunate in the extreme. The ruthless depredations of Ali Pasha were swiftly succeeded by savage reprisals from the Porte. When local pashas threatened rebellion after Ali's death, the Ottoman authorities invited a thousand Albanian leaders to a meeting in Monastir where, summoned to a grand assembly, they were massacred by Turkish troops. Sporadic uprisings like the one recorded by Lear were dealt with in a similar spirit and all signs of national identity rigidly suppressed. The Albanians, who had experienced under Ali Pasha both a brutally efficient government and a proud notoriety, were reduced once again to the reluctant subjects of a tottering empire.

Albanian Journal

26 September 1848

I set off early, to make the most of a whole day at Elbassan – a town singularly picturesque, both in itself and as to its site. A high and massive wall, with a deep outer moat, surrounds a large quadrangle of dilapidated houses, and at the four corners are towers, as well as two at each of the four gates: all of these fortifications appear of Venetian structure. Few places can offer a greater picture of desolation than Elbassan; albeit the views from the broad ramparts extending round the town are perfectly exquisite: weeds, brambles, and luxuriant wild fig overrun and cluster about the grey heaps of ruin, and whichever way you turn you have a middle distance of mosques and foliage, with a background of purple hills, or southward, the remarkable mountain of Tomhor, the giant Soracte of the plains of Berat.

No sooner had I settled to draw – forgetful of Bekir the guard – than forth came the populace of Elbassan; one by one and two by two to a mighty host they grew, and there were soon from eighty to a hundred spectators collected, with earnest curiosity in every look; and when I had sketched such of the principal buildings as they could recognise a universal shout of 'Shaitan!' burst from the crowd; and, strange to relate, the greater part of the mob put their fingers into their mouths and whistled furiously, after the manner of butcher-boys in England. Whether this was a sort of spell against my magic I do not know; but the absurdity of sitting still on a rampart to make a drawing while a great crowd of people whistled at me with all their might struck me so forcibly that, come what might of it, I could not resist going off into convulsions of laughter, an impulse the Gheghes seemed to sympathise with, as one and all shrieked with delight, and the ramparts resounded with hilarious merriment. Alas! this was of no long duration, for one of those tiresome Dervishes – in whom, with their green turbans, Elbassan is rich – soon came up, and yelled, 'Shaitan scroo! – Shaitan!'† in my ears with all his force; seizing my book also, with an awful frown, shutting it, and pointing to the sky, as intimating that heaven would not allow such impiety. It was in vain after this to attempt more: the 'Shaitan' cry was raised in one wild chorus – and I took the consequences of having laid by my fez for comfort's sake – in the shape of a horrible shower of stones which pursued me to the covered streets, where, finding Bekir with his whip, I went to work again more successfully about the walls of the old city.

Knots of the Elbassaniotes nevertheless gathered about Bekir, and pointed with angry gestures to me and my 'scroo'. 'We will not be written down,' said they. 'The Frank is a Russian, and he is sent by the Sultan to write us all down before he sells us to the Russian Emperor.' This they told also to Giorgio and murmured bitterly at their fate, though the inexorable Bekir told them they should not only be scroo'd, but bastinadoed, if they were not silent and obedient. Alas! it is not a wonder that Elbassan is no cheerful spot, nor that the inhabitants are gloomy. Within the last two years one of the most serious rebellions has broken out in Albania, and has been sternly put down by the Porte. Under an adventurer named Zuliki, this restless people rose in great numbers throughout the north-western districts; but they were defeated in an engagement with the late Seraskier Pasha. Their Beys, innocent or accomplices, were exiled to Koniah or Monastir, the population was either drafted off into the Sultan's armies, slain, or condemned to the galleys at Constantinople, while the remaining miserables were and are more heavily taxed than before. Such, at least, is the general account of the present state of these provinces: and certainly their appearance speaks of ill fortune, whether merited or unmerited . . . At half past six a.m. we left Elbassan, Giorgio growling at all the inhabitants and wishing they might be sold to the Czar, according to their fears. In any case, attachment to Abdul Medjid is not the reigning characteristic of this forlorn place. It

Illustration to John Cam Hobhouse's A Journey through Albania

AN ALBANIAN.

London, Published by James Cawthorn, 24, Cockspur Street, 1812.

---

† The Devil draws! – the Devil!

was long before we left walls and lanes ... till we began to climb the sides of the high mountain which separates the territory of Elbassan from that of Tirana.

In Lear's notes to his drawings, in his diaries and occasionally, as here, in his journals, splendid scenery evoked memories of a favourite childhood book, a copy of Robinson Crusoe *illustrated with engravings by Thomas Stothard, 'so knit with my earliest ideas of landscape' and no doubt also with the first intimations of exile. The coast of Coromandel and the sea-coast of Illyria shared the same desolate allure; those who tempted the outback of Albania or sailed to sea in a sieve needed a similar courage and tenacity, an eye for wild beauty and an unusual tolerance for solitude.*

Albanian Journal

27 September 1848

How glorious, in spite of the dimming sirocco haze, was the view from the summit, as my eyes wandered over the perspective of winding valley and stream to the farthest edge of the horizon – a scene realising the fondest fancies of artist imagination! The wide branching oak, firmly rivetted in crevices, all tangled over with fern and creepers, hung halfway down the precipices of the giant crag, while silver-white goats (which chime so picturesquely in with such landscapes as this) stood motionless as statues on the highest pinnacle, sharply defined against the clear blue sky. Here and there the broken foreground of rocks piled on rocks, was enlivened by some Albanians who toiled upwards, now shadowed by spreading beeches, now glittering in the bright sun on slopes of the greenest lawn, studded over with tufted trees, which recalled Stothard's graceful forms, so knit with my earliest ideas of landscape. These and countless well-loved passages of auld lang syne, crowded back on my memory as I rested, while the steeds and attendants reposed under the cool plane-tree shade, and drank from the sparkling stream which bubbled from a stone fountain. It was difficult to turn away from this magnificent mountain view – from these chosen nooks and corners of a beautiful world – from sights of which no painter-soul can ever weary: even now, that fold beyond fold of wood, swelling far as the eye can reach – that vale ever parted by its serpentine river – that calm blue plain, with Tomhor in the midst, like an azure island in a boundless sea, haunt my mind's eye and vary the present with visions of the past. With regret I turned northwards to descend to the new district of Tirana, the town (and it is now past eleven) being still some hours distant.

Illustration to John Cam Hobhouse's A Journey through Albania

A DANCING GIRL.

London, Published by James Cawthorn, 24 Cockspur Street, 1813.

*I*n the nineteenth century Tirana was a small town notable for its beautiful
mosques, its approach signalled by a myriad of minarets among olive and
cypress groves. Its transformation into the bureaucratic capital of Albania is a
modern invention.

Albanian Journal

27 September 1848

Wavy lines of olive – dark clumps of plane, and spiry cypresses marked the
place of Tirana when the valley had fully expanded into a pianura, and the
usual supply of white minarets lit up the beautiful tract of foliage with the
wonted deceptive fascination of these towns. As I advanced to the suburbs
I observed two or three mosques mostly highly ornamented, and from a
brilliancy of colour and elegance of form by far the most attractive of any
public building I had yet beheld in these wild places; but though it was
getting dark when I entered the town (whose streets, broader than those of
Elbassan, were only raftered and matted half-way across) it was at once
easy to perceive that Tirana was as wretched and disgusting as its fellow
city, save only that it excelled in religious architecture and spacious market-
places.

Two khans, each abominable, did we try. No person would undertake
to guide us to the palace of the Bey (at some distance from the town), nor
at that hour would it have been to much purpose to have gone there. The
sky was lowering; the crowds of gazers increasing – Albanian the only
tongue; so, all these things considered, I finally fixed on a third-rate khan,
reported to be the Clarendon of Tirana, and certainly better than the other
two, though its horrors are not easy to describe nor imagine. Horrors I had
made up my mind to bear in Albania, and here, truly, they were in earnest.

Is it necessary, says the reader, so to suffer? And when you had a Sultan's
Bouyourdi could you not have commanded beys' houses? True; but had I
done so, numberless arrangements become part of that mode of life, which,
desirous as I was of sketching as much as possible, would have rendered the
whole motives of my journey of no avail. If you lodge with Beys or Pashas,
you must eat with them at hours incompatible with artistic pursuits, and
you must lose much time in ceremony. Were you so magnificent as to
claim a home in the name of the Sultan, they must needs prevent your
stirring without a suitable retinue, nor could you in propriety prevent such
attention; thus, travelling in Albania has, to a landscape painter, two
alternatives; luxury and inconvenience on the one hand, liberty, hard living,
and filth on the other; and of these two I chose the latter, as the most
professionally useful, though not the most agreeable.

Nasticreechia Krorluppia

O the khan of Tirana! with its immense stables full of uproarious horses, its broken ladders, by which one climbed distrustfully up to the most uneven and dirtiest of corridors, in which a loft some twenty feet square by six in height was the best I could pick out as a home for the night. Its walls, falling in masses of mud from its osier-woven sides (leaving great holes exposed to your neighbour's view, or, worse still, to the cold night air); its thinly raftered roof, anything but proof to the cadent amenities resulting from the location of an Albanian family above it; its floor of shaking boards, so disunited that it seemed unsafe to move incautiously across it, and through the great chasms of which the horses below were open to contemplation, while the suffocating atmosphere produced thence are not to be described!

O khan of Tirana! when the Gheghe Kanji strode across the most rotten of garrets, how certainly did each step seem to foretell the downfall of the entire building; and when he whirled great bits of lighted pitch-torch hither and thither, how did the whole horrid tenement seem about to flare up suddenly and irretrievably!

O khan of Tirana! rats, mice, cockroaches, and all lesser vermin were there. Huge flimsy cobwebs, hanging in festoons above my head; big frizzly moths, bustling into my eyes and face, for the holes representing windows I could close but imperfectly with sacks and baggage: yet here I prepared

Albanian khan

to sleep, thankful that a clean mat was a partial preventive to some of this list of woes, and finding some consolation in the low crooning singing of the Gheghes above me, who, with that capacity for melody which those Northern Albanians seem to possess so essentially, were murmuring their wild airs in choral harmony.

28 September 1848

Though the night's home was so rude, fatigue produced sound sleep. The first thing to do was to visit Machmoud Bey, Vice-Governor of Tirana, to procure a Kawas as guardian during a day's drawing, and a letter to his nephew, Ali Bey, of Kroia, for to that city of Scanderbeg I am bent on going . . .

But even with a guard it was a work of trouble to sketch in Tirana: for it was market or bazaar day, and when I was tempted to open my book in the large space before the two principal mosques (one wild scene of confusion, in which oxen, buffaloes, sheep, goats, geese, asses, dogs, and children were all running about in disorder) a great part of the natives, impelled by curiosity, pressed closely to watch my operations, in spite of the Kawas, who kept as clear a space as he could for me; the women alone, in dark feringhis, and ghostly white muslin masks, sitting unmoved by their wares.

Fain would I have drawn the exquisitely pretty arabesque-covered mosques, but the crowds at last stifled my enthusiasm. Not the least annoyance was that given me by the persevering attentions of a mad or fanatic dervish, of most singular appearance as well as conduct. His note of 'Shaitan' was frequently sounded; and as he twirled about, and performed many curious antics, he frequently advanced to me, shaking a long hooked stick, covered with jingling ornaments, in my very face, pointing to the Kawas with menacing looks, as though he would say, 'Were it not for this protector you should be annihilated, you infidel!' The crowd looked on with awe at the holy man's proceedings, for Tirana is evidently a place of great attention to religion. In no part of Albania are there such beautiful mosques and

Tirana

nowhere are collected so many green-vested dervishes. But however a wandering artist may fret at the impossibility of comfortably exercising his vocation, he ought not to complain of the effects of a curiosity which is but natural, or even of some irritation at the open display of arts which, to their untutored apprehension, must seem at the very least diabolical.

The immediate neighbourhood of Tirana is delightful. Once outside the town and you enjoy the most charming scenes of quiet, among splendid planes and the clearest of streams. The afternoon was fully occupied on the road from Elbassan, whence the view of the town is beautiful. The long line of peasants returning to their homes from the bazaar enabled me to sketch many of their dresses in passing; most of the women wore snuff-coloured or dark vests trimmed with pink or red, their petticoats white, with an embroidered apron of chocolate or scarlet; others affected white capotes; but all bore their husband's or male relative's heavy black or purple capote, bordered with broad pink or orange, across their shoulders. Of those whose faces were visible – for a great part wore muslin wrappers (no sign hereabouts of the wearer being Mohammedan, for both Moslem and Christian females are thus bewrapped) – some few were very pretty, but the greater number had toil-and-careworn faces. There were many dervishes also, wearing high white felt steeple-crowned hats, with black shawls round them.

No sooner, after retiring to my pigsty dormitory, had I put out my candle and was preparing to sleep, than the sound of a key turning in the lock of the next door to that of my garret disturbed me, and lo! broad rays of light illumined my detestable lodging from a large hole a foot in

Tirana

Tirana
Lithograph from Journals of a Landscape Painter in Albania &c

diameter, besides from two or three hours, just above my bed; at the same time a whirring, humming sound, followed by strange whizzings and mumblings, began to pervade the apartment. Desirous to know what was going on, I crawled to the smallest chink, without encountering the rays from the great hiatus, and what did I see? My friend of the morning – the maniac dervish – performing the most wonderful evolutions and gyrations; spinning round and round for his own private diversion, first on his legs, and then pivot-wise, *sur son séant*, and indulging in numerous other pious gymnastic feats. Not quite easy at my vicinity to this very eccentric neighbour, and half anticipating a twitch from his brass-hooked stick, I sat watching the event, whatever it might be. It was simple. The old creature pulled forth some grapes and ate them, after which he gradually relaxed in his twirlings and finally fell asleep.

29 September 1848

I was glad enough to leave Tirana, and rejoiced in the broad green paths,

or roads, that lead northwards, through a wide valley below the eastern
range of magnificent mountains, on one of which, at a great height from
the plain, stands the once formidable Kroia [Kruje], so long held out against
the conquering Turk, by Iskander Bey. Certain of its historical interest, I
was now doubly anxious to visit, from its situation, which promised
abundance of beauty . . .

*I*n Illustrated Excursions in Italy *Lear recounted the discovery of a colony of*
Albanians in the Abruzzi. Variously known as Albanesi, Greci, Epiroti or
Schiavoni, they were descended from refugees of the great national rebellion
led by Scanderbeg in the fifteenth century. From his mountain stronghold in Kroia
he had resisted the Porte for twenty-four years, uniting his countrymen in a common
cause and, against extraordinary odds, maintaining his defence against an army one
hundred thousand strong and led by the Sultan himself. The nationalist cause died
with Scanderbeg, but in his day he was hailed throughout Europe as a hero, a
Christian champion against the Infidel invader. The subject of numerous biographies
and epic poems, he was praised by Voltaire, and Vivaldi wrote an opera in his
honour. Four hundred years later, at the time of Lear's visit, Kroia was reduced to
a remote feudal court and in the citadel of the great military leader there reigned a
young Bey with time on his hands.

Albanian Journal

29 September 1848

Ascending through the dark-roofed bazaars – the huge crags towering over
which reminded me of Canalo in Calabria – we arrived at Ali Bey's palace –
a singularly picturesque pile of building, composed of two-storied, painted
galleries, with irregular windows, projecting roofs, and innumerable novelties of architecture – all in a dreary courtyard, the high walls of which shut
out effectually the glorious landscape below.

In the arabesqued and carved corridor, to which a broad staircase con-
ducted me, were hosts of Albanian domestics; and on my letter of introduction being sent in to the Bey, I was almost instantly asked into his room
of reception – a three-windowed, square chamber (excellent, according to
the standard of Turkish ornament, taste, and proportion) – where, in a
corner of the raised divan sat Ali, Bey of Kroia – a lad of eighteen or
nineteen, dressed in the usual blue frock-coat now adopted by Turkish
nobles or officers. A file of kilted and armed retainers were soon ordered
to marshal me into a room where I was to sleep, and the little Bey seemed

greatly pleased with the fun of doing hospitality to so novel a creature as a Frank. My dormitory was a real Turkish chamber; and the raised cushions on three sides of it; the high, square, carved wooden ceiling – the partition screen of lofty woodwork, with long striped Brusa napkins thrown over it – the guns, horse-gear, etc., which covered the walls; the fireplace-closets-innumerable pigeonholes; green, orange, and blue stained-glass windows – all appeared so much the more in the light of luxuries and splendours when found in so remote a place as Kroia. It was not easy to shake off the attentions of ten full-dressed Albanian servants, who stood in much expectation, till, finding I was about to take off my shoes, they made a rush at me as the Jews did at Salonica and showed such marks of disappointment at not being allowed to make themselves useful that I was obliged to tell Giorgio to explain that we Franks were not used to assistance every moment of our lives and that I should think it obliging of them if they would leave me in peace. After changing my dress, the Bey sent to say that supper should be served in an hour, he having eaten at sunset, and in the meantime he would be glad of my society; so I took my place on the sofa by the little gentleman's side, and Giorgio, sitting on the ground, acted as interpreter. At first Ali Bey said little, but soon became immensely loquacious, asking numerous questions about Stamboul and a few about Franks in general – the different species of whom he was not very well informed. At length, when the conversation was flagging, he was moved to discourse about ships that went without sails and coaches that were impelled without horses; and to please him I drew a steamboat and a railway carriage; on which he asked if they made any noise; and I replied by imitating both the inventions in question in the best manner I could think of – 'Tik-tok, tik-tok, tik-tok, tokka, tokka, tokka, tokka, tokka-tok' (crescendo), and 'Squish-squash, squish-squash, squish-squash, thump-bump' – for the land and sea engines respectively – a noisy novelty, which so intensely delighted Ali Bey that he fairly threw himself back on the divan and laughed as I never saw Turk laugh before.

For my sins, this imitation became fearfully popular, and I had to repeat 'squish-squash', 'tik-tok', till I was heartily tired, the only recompense this wonderful little pasha offered me, being the sight of a small German writing-box (when new it might have cost three or four shillings), containing a lithograph of Fanny Ellsler† and two small looking-glasses in the lid. This was brought in by a secretary, attended by two Palikari, at the Bey's orders, and was evidently considered as something uncommonly interesting. So, when this very intellectual intercourse was over, I withdrew to my wooden room, and was glad of a light supper before sleeping.

K was a very small King
Who wore a prodigious crown;
His cloak was of scarlet velvet,
Spotted with blue & brown.

† The celebrated Viennese dancer.

30 September 1848

But one day can be allotted to Kroia, so how to make the best of that day? Little liberty do I look for, the more that while I take my café an Albanian stands at the door who shies off his slippers if I only move a finger – rushing forward to know if I want anything. However, I have caused it to be known through Giorgio, that I only require a single attendant, and that that one should be well paid. Spite of forebodings, I actually escaped from the palace, and having repassed the bazaars was at work on a drawing of the castle rock, one of the most imposing of subjects, ere yet the sun had risen over the eastern hills. Above the town the view is still more majestic, and although many of the inhabitants came and sat near me, yet no one annoyed me in the least, and I drew comparisons between these well-bred people and the rude men of Elbassan and Tirana. At eleven I returned to dine with Ali Bey, an amiable little fellow, who was evidently anxious to make my stay agreeable, though he could not long control his childish curiosity from bidding Giorgio (who could ill keep his gravity) to ask me to imitate the noises of the steamboats and coaches. So I again went through, 'Tik-tok, tokka, tokkey', and 'Squish-squash, squash, squash', to the great delight of the Bey and his retinue.

The routine of dinner was as follows: ten servants, in full Albanian dress came in at once, for all the world like in an opera ballet. One of them places a little stool on the ground, upside down, as much as to say that it is not to be sat upon; others fix thereon a large flat plate of tin, or some similar metal, with a spoon, or piece of bread, to each diner (there were two guests beside myself); then an ewer with water is handed to each person by one of the domestics, who kneels until you have used it and the Brusa towel. Soup, somewhat like sago and vinegar, was the first dish placed before us: and here my good genius basely forsook me, for endeavouring to sit cross-legged like my entertainers I somehow got my knees too far below the pewter table-top, and an ill-conditioned violent cramp seizing me at the unlucky moment in which the tureen was placed on the table, I hastily endeavoured to withdraw the limb, but unsuccessfully – gracious! – sidelong went the whole table and all the soup was wasted on the ground! Constantly as a Frank is called on to observe the unvarying good breeding and polite case of Turkish manner, this was a most trying proof of the endurance of those qualities. Nobody spoke, or even looked, as if anything had gone amiss; one of the corps de ballet wiped up the catastrophe and others soon brought in a new bowl ... as if nothing had happened. Nor was my awkwardness alluded to except by Giorgio, who, by my orders, offered a strong apology for the stiffness of Franks' legs in general and of mine in particular.

But I took care not to commit myself by unexpected cramps any more, and sprawled sideways through the rest of the dinner as I best could. A pilaf of fowls, full of spices and bones, kebabs, a paste of rice, onions, and pie-crust, and some round balls of chopped meat concluded the repast, some grapes excepted. Nobody drank anything, and abstemiousness was the order of the day, a virtue I was compelled to practise, even more than my companions, seeing that I was unskilled at selecting proper bits from the dishes with my fingers, and not only caught at unsatisfactory bones, but let half of what I did catch fall midway between my mouth and the single bowl into which we dipped in rotation. So ended my first Turkish dinner . . .

Later, Ali Bey showed me the rooms of his harem (the first and last I am most probably destined to see), which he was repairing with an indistinct view to future matrimony. Very picturesque and Arabian-night-like chambers they were, with a covered gallery, looking down on the (now) still bazaars and the tall minarets, to the rocks and the oak woods sloping down, down by undulating hills to the boundless plains, moonlit sea, and far faint hills of Skodra. Imagination peopled this gallery with houri tenants, waving feringhees, and laughing faces, but the halls of Ali Bey were silent for the present.

*F*rom Kroia Lear travelled to Alessio (Lezhe) and thence to the northern *limits of Albania, arriving at Shkoder (the Venetian Scutari) on the Mon- tenegrin border. A trading town of fine houses and orchards stretched along Lake Skodra which, in the nineteenth century, was the capital of upper Albania and the seat of the governing pasha. Accompanied by Signor Bonatti, the English*

The bridge at Scutari

Vice-Consul, Lear endured a memorable feast at the provincial palace. His description of this elaborate and indiscriminate repast is confirmed by the complaints of other travellers; Hobhouse protested as well at the 'violent eructations' 'expected by visitants as a compliment to show their host they have digested his good fare.' Perhaps Lear recalled his experience of Albanian haute cuisine when he ventured into the novel field of 'Culinary Science'. His receipt for Amblongus Pie should have been derived from a traditional Skipetar source:

> *Take 4 pounds (say 4½ pounds) of fresh Amblongusses, and put them in a small pipkin.*
> *Cover them with water and boil them for 8 hours incessantly, after which add 2 pints of new milk, and proceed to boil for 4 hours more . . .*
> *Grate some nutmeg over the surface, and cover them carefully with powdered gingerbread, curry-powder, and a sufficient quantity of cayenne pepper . . .*
> *Shake the pan violently till the Amblongusses have become of a pale purple colour . . .*
> *Serve up in a clean dish, and throw the whole out of the window as soon as possible.*

Albanian Journal

5 October 1848

It rained hard all night and at 10 a.m. (when we should have been going up to the Pasha's dinner) torrents descended, with violent thunder and hail. Towards eleven it held up a little, so as the invitations of three-tailed Pashas are not to be neglected, I set off to the Vice-Consul's, taking Giorgio, with a supply of shoes, linen, and cloth clothes as a remedy against the wetting there was small chance of escaping. Whereupon, fresh storms commencing, Signor Bonatti, myself, the Dragoman Pazzini and a Kawas, all rushed desperately through the falling torrents, by odious paved paths to the castle, arriving there in a perfect deluge. Having changed our dress, the time till dinner was served (about noon) passed in continual repetitions of sherbet, sweetmeats, pipes, and coffee, the Pasha being always very lively and merry.

Osman Pasha affects European manners, and (to my great relief) we all sat in chairs round a table; a Bimbashi (or captain on guard) appearing about as much at ease in his new position as I had done when in that of the natives. As for the legion dinner, it is not to be described. I counted up thirty-seven dishes, served, as is the custom in Turkey, one by one in succession, and then I grew tired of reckoning (supposing that perhaps the feast was going on all day) though I think there were twelve or fourteen more. But nothing was so surprising as the strange jumble of irrelevant food offered: lamb, honey, fish, fruit; baked, boiled, stewed, fried; vegetable, animal; fresh, salt, pickled; solid; oil, pepper; fluid; sweet, sour; hot, cold – in strange variety, though the ingredients were often very good. Nor was there any order in the course according to European notions – the richest pastry came immediately after dressed fish and was succeeded by beef, honey, and cakes; pears and peaches; crabs, ham, boiled mutton, chocolate cakes, garlic, and fowl; cheese, rice, soup, strawberries, salmon-trout, and cauliflowers – it was the very chaos of a dinner! Of those who did justice to the repast I was not one; and fortunately it is not considered necessary, by the rules of Turkish etiquette, to do more than taste each dish; and although the Pasha twice or thrice helped me himself, it is sufficient to eat the smallest atom, when the attendant servant removes your plate. As for drink, there were marsala, sherry, hock, champagne, Bass's pale ale, bottled porter, rakhi, and brandy – a large show of liquor in a Mohammedan house, nor did the faithful seem to refrain particularly from any fluid; but there was no unbecoming excess, and as is remarkably the case with Turkish manners, quiet and order was observable throughout the festivity. Only the Bimbashi, a heavy, dull man, seemed marked out for practical jokes, and they made him take an amazing mixture of porter and champagne, assuring him it was a species of Frank soup, which he seemed to like little enough. As the entertainment draws to a close it is polite to express your sense of the host's hospitality by intimating a sense of repletion, and, by pointing to your throat, the utter impossibility of eating any more; and perhaps the last delicate act of complimentary acknowledgement, which it is not easy to describe otherwise than as a series of remarkable choral ventriloquism, was the queerest and most alarming trait of the whole fête.

6 October 1848

An April day of sun and showers. Early I went to the Consul's, to make a drawing of Calliope Bonatti, the Consul's second daughter, a very pretty girl, who good-naturedly sat to me in a bridal Scutarine dress which Madame Bonatti had most obligingly borrowed. No toilet can be more splendid; purple silk and velvet, elaborately embroidered in gold and silver, form the outer garment, the patterns worked by hand with the greatest taste; two or three undervests covered with embroidery, full purple trousers, innumerable chains of gold and silver coins and medals, with a long white veil, complete the costume, excepting several coloured silk handkerchiefs which are sewn inside the outer vest and have a tawdry and ill-arranged look when compared with the rest of the dress. This gay attire is only

Calliope Bonatti in Scutarine bridal dress

worn on great fête days, or on marked occasions, such as marriages and christenings.

At four we adjourned to the house of [the merchant] Antonio Summa – a substantial building in a large courtyard, all the appurtenances about which indicated opulence and comfort. The usual compliments of pipes, coffee, and lemonade were gone through, and I made a drawing of the worthy merchant in his Skodra costume, but on his younger brother coming in (both were men of about forty years of age), and requesting to be sketched also, I, for want of paper, was obliged to make a small though accurate portrait of him on the same page as that on which I had drawn his eldest brother, on a larger scale.

'O, canto cielo!' said the younger, in a fury of indignation, when he saw the drawing: 'why have you done this? It is true I am the youngest, but I am not smaller than my brother, and why should you make me so diminutive? What right have you thus to remind me of my inferior position? Why do you come into our house to act so insultingly?'

I was so amazed by this afflicting view of my innocent mistake that I could hardly apologise when the elder brother took up the tale.

'I, too,' said he, 'am vexed and hurt, O Signore! I thought you meant well; but if you think that you win my esteem by a compliment paid at the expense of the affection of my brother, you are greatly mistaken.'

What could I say? Was there ever such a lesson to unthinking artists in foreign lands? I had made two enemies by one sketch, and was obliged to take a formal addio, leaving the injured brothers bowing me out with looks of thunder.

*A*pproaching Berat, Lear paused to analyse his impressions of the Albanian language while his baggage horse was being extracted from a ditch. 'Among the clatter of strange monosyllables – dort beer, dort bloo, dort hitch, hitch beer, blue beer, beer chak, dort gatch' were notable. Victorian philologists claimed – on scant evidence – the unbroken descent of Albanian from the ancient Illyrian; some heard echoes of a distant heroic past, identifying in ordinary Albanian expressions entire phrases from Homer. 'That I do not speak the language, and that I had not previously studied figure drawing are my two great regrets in Albania', Lear noted in his Journal.

Albanian Journal

14 October 1848

At length the celebrated fortress of Berat appeared – dark blue and diminutive on a pointed hill. Approaching the capital of Central Albania – a place I had so long desired to see – every step leads into grander scenes . . .

Passing below the cliffs of the gorge and entering the street of bazaars which runs quite through the town, I was at once struck by the entire change of costume in this district – that of the Toskidhes. Instead of the purple frock, scarlet vest, black waistcoat, and short kilt of Ghegheria, here all is white, or spruce fluffy grey cloth, with long, many-fluted fustianells, while the majority, instead of the red fez, wear white caps. Beyond the bazaars, which are extensive and well filled, is a wide open space by the river, whence the view of the dark gorge of the Beratino, the town, and castle are truly wondrous. On one side of this piazza or market-place is a large new khan, and here I took possession of a corner room looking out on to the busy scene that extends to the foot of the hill – a space in which hundreds of figures sat continually before me for their pictures without suspicion or restraint. This was a khan arrangement which pleased me not a little, besides the comfort of the room, which was new and clean, and had well-glazed windows. Nothing could be more amusing than the variety of life below. There was the Dervish with white or green caps – the Mohammedan, as well as most of the Christian women, in loose blue feringhis and closely veiled – while infinite numbers of carts drawn by coal-black buffali – Greeks, Turks, Albanians, mingled and moved in profusely changing groups.

Having a letter to the Pasha (Berat, with Skodra and Ioannina, are the three existing Pashaliks of Albania), I sent Giorgio with a request for a Kawas, who shortly arrived, and after early dinner I began to sketch (there is no time to be lost in places so full of interest) on the riverside below the castle, hundreds of people pouring forth to see my operations; but all were violently repelled by the active guardian Kawas with a stick, which he threw with all his force at the legs of such unlucky individuals as pressed too closely on me or interfered with the view. When this club was ejected from the incensed authority's hand the rush to escape was frightful and the yells of those who received the blows very disagreeable to my feelings. After a time my guard got tired of his work, and sitting down calmly to smoke, delegated his power to a young pickle of a boy, who took infinite delight in using his temporary dignity to the utmost, greatly to the disgust of his elders, who durst not complain.

Berat

*L*eaving Berat with regret, 'for an artist may go easily enough at any time of his life to Rome or the Rhine, Matlock, Constantinople, Jerusalem, Killarney or Calcutta, but Berat and Illyria are not easy places to revisit', Lear stopped at Apollonia to see the ruins of the great Roman city whose marbles *had been plundered by Ali Pasha for his palaces; a solitary column survived in the wilderness.*

In Avlona (Vlore) his German hosts arranged for a guide to accompany him to Khimara (Himare), the most savage and·sublime district of Albania, still terra incognita *to the English traveller. Conversation at dinner was devoted to news of revolution and counter-revolution in the civilised world, which had recently witnessed the dramatic downfall of Prince Metternich, the Emperor Franz Josef, King Ludwig of Bavaria and Lola Montez.*

Albanian Journal

19 October 1848

Avlona is but a poor place now, and having suffered in the latest Albanian (or Zukili's) rebellion, exhibits a mournful air of decay. Passing through the town, I made my way to the residence of a merchant, Herr J——, who, with Herr S——,† a doctor of quarantine in these coasts, lives in a two-storied wooden house overlooking town, plain, and sea; and by means of a walled courtyard, a broad veranda, a gallery, and some inner rooms, had made himself a very comfortable place for such an out-of-the-way part of the world. I was received, on presenting a letter from Signor Bonatti of Skodra, with courtesy, though with an eternity of fuss and compliment I would have dispensed with. A good room, used as an office, was given me to abide in, but the difficulty of attaining the usual degree of travelling cleanliness was greater here than at the houses of either Greeks or Turks, seeing that the masters of this continually came in and out, and scrutinised with infantine curiosity all their guests' acts and property. Having read with avidity some German papers conveying the latest intelligence of the past six weeks (news of the most extraordinary events occurring throughout all Europe), I sat with my hosts till their supper-time, conversing about parts of Albania, especially Acroceraunia or Khimara, with which the doctor is well acquainted. They advise me to visit that coast and its unknown villages, and offer their servant as guide – a trustworthy Khimariote, who speaks Italian well and is known throughout his native territory. At supper time Herr S—— held forth on German and European politics with alarming enthusiasm. Prophecy succeeded prophecy, as to all the royal and noble heads to be cut off; and the plates and salt-cellars jingled to the thumps which accompanied each denunciation of tyrants and each appeal to liberty. Not thinking it well-bred to expostulate with my host on the length of his

† Lear had a particular prejudice against 'Ger-men', 'Ger-women' and 'Ger-children'.

monologue, and not quite agreeing with all his sentiments, I wished he was a silent Turk, and entreated to retire to sleep.

*O*n 21 October Lear set off for a week's tour of Khimara, the ancient Acroceraunia and one of the wildest outposts of Europe. This was, at last, the Albania of Gothick romance, refuge of outlaws, home of the blood feud and the vendetta, nominally Christian but governed by an implacable tribal code. Accompanied by an armed guard, Anastasio Kanetzi of Vuno, and carrying a small knapsack containing 'the fewest articles of toilet ever known to have been taken by a Milordos Ingliz', Lear turned towards the snow-topped interior and as they reached their first mountain pass Anastasio brandished his pistols and fired a feu de joie.

Albanian Journal

21 October 1848

Presently we came to the oak-clad hills immediately below the town, where narrow winding paths led upwards among great rocks and spreading trees worthy of Salvator Rosa and not unlike the beautiful serpentara of Olevano. I have never seen more impressively savage scenery since I was in Calabria. Evening or early morn are the times to study these wild southern places to advantage; they are then alive with the inhabitants of the town or village gathering to or issuing from it; here were sheep crowding up the narrow rock-stairs – now lost in the shade of the foliage – now bounding in light through the short lentisk – huge morose dogs, like wolves, walking sullenly behind – shepherds carrying lambs or sick sheep, and a crowd of figures clad in thick large trousers and short jackets and bearing immense burdens of sticks or other rustic materials. These last are the women of Draghiadhes, for here, and at the next village (Dukadhes [Dukat]), the fair sex adopt male attire, and are assuredly about the oddest-looking creatures I ever beheld. Worn and brown by hard labour in the sun, they have yet something pensive and pleasing in the expression of the eye, but all the rest is unfeminine and disagreeable. They are, as far as I can learn, the only Mohammedan women in these regions who do not conceal their faces – whether it be that their ancestors were Christians and turning to the faith of the Prophet did not think it worth while in so remote a place as Khimara to adopt articles of such extra expense as veils, I know not – but such is the fact, and they are the only females of their creed whose faces I ever saw. 'But,' said Anastasio, 'when we have passed Tchika, and are in true Khimara, out of the way of these Turks, then you will see women and not like pigs. Ah, Signor mio! these are not women! – these are pigs, pigs – Turks – pigs, I say! For all that, they are very good people, and all of them my intimate friends. But, Signore, you could not travel here alone.' And, although Anastasio certainly made the most patronising use of his position as interpreter, guide, and guard, I am inclined to believe that he was, in this, pretty near the truth, for I doubt if a stranger could safely venture through Acroceraunia unattended. Assuredly also all the world hereabouts seemed his friends, as he boasted, for the remotest and almost invisible people on far-away rocks shouted out 'Capitano' as we passed, proving to me that I was in company with a widely known individual.

The musical talents of the Skipetars and the tradition of the klephtic ballad were in the nineteenth century and are still today a subject of scholarly study, but the most memorable accounts of Albanian artistry are often those of travellers. The Swedish artist Otto Magnus von Stackelberg, kidnapped by Albanian bandits in northern Greece, recorded the rousing chorus of his captors:

> *There were forty brigands, sitting on Olympus*
> *   forty cold nights long,*
> *Their jackets rotting on their bodies*
> *   were smeared with black blood.*
> *Bo! Bo! the night and the moon.*

Byron included a Skipetar song in 'Childe Harold's Pilgrimage' and Hobhouse described 'a scene from the Mysteries of Udolpho', klephts bounding around a bonfire to 'wild and monstrous music' as they roared out the refrain, 'Robbers all at Parga!' Lear's Albanian entertainments were rather more subdued.

Albanian Journal

22 October 1848

My arrival at Dukadhes seemed the signal for a sort of universal soirée; and I was to promote the general hilarity by the gift of an unlimited quantity of wine – an arrangement I willingly acceded to for the sake of witnessing 'life in Khimara' . . .

Presently the company came, and queer enough it was! The two Messieurs Zingari, or gipsies, are blacksmiths by profession and are clad in dark-coloured garments, once white, now grey-brown; the contrast between them and the Albanians round them, nearly all of whom have light hair and florid complexions, is very striking. The gipsy, all grin and sharpness, who plays second fiddle is continually bowing and ducking to me ere he squats down; but the elder, or first performer, is absolutely one of the most remarkable-looking creatures I ever beheld; his great black eyes, peering

below immensely thick arched brows, have the most singular expression
of cunning and ferocity, and his black moustache and beard enclose a mouth
which, when shut, argues all sorts of tragic obstinacies, but on opening
discloses a grin of brilliant ivory from ear to ear. Take him for all in all,
anything so like a diabolical South Sea idol I never yet saw living.

At first the entertainment was rather slow. The gipsies had two guitars,
but they only tinkled them with a preparatory coquettishness, till, another
friend dropping in with a third mandolino, a pleasing discord was by
degrees created and increased to a pitch of excitement that seemed to
promise brilliant things for the evening's festivities. Anastasio, also, catching
the melodious infection, led the performers by his own everlasting Greek
refrain – sung at the full power of a tremendous voice and joined in by all
present in the first circle – for now many more than the chorus had entered

Dukadhes

the room, remaining seated or standing behind, and the whole formed, in the flickering light of the wood torches, one of the most strange scenes imaginable. Among the auditors were the padrona of the house (a large lady in extensive trousers), her daughter (a nice-looking woman), and two pretty little girls, her grandchildren – all unveiled, as is the mode in Dukadhes. As the musical excitement increased, so did the audience begin to keep time with their bodies, which this people, even when squatted, move with the most curious flexibility. An Albanian, in sitting on the ground, goes plump down on his knees, and then bending back crosses his legs in a manner wholly impracticable to us who sit on chairs from infancy. While thus seated he can turn his body half round on each side as if on a pivot, the knees remaining immovable; and of all the gifted people in this way that I ever saw, the gipsy guitarist was pre-eminently endowed with gyratory powers equal almost to the American owl, which, it is said, continues to look round and round at the fowler as he circles about him till his head twists off.

Presently the fun grew fast and furious, and at length the father of song – the hideous idol-gipsy – became animated in the grandest degree; he sang and shrieked the strangest minor airs with incredible accompaniments, tearing and twangling the guitar with great skill and energy enough to break it into bits. Everything he sang seemed to delight his audience, which at times was moved to shouts of laughter, at others almost to tears. He bowed backwards and forwards till his head nearly touched the ground and waved from side to side like a poplar in a gale. He screamed – he howled – he went through long recitatives and spoke prose with inconceivable rapidity; and all the while his auditors bowed and rocked to and fro as if participating in every idea and expression. I never saw a more decided instance of enthusiastic appreciation of song, if song it could be called, where the only melody was a wild repetition of a minor chorus – except at intervals, when one or two of the Toskidhes' characteristic airs varied the musical treat.

The last performance I can remember to have attended to appeared to be received as a *capo d'opera*: each verse ended by spinning itself out into a chain of rapid little Bos, ending in chorus thus: 'Bo, bo-bo-bo, BO! – bo, bobobo, BO!' – and every verse was more loudly joined in than its predecessor, till at the conclusion of the last verse, when the unearthly idol-gipsy snatched off and waved his cap in the air – his shining head was closely shaved, except one glossy raven tress at least three feet in length – the very rafters rang again to the frantic harmony: 'Bo, bo-bo-bo, bo-bo-bo, bo-bo-bo, bobobo, BO!' – the last 'BO!' uttered like a pistol-shot and followed by a unanimous yell.

Fatigue is so good a preparation for rest that after this savage mirth had gone on for two or three hours I fell fast asleep and heard no more that night.

23 October 1848

I am awaked an hour before daylight by the most piercing screams. Hark! – they are the loud cries of a woman's voice, and they come nearer – nearer – close to the house. For a moment the remembrance of last night's orgies, the strange place I was lying in and the horrid sound by which I was so suddenly awakened made a confusion of ideas in my mind which I could hardly disentangle, till, lighting a phosphorus match and candle, I saw all the Albanians in the room sitting bolt upright and listening with ugly countenances to the terrible cries below. In vain I ask the cause of them; no one replies; but one by one, and Anastasio the last, all descend the ladder, leaving me in a mystery which does not make the state of things more agreeable; for though I have not 'supped full of horror' like Macbeth, yet my senses are nevertheless 'cooled to hear so dismal a night shriek' . . .

After a short time Anastasio and the others returned, but at first I could elicit no cause for this startling the night from its propriety. At length I suppose they thought that, as I was now irretrievably afloat in Khimara life, I might as well know the worst as not; so they informed me that the wailings proceeded from a woman of the place whose husband had just been murdered. He had had some feud with an inhabitant of a neighbouring village (near Kudhesi) nor had he returned to his house as was expected last night; and just now, by means of the Khimariot dogs, whose uproar is unimaginable, the head of the slain man was found on one side of the ravine, immediately below the house I am in, his murderers having tossed it over from the opposite bank, where the body still lay. This horrid intelligence had been taken (with her husband's head) to his wife, and she instantly began the public shrieking and wailing usual with all people in this singular region on the death of relatives. They tell me this screaming tragedy is universal throughout Khimara, and is continued during days, commonly in the house of mourning, or when the performers are engaged in their domestic affairs. In the present instance, however, the distressed woman, unable to control her feelings to the regular routine of grief, is walking all over the town, tearing her hair and abandoning herself to the most frantic wretchedness . . .

No English travellers failed to remark on the Albanian treatment of women, who were used with considerably less kindness than ordinary beasts of burden and brutally beaten for their labours. The relationship between the sexes was not one conforming to Victorian canons of propriety; love and loyalty were confined to masculine society. Hobhouse commented, 'they have, in truth, rather a contempt, and even an aversion for their females, and there is nothing in any of their occasional inclinations which can be said to partake of what we call the tender passion. Yet all of them get married who can, as it is a sign of wealth and they wish to have a domestic slave.'

Albanian Journal

23 October 1848

At half past ten we began to descend, and soon emerged from the clouds into bright sunlight, which lit up all the difficulties of what is called the Strada Bianca or Aspri Ruga – a zigzag path on the side of the steepest of precipices, yet the only communication between Khimara and Avlona towards the north … Lower down in the descent a migration of Khimariotes – the most restless of people – met us; some eighty or one hundred women laden as never women were elsewhere – their male relations taking it easy up the mountain – the ladies carrying the capotes as well as babies and packages.

Heavens!' said I, surprised out of my wonted philosophy of travel, which ought not to exclaim at anything, 'how can you make your women such slaves?' 'O Signore,' said Anastasio, 'to you, as a stranger, it must seem extraordinary; but the fact is we have no mules in Khimara – that is the reason why we employ a creature so inferior in strength as a woman is (*un animale tanto poco capace*); but there is no remedy, for mules there are none and women are next best to mules. *Vi assicuro, Signore*, although certainly far inferior to mules, they are really better than asses, or even horses.' That was all I got for my interference.

24 October 1848

[At Vuno] there arose the wail for the poor girl, the cousin of the Kasnetzi, who died three days ago. It was, as at Dukadhes, a woman's cry, but more mournful and prolonged, with sobs between nearly each cry; and when the first wail was over a second female took it up in the same strain. Nothing can be more mournful than this lament for the dead, yet there seems to be a sort of pride in executing the performance well and loudly, for when I spoke of the sadness of the sound – 'Ah, Signore!' said Anastasio, '*ci sono altre chi piangono assai meglio di quella!*'† The death of this cousin led the eldest brother to apologise much for the curtailed hospitality which iron custom compelled them to show to me under the circumstances: they

---

† Ah, sir, there are others who cry ever so much better!

should have killed a sheep – they would have had a dance, and all sorts of fêtes, etc. etc., but on the decease of near relatives no allegria is ever permitted for nine days...

The Khimariotes appear to have a code of some very severe laws, and all tell me that they know no instance of their ever having been broken through. Those, for instance, for the punishment of conjugal infidelity insist on the death of the woman and the cutting off ears and nose of the other offending party. Two or three instances have occurred among the various towns in the memory of my informers, and one gentleman whose head is unadorned with ears or proboscis, I have myself seen. Another was pointed out to me today, as a man who made a great disturbance in Vuno by destroying the peace of one of its best families: the wife was instantly put to death, but her paramour escaped and remained abroad for two years, when he returned and is now settled here. 'But,' said I, 'how did he remain unpunished?' 'Because he escaped.' 'But why, since your severity in these cases is so extreme, why was he allowed to return?' 'Because we killed his father instead of him!' 'O, cielo, but what had his father done?' 'Niente! Ma sempre ci vuol qualchuno ammazzato in queste circonstanze; e cosi, abbiam preso il padre. Somebody must have been killed. E lo stesso – basta cosi'† – an obliquity of justice alarming to parents with unruly offspring.

25 October 1848

At half past seven, I set out for Khimara: the town so called is considered as the capital of this district, to which it gives its name ...   Khimara‡ is now a ruined place, since its capture by the overwhelming Ali Pasha, but it still retains its qualities of convenient asylum for doubtful or fugitive characters: for what force can penetrate the fastnesses by which the rock is surrounded without time being given to the pursued to escape beyond the possibility of capture? ...

As I walked slowly up the zigzag path to the entrance of the town, I had leisure to examine my numerous new acquaintance, whom I thought by far the most wild and most typical of Albanian character that I had yet seen; the men wear their hair extremely long, and walk with the complete strut of Albanian dignity – the loftiest and most sovereign expression of pride and independence in every gesture. As for the females, I saw none, except a few of the heavy stick-laden, who were toiling up the hill, clad in dark blue dresses with red aprons (worn behind), and red-worked hose. Guided by Anastasio, who seemed here, as elsewhere, a general acquaintance and was greeted with excessive hilarity, we proceeded to a house where, in

† Nothing at all, but somebody must be killed under these circumstances, so we killed the father, it is all one.
‡ Khimara, anciently Chimaera.

a dark room of great size, a mat and cushions were spread for me and there was no lack of company. A very aged man, more than a century old, occupied a bed in one corner; a screaming baby in a cradle on the opposite side illustrated another extreme point of the seven ages of the family; two or three women, retiring into the obscurest shade, seemed to be knitting, while circles of long-haired Khimariotes thronged the floor.

Many of these, both outside and in the house, extended their hands for mine to shake, I supposed from being aware of Frank modes of salutation; but among them three or four gave me so peculiar a twist or crack of my fingers that I was struck by its singularity; though it was not until my hand had been held firmly for a repetition of this manœuvre, accompanied by a look of interrogation from the holder, that the thought flashed on my mind, that what I observed was a concerted signal. I shortly became fully aware that I was among people who, from some cause or other, had fled from justice in other lands.

Of these was one who, with his face entirely muffled excepting one eye, kept aloof in the darker part of the chamber, until having thoroughly scrutinized me he came forward, and dropping his capote discovered to my horror and amazement features which, though disguised by an enormous growth of hair, I could not fail to recognize. 'The world is my city now,' said he; 'I am become a savage like those with whom I dwell. What is life to me?' And covering his face again, he wept with a heart-breaking bitterness only life-exiles can know.

Alas! henceforth this wild Alsatia of the mountains – this strange and fearful Khimara – wore to my thoughts a tenfold garb of melancholy, when I considered it as the refuge during the remainder of a weary life of men whose early years had been passed in far other abodes and society . . .

Far up the ravine [on the retreat to Vuno] there is a detached rock, covered with Greek inscriptions; I mean modern names, inscribed in Romaic. 'Tutti scrivono,' said Anastasio, 'scrivete anche voi'† so as I defaced nothing by the act I added my name to the visitors' book of the Pass of Khimara, the only Englishman's there, and it will be long before there are many more. Much time must elapse ere Khimara becomes a fashionable watering-place, and before puffing advertisements of 'salubrious situation, unbroken retirement, select society, and easy access from Italy', meet the eye in the daily papers of England.

In the stony river-bed we fell in with three armed Albanians, of Delvino, and they instantly commenced a sham fight with Anastasio, as did the Kawas of Berat, by seizing throats, firing pistols, laughing and screeching

---

† Everybody writes – write your name also.

'The Palace of Ali Pacha at Tepaleen'
From Finden's ... Illustrations to the Life
and Work of Byron

uproariously. I left them at this pastime, and wound up the path of the
ravine, whence, looking down, I perceived the men of war examining my
three-legged sketching-stool, carried by Anastasio, with every kind of
experimental sitting. The sun was low by the time all the precipices and
chasms were past; and as we entered Vuno, it seemed, by comparison with
Khimara, a city of palaces ...

The poor woman next door is still wailing, filling the air with her
monotonous cry.

*L*ear's Albanian tour was ending. From Khimara he returned to Avlona,
then turned south toward Tepelene, Arghyro Kastro (Girjokaster) and the
Greek province of Epirus. This was the land made famous by Byron, where
anecdotes of the poet were eagerly and too easily offered; but the splendid palace of
Ali Pasha at Ioannina, described in 'Childe Harold's Pilgrimage', had vanished
in vainglorious ruin. The painted chambers of the Seraglio, compared by travellers
to a scene from the Arabian Nights, *were a blackened waste, and the court which*
Byron and Hobhouse saw filled with an imperial assembly of pashas and petitioners,
ministers, merchants, Turkish and Moorish soldiers, Greek secretaries, Tartar
couriers and black slaves had disappeared without a trace.

Albanian Journal

29 October 1848

At sunrise I went down into the plain with the Black Margiann,† and drew
Avlona from the level ground near the sea, returning to dinner before
noon. At this meal, the overbearing and violent political thunderings of

---

† The Nubian servant of his German hosts.

Herr S— against all monarchs, tyrants, kings, autocrats, etc. (they had received new gazettes from Austria) was so profoundly disagreeable, that I was rejoiced to know that two horses had arrived, with which, the Black being my guide, I was to visit the monastery of Aghia Marina di Svernez, in a little island about two miles from Avlona.

We had soon passed the border of olives that surround the town and were trotting over the wide plain, almost impassable with mud when I had arrived, but now hard and dry; and beyond this, always making for a little woody peninsula which projects into the sea, we came to the salt works. Here they take a sort of mullet, from which is prepared the roe called *bottarga*, for which Avlona is famous. As we skirted these salt lagunes I observed an infinite number of what appeared to be large white stones, arranged in rows with great regularity, though yet with something odd in their form not easily to be described. The more I looked at them, the more I felt they were not what they seemed to be, so I appealed to Blackey, who instantly plunged into a variety of explanations, verbal and active, the chief of which consisted in flapping his arms and hands, puffing and blowing with most uncouth noises, and putting his head under one arm, with his eyes shut; as for his language, it was so mixed a jargon of Turkish, Italian, Greek and Nubian that little more could be extracted from it than that the objects in question ate fish and flew away afterwards; so I resolved to examine these mysterious white stones forthwith, and off we went, when – lo! on my near approach, one and all put forth legs, long necks, and great wings, and 'stood confessed' so many great pelicans, which, with croakings expressive of great disgust at all such ill-timed interruptions, rose up into the air in a body of five or six hundred and soared slowly away to the cliffs north of the gulf.

These birds frequent the coast around Avlona in great numbers, breeding in the rocky inlets beyond the bay and living on fish and refuse in the salt lagunes. Pleased with these ornithological novelties, hitherto only seen in zoological gardens or at Knowsley, I followed the faithful Margiann (who nearly fell off his horse with laughter at my surprise at the transmutation of the white stones) through levels of deep sand, by tracts of sedge and rushes and groups of salt-kilns . . . Then we galloped across to marshy sand waste, pursued now and then by ravenous howling dogs, and by half an hour after dark were at the gate.

The party there was increased by a Vuniote who had been one of Lord Byron's guards at Missolonghi. He told me some anecdotes of the poet, but on such slight authority, I write them not down. As for my hosts, the news of the Emperor's flight from Vienna had made them more full of political excitement than ever; between their pipes they thumped their

Avlona
Lithograph from Journals of a Landscape
Painter in Albania &c

table destructively, predicting with sinister glee all sorts of bloodshed and downfall of tyrants. In vain did I attempt to change the current of discourse; but when they proceeded to some long and violent tirades against 'England and the English', I broke through my role of passive listener, and having much the advantage of my hosts in fluency of Italian, took the liberty of telling them what I thought of their illbreeding in thus victimizing a guest who might by possibility not quite agree with all their opinions – requesting earnestly that we might henceforth talk about pelicans, or red mullet, or whatever they pleased, so that we eschewed politics.

31 October 1848

Nearer Tepelene we met many peasants, all in white caps and kilts and of a more squalid and wretched appearance than any I had yet seen; the whole of this part of Albania is indeed most desolate and its inhabitants broken and dejected. Their rebellion under Zuliki seems to have been the last convulsive struggle of this scattered and disarmed people, and the once proud territory of Ali Pasha is now ground down into a melancholy insignificance, and wellnigh deprived of its identity. It was nearly 3 p.m. ere the last tedious windings of the valley disclosed . . . the long promontory

Pelican (Pelecanus Onocrothalus)
From John Gould's Birds of Europe

of Tepelene, whose ruined palace and walls and silver-toned mosque give a strange air of dreamy romance to this scene, one of the most sublime and simple in Albania and certainly one most fraught with associations ancient and modern.

My curiosity had been raised to its very utmost to see this place, for so many years full of the records of one of the most remarkable of men; yet it seemed so strange, after all one had read of the 'no common pomp' of the entertainer of Lord Byron and Sir J. C. Hobhouse, to find a dreary, blank scene of desolation, where once, and so recently, was all the rude magnificence of Oriental despotism!

Giorgio went on to find a lodging in this fallen stronghold of Albania, and I, meanwhile, sat down above the [River] Bantja, to sketch the town, which, on its rocky peninsula seems a mere point in comparison with the magnificent mountain forms around ... The sun was sinking as I sat down to draw in what had been a great chamber, below one of the many crumbling walls – perhaps in the very spot where the dreaded Ali gave audience to his Frank guests in 1809 – when Childe Harold was but 24 years old† and the Vizir in the zenith of his power. The poet is no more; the host is beheaded, and his family nearly extinct; the palace is burned, and levelled with the ground; war and change and time have, perhaps, left but one or two living beings who, forty years back, were assembled in these gay and sumptuous halls. It was impossible not to linger in such a site

†Byron was 21 in 1809.

and brood over such images, and of all the scenes I have visited the palace of Ali Pasha at Tepelene will continue most vividly imprinted on my recollection.

But the desert chambers and the rushing wide river below and the majestic peaks above are grown cold and grey as the last crimson of daylight has faded. A solitary Cogia, having cried a mournful cry from the minaret opposite, sits motionless on the battlements – the only living object in this most impressive scene. Of all days passed in Albania, this has most keenly interested me.

2 November 1848

Arghyro Kastro   Of all surprising novelties, here or anywhere else, commend me to the

Arghyro Kastro
Lithograph from Journals of a Landscape
Painter in Albania &c

costume of the Arghyro Kastro women! The quaintest monsters ever portrayed or imagined fall short of the reality of these most strange creatures in gait and apparel; and it is to be wondered at when and by whom the first garb of the kind was invented, or how human beings could submit to wear it. Suppose first a tight white linen mask fixed on the face, with two small slits cut in it for the eyes to look through. Next a voluminous wrapper of white, with broad buff stripes, which conceals the whole upper part of the person, and is huddled in immense folds about the arms, which are carried with the elbows raised, the hands being carefully kept from sight by the heavy drapery; add to these, short, full, purple calico trousers, and canary-coloured top-boots, with rose-coloured tassels – and what more amazing incident in the history of female dress can be fancied?

4 November 1848

We halted at the khan of Episkopi [Peshkopi], close to a little stream full of capital watercresses which I began to gather and eat with some bread and cheese, an act which provoked the Epirote bystanders of the village to ecstatic laughter and curiosity. Every portion I put into my mouth, delighted them as a most charming exhibition of foreign whim, and the more juvenile spectators instantly commenced bringing me all sorts of funny objects, with an earnest request that the Frank would amuse them by feeding thereupon forthwith. One brought a thistle, a second a collection of sticks and wood, a third some grass, a fourth presented me with a fat grasshopper – the whole scene was acted amid shouts of laughter, in which I joined as loudly as any. We parted amazingly good friends, and the wits of Episkopi will long remember the Frank who fed on weeds out of the water.

A t the British Consulate in Ioannina Lear collected his letters, among them an invitation from a North Country friend, John Cross, to visit Egypt at his expense. Egypt had always been one of Lear's ambitions, and, in any case, it was time to leave Albania where 'the cold-Cumberland feeling of these mountains savours too much of fever to allow of sitting long to draw.' He decided to return in the spring to 'finish' Epirus; 'My journey', he wrote to Ann, '... has placed me in a position to publish a most magnificent work.' On 2 November he sailed from Prevesa to Santa Maura (Lefkas) where he entered a nine-day quarantine. He described his Albanian tour in several letters to Charles Church and sent an ornithological account to his former employer, Lord Derby, and a note to Ann from his 'qualmish & quiet-quelling querulous quarantine'.

Letter to the 14th Earl of Derby

Cairo. 12 January 1849

I have been thinking more than commonly of Knowsley during my 3 month's tour in Albania, for – for many reasons – Albania is much like a great Zoological Gardens than any country I ever saw: the first of these reasons is that the Turks never kill any animal if they can help it – (I wish to goodness they would kill their dogs who eat up the calves of my legs

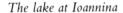
The lake at Ioannina

continually,) – & another cause is that the Albanians, ever since their last rebellion have been denied the use of all firearms: consequently creatures of all sorts abound and flourish. Beginning from Salonica, the great plains below Olympus are *full of birds*: Hoopoes – numberless – Hawks so tame that they allow you to come within 2 or 3 yards of them – eagles & vultures – all sorts of crows in multitudes – pigeons, quails – in fact it is a wide aviary, though I did not see any bird that I did not know. When I got up to Ochridia (beyond Monastir), the White Egret was as common all round the lake as the coot or the duck – & just as little alarmed. I should have liked much to have sent one to Knowsley, but I did not know how to get it away & could I have done so, the Turks there would hardly have allowed me …

Letter to Ann Lear

Quarantine. Santa Maura. 13 November 1848

I have never been in quarantine before; the regulations are very funny. The governor here – Major Williams – who knows me – is exceedingly kind & sends all sorts of good things – beer – and wine – newspapers – books etc., & I have hot dinners from the garrison table – so as far as that goes all is well; & as this little room is light, I can employ myself in writing, reading, or drawing – so that the day is never too long. The worst is my man Giorgio is obliged to sleep in a tent – & I fear may get fever – which I should be sorry for as he has been a most excellent servant for the past 2 months he has travelled with me & has contributed immensely to my comfort. I mean to give him £5 over his pay, & expenses back – which I do not think too much – because I give more trouble than ordinary travellers …

Zante. 9 December 1848

This long letter … will not end so beautifully. I got so tired of my 'prison' in quarantine, & so unwell from want of exercise that I did not write any more …

*L*ear *joined John Cross in Cairo at the beginning of February and a week later they set out for Mount Sinai. It was Lear's first encounter with a camel, a creature he described with a characteristic compound of amusement, horror and disgust. 'Cross's camel we call a "Dowager" – mine is "Miss Woolly"',* he wrote to Ann from the desert. *'They* are *quite harmless & quiet, but* seem *the most odious beasts – except when they are moving. The sort of horrible way in* which they growl & snarl if you only go 6 feet near them – is just frightful – & if you did not know them – you would suppose they were going to eat you ... Most of them make a nasty noise as if they were sick all night long.'

They reached Mount Sinai, spending three nights at the monastery there, but Lear was seized by another attack of fever, and had to abandon the expedition; while Cross continued to Palestine, he convalesced at Suez, defeated and disappointed by his relapse. At the end of the month he left Egypt and returned to quarantine in Malta, where he enlisted yet another travelling companion, a young barrister named Franklin Lushington, the brother of the government secretary there; over the next forty years, Lushington remained one of Lear's dearest friends and the oblivious object of his unreturned affections.

4

In Arkady

The tour which Lear and Lushington made through classical Greece was the happiest of Lear's life. During his subsequent decades of wandering, the fleas and frostbite and belligerent little boys were forgotten; just as the real Arcadia through which they passed had been transformed by poets and painters into a spiritual landscape, so the six-week tour with Lushington always inspired images of a Golden Age, of youth and springtime, the joy of friendship and the enchantments of the Greek countryside. From deepest Arkady Lear wrote to Ann, 'we gathered enormous bunches of Hepaticas, Narcissus, Anemones of all colours & Blue Bells ... Cistus & Orchids & wild Roses & May ... No one can form any idea of what the spring is in Greece –; it is all very well to say that here is a mile of scarlet ground, then half a mile of blue or pale pink – but it is difficult for you to realise that the whole earth is like a rich Turkey carpet. As for Lushington & I, equally fond of flowers, we gather them all day like children, & when we have stuck our hats & coats & horses all over with them – it is time to throw them away, & get a new set.'

For Lushington the tour was a brief moment of freedom in a conventional and overly conscientious career. As an old man he fondly recalled Lear's surprising energies and unquenchable humour, particularly during an incident in which he mistakenly bedded down on a 'dark bovine quadruped'. Unceremoniously catapulted into the mud, Lear 'suddenly burst into song:

> There was an old man who said now
> I'll sit down on the horns of this cow.'

Lushington, who was not himself a humorous man, noted studiously, 'I am not sure whether the stanza was ever finished or illustrated.' He was otherwise an ideal *travelling companion for Lear, an energetic walker, an accomplished classicist and a prolific draughtsman in a fastidious, old-fashioned style.† Lear himself was sketching constantly, making careful notes on colour and costume and adding his idiosyncratic and evocative aides-mémoire in the margins. At Mycenae he records 'Time & Assfiddle [Thyme and Asphodel]'; in the corner of a drawing of Kineta he regrets, 'the brightest yellow in the world can never equal these pines'; at Plataea he sees '10,000,000,000 gotes'; and on a chill morning near Mount Parnassus he neatly pencils across a horizon the words: 'palest yellow clouds fainting into lilac hills', 'sky blue', 'blu', 'blew', 'bloo'.*

At Patras Lear and Lushington took on a servant named Nicolo and 'a good steady old guide', Andrea Vindisi, 'who is perfectly to be trusted as a cook and doctor'. On 9 March they set off for a tour of the Morea, following the traditional route of Bassae, Sparta, Mycenae and Corinth, then turning north towards Athens, Mount Parnassus and Delphi. Modern archaeological excavation has transformed most of the ancient sites recorded by earlier explorers. In the mid-nineteenth century, visitors to Delphi could gaze at the awesome scenery or quaff an inspiring cup at the Castalian Spring of the Muses, but the site of the sanctuary of Apollo was

† A collection of over two hundred of Lushington's drawings from this tour is now in the Benaki Museum in Athens.

The Temple of Apollo at Bassae Illustration to Tennyson's poem 'You Ask Me Why'

Temple of Apollo at Bassae

hidden by the modern village of Kastri. At Mycenae the main outline of the citadel and its monumental entrance, the Lion Gate, could be traced, but it was not until 1875 that Heinrich Schliemann discovered the golden masks in the royal tombs and sent his telegram proclaiming, 'I have gazed on the face of Agamemnon.' For the Victorian traveller the most impressive antiquity of all was the Temple of Apollo at Bassae,† the work of Ictinus, architect of the Parthenon. In its sublime and lonely setting on a mountain plateau high above the village of Andritsena, its very existence had been forgotten until it was rediscovered by a Frenchman in the eighteenth century. Lear arrived at Andritsena on a gusty spring day, the 'thermometer 400 below zero' and reached Bassae in a snowstorm.

---

† The subject of one of Lear's most ambitious oils which was presented by subscription to the Fitzwilliam Museum in Cambridge.

Journal of Tour to the Morea with Franklin Lushington

18 March 1849

Although I woke at 3 a.m. and read, and half dressed, I fell asleep again, and Andrea did not call us till past 6! So we hurried over breakfast and got off by 7. The cold was piercing, – but there was little or no wind … By degrees, as we ascended, we came to hills covered with mingled ilex and old oak trees, and were it summer and these latter in leaf, nothing more beautiful could be imagined: – huge rocks, fringed with foliage, – deepest glens full of black armed oaks, – the distant wide sea, all bright beyond the canopy of grey cloud immediately above us, – Zante on the horizon afar, gleaming with touches of bright pink light, – and the snowy mountains over the plains of Elis on our right.

So, after three hours from leaving Andritsena we reached the top of the mountain Phigaleia – oh! oh! – how horrible was the cold! But the Temple of Bassae, and its position, much as I had expected were far beyond my expectations of beauty and Arcadian landscape. The columns are of a light blue grey-white, and stand as if placed for a picture in front of the finest scenery it is possible to fancy, – including Mt. Ithome, (if so it be Ithome,) – the sea and gulfs beyond, – the infinitely well-drawn lines of interwoven hills, – the rich oakwoods on all sides, – the intense depth and variety of the vallies around, – and the magnificent horizon of Spartan mountains!!!!! I drew once, twice, three times; – and then, at noon, we had a hasty lunch. At 12.30 p.m. it began to snow hard, – a peppery white sleet, – snow storms had been veering all over the landscape through the day, – and the cold became intense. Nevertheless I made some more efforts to carry away memories of this wonderfully beautiful place; but by 1.30 p.m. – although indeed we had done a good deal hastily, – we were fairly beaten, and began to walk downwards towards Paulitza.† Thus we left Bassae …

For dinner we had capital soup, boiled fowl and potatoes, and a roast suckling pig, – and somehow are tolerably jolly, – spite of circumstances. It is in fact, funny enough, how one can make oneself so comfortable in these very queer places! All the world is wrapped in rags, – a-sleeping about the embers quietly; Andrea alone is snoring terribly. L. and I have made our beds, and I have besides unpacked and repacked my case of drawings. Now we have quietly down-sate to read and write; the barking of dogs, and the Dutch-clock-like tinkling of a mule bell hardly disturbing us. Anyone – it is certain, – more quiet and good and full of all sorts of intelligences and knowledges than Lushington, a man could not travel with. Charles M. Church, John E. Cross and F. Lushington are three companions

---

† A modern village built into the ruined walls of the ancient Phigaleia.

within 12 months such as few could fall in with. How this fly got into all that amber I can't understand, – 'one wonders how the devil it got there.'

20 March 1849

The plain towards Kalamata is wide, and unimaginably rich in tone and colour. The way down to Mauromati was a succession of pure Claude pictures. The quiet 'Arcadian' softness of the whole scene! ... The Priest's house, – also overlooking a Claude Landscape, had been made all comfortable for us; and as usual, Andrea gave us a capital dinner; Andrea is a famous man. I, however, by reason of eating curds and honey, was by no means well.

23 March 1849

We enjoyed Sparta most thoroughly. The Theatre overlooks all the plain, and the vast Taygetus range is fully before it. The purple tone of the lower part of the range is extraordinary, – contrasted with the brilliant shivery-

Mount Ithome

sparkly silver of the white snow above. Mistra seems a wondrous place, and reminds me of Amalfi, with a plain below it instead of sea. The solitary wild quiet of this spot, – the immensity of grandeur all around, – the ancient associations of the place, and the charm of climate, – have made this day a very delightful one. At sunset we came up to the modern town of Sparta, where there seem more better-constructed houses than these places generally possess. We were housed in a 'Café', and at 6.45, dined sumptuously in a sort of Trattoria. The wine also, strange to say, was very good. Wonderfully swell Spartans in magnificent toggery keep circulating about, or are supping in the Trattoria room.

24 March 1849

Sparta   After breakfast – cold lamb and excellent honey! – we followed our Mistra

guide up to the Kastro ... It was surprising to find oneself in a large town entirely ruined; – several good churches, (apparently Latin, i.e. they had square Campanili though of Byzantine details of workmanship;) and endless shells of houses and castles of Venetian times, gorgeous with ivy and creepers. The top of the castle was a sell, seeing we could see nothing for cloud. So we returned, drawing often, i.e. as well as we could, for no outline beyond Mistra was visible, and the plain was a weary dilution; and presently joined Andrea, whom we found in a stable where we lunched on Spartan wine, bread, and cheese, bacon, and cold pudding ... Several impyous children came and sate about us, and as soon as we left, stoned us horribly with showers of stones, – the foul little beasts.

There was an Old Person of Sparta, who had twenty-five sons and one "darter

13 April 1849

We had determined on making one day at Cheronoea, and on going to Daulia tomorrow. A horrid paved road led to the lower part of the valley, and on the high ground beyond this I sate down to draw the town of Livadia. It was Bazaar day, and hundreds of peasants were passing – all of whom said emphatically, 'Καλημερα [Good-day].' The costumes were truly wonderfully beautiful; most of the women had capotes edged or bordered with pink; hcaddress or white handkerchief; belts, brown, or blue striped; aprons, white, scarlet, or yellow; sometimes blue shifts, exquisitely embroidered with pale pink and blue; often the outer vest was tufted with chocolate, or lilac, or purple, or madder-brown; – fronts of shifts embroidered deeply and beautifully. Women ruddy and robust generally, and tolerably good looking, but I did not observe any very beautiful ... Men with black or yellow handkerchiefs round their Fezzes.

The day became quite grey, at first it was very cloudy; but Parnassus always remained clear. About 9.15. – some two hours after leaving Livadia we reached the little plain of Cheronoea. Its simple outline, (its Acropolis and Parnassus) is most delightful; the foreground of this picture is made by the broken lion,† lying in a hollow of [a] sand bank, covered with Asphodel, and alive with goats.

15 April 1849

A disagreeable night, – the one glass I took of Arachova wine, having brought on a horrid diarrhoea, but with a hot bottle, and rice, I got better. From 8.15 to 11 a.m. Lushington and I drew ... but there were such odious

---

† This remarkable sculpture once guarded the common tomb of Theban soldiers. It was discovered, almost buried in the ground, by a party of English travellers in 1818 and was smashed during the War of Independence because it was thought to contain treasure.

crowds of boys about that I could not [continue] … At 2 p.m. the whole
village world began to dance: I think–nay–I am sure I never before saw so
beautiful a fête as this. The dresses of the women were very remarkable;
the heads of some were quite covered with gold and silver coins. Men and
women danced together, but mostly by twenties or thirties of either sex
alternately, – 20 men – then 20 women. Many of these village women are
absolutely beautiful, not only as to complexion and fine contour of head
and figure, but as to real Greek outline of feature. The Arachova people
seem a nice lot, though the little boys bored me terribly.

17 April 1849

Delphi

Alas! alas! the Greek tour closes! We drew by the Fountain, and afterwards
by the Pythons' cave – but the place was cold, and I within an ace of fever.

Self-portrait, Delphi
Detail

We dawdled about the Panaghia† olives . . . when I set off, getting a Palikari to see me safely by the dogs; Lushington joined me under the Cypress of St. Elia.‡ A drove of boys as usual bored us horribly, and ended by throwing showers of stones. So we went our way down the hill, with Andrea and mules, – beasts I detest, so therefore I walked. Near Crisso, the views of the Gulf, and of the olive plains, are highly exquisite; – the hills are so cleanly and clearly cut and drawn, and the plains so beautifully level. Above Crisso we drew, pestered by horrid troops of boys, who finally pelted us into the town, whence the Elders came forth and rebuked them.

18 April 1849

At 5 or 6 p.m. we got to Pentornea, a little village full of dogs, fleas, and dirty people. I drew, solus, till sunset, plagued by diabolical little boys as usual. We had a room, – windy enough! – in a peasant's house; the wind is very high and they say portends rain. Good dinner, and lots of quinine, – but a long struggle against fever, (for it is the 21st day!) before I could sleep. Slept tolerably – O dogs!

It was past 8 p.m. before we attained to the desired place, Omareffendi: – we were a long weary time, I utterly dead tired, poking about in the dark

---

† The monastery of Panayia near Delphi.
‡ A nearby chapel.

to find it, and when we did it was only a wretched collection of some 6 or 7 houses so to speak! The first was 'too' full of Gran Turco,† – no room: – then we had to grope and feel our way to another – I getting more and more faint and tired. And here, in the black darkness I sate down – glad of any chance to rest – on what I thought was a white stone, but it was the white head of a black cow – happily hornless – who suddenly and disagreeably rose up and threw me into the mud among other bulls and cows, imperceptible in the obscurity. A third house contained an ammalato with some 'contagious disease' they said; so there we refused to go. At last – more asleep than awake – we were put into one end of a long room full of people and convulsive babies. In spite of our falling at once to sleep, Andrea the energetic insisted on our dining at 9.30 p.m.!! and turned out a capital dinner. Finalmente we got to bed, but not to sleep. 100,000,000 fleas forbade.

20 April 1849

Rose before light, in great haste; ... Morning quite grey and soft to look at. We went on for an hour before we reached a great river, forded in three divisions, a horrid operation and odious to me, whom running water always bedizzes and distracts. Then, by brambly lanes, – ever by flat ground, – we reached Lepanto [Nafpaktos] and now we are 'waiting', I within half an ace of fever.

(We witnessed intanto a strange scene; – 3 gypsies playing a pipe and drum, and all the Townpeople frantically proceeding to pluck up Euphorbiae, and nettles and mallows, as producing Malaria! This, performed by great swells among others, was immensely funny.)

A very dummy place is Lepanto. What next? We waited, and waited, and waited.

*T*he next day the friends parted at Patras, Lushington to begin his journey back to England and Lear to 'finish' Epirus, Thessaly and Mount Athos. With his elderly guide Andrea, he travelled up the coast to Prevesa and the great Roman ruins of Nicopolis, his mind on modern tragedy rather than ancient history. At Nicopolis he mused on the evil ambitions of Ali Pasha; at Suli, the mountain refuge of Christian klephts who had long resisted both Ali and the Turks, he thought of the mothers who had flung themselves and their children from a precipice to avoid capture; and at Parga he remembered the British betrayal of this Christian stronghold to Ali Pasha and the desperate flight of the entire population on an April day in 1819.

---

† Maize.

Albanian Journal

1 May 1849

The ruins of [Nicopolis], founded by Augustus after the battle of Actium, lie not above three miles from Prevesa, and the walk thither is very pleasant, through plantations of olive trees.

The scattered remains of Palaio-Kastro (so the peasants call the site of Nicopolis) occupy a large space of ground; and although there are here and there masses of brickwork, which forcibly recall to my memory those on the Campagna of Rome, yet the principal charm of the scene consists in its wild loneliness, and its command of noble views over the Ionian sea as well as of the Gulf of Arta and the mountains of Agrafa. My principal object was to obtain correct drawings from the great theatre, as well as from the Stadium and the lesser theatre; but at this season of the year I found many impediments which in the late autumn of 1848 had not presented themselves. Vegetation had shot up in the early spring to so great a size and luxuriance, that a choice of position was difficult to find among gigantic asphodel four or five feet high – foxgloves of prodigious size, briars and thistles of obstinate dignity. Nor was the passing from one point of the ruins to another, through the fields of beans and Indian corn which cover the cultivated portions of the soil, a light task; there were snakes too in great numbers and size, so that when the sun's heat became powerful, I found the operation of exploring the whole of the Augustan city too nearly allied with risk of fever-fits to prolong it. Great as was the destruction of Nicopolis by Ali Pasha, who carried off vast portions of it for the construction of his palace at Preveza . . . The great palace of Ali Pasha exists no more – it is utterly destroyed – and the whole place has an air of melancholy desolation, increased possibly by one's knowledge of its past history and evil destiny.

5 May 1849

Descending the hill of Zermi we came in less than an hour to the vale of Tervitziana, through which the river of Suli† flows ere, 'previously making many turns and meanders as if unwilling to enter such a gloomy passage', it plunges into the gorge of Suli. We crossed the stream, and began the ascent on the right of the cliffs, by narrow and precipitous paths leading to a point of great height, from which the difficult pass of the Suliote glen commences. And while toiling up the hill, my thoughts were occupied less with the actual interest of the scenery, than with the extraordinary

---

† The river Suli is the Acheron of antiquity.

recollections connected with the struggles of the heroic people who so lately as forty years back were exterminated or banished by their tyrant enemy. Every turn in the pass I am about to enter has been distinguished by some stratagem or slaughter: every line in the annals of the last Suliote war is written in characters of blood . . .

I shall not soon forget the labour it cost to convey our horses through this frightful gorge. In many places the rains had carried away even what little footing there had originally been, and nothing remained but a bed of powdered rock sloping off to the frightful gulf below; and all our efforts could hardly induce or enable each horse to cross singly. The muleteer cried, and called on all the saints in the Greek calendar; and all four of us united our strength to prevent the trembling beast from rolling downwards. There were three of these passi cattivi, and the sun was setting. I prepared to make up my mind, if I escaped the Acheron, at least to repose all night in the ravine.

Suli
Lithograph from Journals of a Landscape Painter in Albania &c

At sunset we reached the only approach on this side of 'the blood-stained Suli' – an ascent of stairs winding up the sides of the great rocks below Avariko – and very glad was I to have accomplished this last and most dangerous part of the journey. Before me is the hollow vale of Avariko, Kiafa, and Suli – places now existing little more than in name; and darkly looking against the clear western sky stands the dread Trypa – the hill of Thunderbolts – the last retreat of the despairing Suliotes.

Here, at the summit of the rock, Ali Pasha built a castle, and within its walls I hope to pass the night. I reached it at nearly two hours after sunset, the bright moon showing me the Albanian governor and his twenty or thirty Palikari sitting on the threshold of the gate. But as unluckily I had not procured any letter from the Turkish authorities at Preveza, the rough old gentleman was obdurate, and would not hear of my entering the fortress. '*yok*,' said he, frowning fiercely, '*yok, yok*.' And had it not been for the good nature of a Turkish officer of engineers who had arrived from Ioannina on a visit of inspection, I must have passed the night supperless and shelterless. Thanks to him, men and horses were at length admitted to the interior of the fort . . .

I gazed on the strange, noiseless figures about me, bright in the moonlight, which tipped with silver the solemn lofty mountains around. For years those hills had rarely ceased to echo the cries of animosity, despair, and agony; now all is silent as the actors in that dreadful drama.

7 May 1849

About nine we arrived at beautiful and extensive groves of olive, for the cultivation of which Parga is renowned; they clothe all the hills around,

Suli

and hang over rock and cliff to the very sea with delightful and feathery luxuriance. At length we descended to the shore at the foot of the little promontory on which the ill-fated palace and its citadel stood; alas, what now appears a town and castle consists of old ruined walls, for Parga is desolate. A new one built since the natives abandoned the ancient site, is, however, springing up on the shore, and with its two mosques is picturesque: this, with the rock and dismantled fortress – the islands in the bay, and the rich growth of olive slopes around, form a picture of completely beautiful character, though more resembling an Italian than a Greek scene; but it is impossible fully to contemplate with pleasure a place, the history of which is so full of melancholy and painful interest.

A dark cloud hangs over the mournful spot. Would that much which has been written concerning it were never read, or that having been written it could be disbelieved!

A lodging was found me in a very decent house and shelter against the heat of midday was grateful. In the afternoon and evening I made many drawings from either side of the promontory of Parga. From every point it is lovely, very unlike Albanian landscape in general, and partaking more of the character of Calabrian or Amalfitan coast scenery. But in spite of the delightful evening, and the sparkling white buildings that crowned the rock at whose feet the waves murmured, the whispering olives above me, the convent islets, and the broad bright sea beyond, in spite of all this, I felt anxious to leave Parga. The picture, false or true, of the 10th of April 1819 was ever before me, and I wished with all my heart that I had left Parga unvisited.

Uncertain weather and the fear of returning fever threatened to unsettle Lear's plans. He returned to Ioannina and spent several days drawing there while he debated his route. On 14 May he crossed the Pindus Mountains into Thessaly, continuing to Metsovo and the Christian sanctuary of Meteora. His description of the monastic eyries and the extraordinary lunar landscape are oddly perfunctory. It was a scene that might have appealed to his sense of the absurd, but the precarious ascent by rickety ladder or frayed pulley was not enticing, and the monasteries and their treasures remained unvisited. After making some unexceptional sketches, he was eager to be off to Larissa and the Vale of Tempe, that celebrated pass between Mounts Ossa and Olympus sacred to Apollo and many generations of minor English poets.

Albanian Journal

11–13 May 1849

The lake at Ioannina

During these days [in Ioannina] time passed rapidly away, for there was

'The Monastery in the Island where Ali Pasha was killed, Ioannina'

full employment for every hour; one moment I would sit on the hill which rises west of the city, whence the great mountain of Mitzikeli on the eastern side of the lake is seen most nobly: at another, I would move with delight from point to point among the southern suburbs, from which the huge ruined fortress of Litharitza, with many a silvery mosque and dark cypress, form exquisite pictures: or watch from the walls of the ruin itself, the varied effect of cloud or sunbeam passing over the blue lake, now shadowing the promontory of the kastron or citadel, now gilding the little island at the foot of majestic Mitzikeli. Then I would linger on the northern outskirts of the town, whence its long line constitutes a small part of a landscape whose sublime horizon is varied by mountain forms of the loftiest and most beautiful character, or by wandering in the lower ground near the lake, I would enjoy the placid solemnity of the dark waters reflecting the great mosque and battlements of the citadel as in a mirror. I was never tired of

There was a Young Person of Janina, whose Uncle was always a-fanning her

walking out into the spacious plain on each side [of] the town, where immense numbers of cattle enlivened the scene, and milk-white storks paraded leisurely in quest of food: or I would take a boat and cross to the little island, and visit the monastery, where that most wondrous man Ali Pasha met his death: or sitting by the edge of the lake near the southern side of the kastron, sketch the massive, mournful ruins of his palace of Litharitza, with the peaks of Olytzika rising beyond. For hours I could loiter on the terrace of the kastron opposite the Pasha's serai, among the ruined fortifications, or near the strange gilded tomb where lies the body of the man who for so long a time made thousands tremble! It was a treat to watch the evening deepen the colours of the beautiful northern hills, or shadows creeping up the furrowed sides of Mitzikeli.

And inside this city of manifold charms the interest was as varied and as fascinating: it united the curious dresses of the Greek peasant – the splendour of those of the Albanian: the endless attractions of the bazaars, where embroidery of all kinds, fire-arms, horse-gear, wooden-ware, and numberless manufactures peculiar to Albania were exhibited – the clattering storks, whose nests are built on half the chimneys of the town, and in the great plane-trees whose drooping foliage hangs over the open spaces or squares: these and other amusing or striking novelties which the pen would tire of enumerating, occupied every moment, and caused me great regret that I could not stay longer in the capital of Epirus. And when to all these artistic beauties is added the associations of Ioannina with the later years of Greek history, the power and tyranny of its extraordinary ruler, its claim to representing the ancient Dodona, and its present and utterly melancholy condition, [it is] no marvel that Ioannina will always hold its place in memory as one of the first in interest of the many scenes I have known in many lands . . .

The unsettled state of the weather, which characterises the spring and early summer in this place . . . made me very undecided as to pursuing my journey eastward; yet it seemed hard to return to England without seeing Meteora, Tempe, Olympus, and Athos; and when on the 13th the wind changed, and there were all sorts of atmospherical signs of permanently fine weather about to set in, I finally resolved on crossing the Pindus into Thessaly and ordered horses for the morrow.

15 May 1849

[Near Metsovo] we passed more than one khan by the road, and usually at these places the Albanian guards asked us questions and insisted on seeing passports which they had not the slightest idea of reading. As a proof of this, on my taking out by mistake the card of a hotel-keeper at Athens, the

Costume studies, Ioannina

Palikar snatched at it hastily, and after gravely scrutinising it, gave it back to me, saying, 'Good; you may pass on!' At the next guardhouse I confess to having amused myself by showing a bill of Mrs Dunsford's Hotel, at Malta, and at another the back of an English letter, each of which documents were received as a Teskerc. So much for the use of the Derveni guards, placed by the Turkish Government to take accurate cognisance of all passers-by.

As the day wore on and the river opened out into a wider valley the eastern horizon suddenly exhibited a strange form in the distance, which at once I felt to be one of the rocks of the Meteora . . .

'Twelve sheets', says Mr Cockerell, in a letter, Feb. 9, 1814, 'would not contain all the wonders of Meteora, nor convey to you an idea of the surprise and pleasure which I felt in beholding these curious monasteries, planted like the nest of eagles, on the summits of high and pointed rocks.'† We arrived at Kastraki, a village nestled immediately below these gigantic crags, at sunset. I do not think I ever saw any scene so startling and incredible; such vast sheer perpendicular pyramids, standing out of the earth, with the tiny houses of the village clustering at the roots.

With difficulty – for it is the time when silk worms are being bred in the houses, and the inhabitants will not allow them to be disturbed – Andrea procured a lodging for me in the upper part of a dwelling, formed as are most in the village, like a tower, the entrance to which, for the sake of defence, was by a hole three feet high. Here, after having gazed in utter astonishment at the wild scenery as long as the light lasted, I took up my abode for the night. The inhabitants of this place, as well as of Kalabaka (or Stagus)‡ are Christians, and every nook of the village was swarming with pigs and little children. 'Πολλα παιδια,' said an old man to me, as the little creatures thronged about me, 'δια του νερόυ καλόυ.'§ What a contrast is there between the precipices, from five to six hundred feet high, and these atoms of life playing at their base! Strange, unearthly-looking rocks are these, full of gigantic chasms and round holes, resembling Gruyère cheese, as it were, highly magnified, their surface being otherwise perfectly smooth. Behind the village of Kastraki, the groups of rock are more crowded, and darkened with vegetation; and at this late hour a sombre mystery makes them seem like the work of some genii, or enchanter of Arabian romance.

---

† Quoted in T. S. Hughes, *Travels in Greece & Albania*, 1820. C. R. Cockerell's account of his tour with Hughes was included in the posthumous *Travels in Southern Europe and the Levant*, 1903.
‡ Anciently Aeginium.
§ 'Many children because of the good water', an obscure remark unless it refers to the popular belief in the beneficent qualities of certain springs.

18 May 1849

I set off with Andrea, two horses and a knapsack, and a steeple-hatted Dervish, at whose convent in Baba, at the entrance to the Pass of Tempe, my night's abode is to be.

They call the Dervish Dede Effendi, and he is the head of a small hospitable establishment, founded by the family of Hassan Bey,† who allows a considerable sum of money for the relief of poor persons passing along the ravine. The Dervish is obliged to lodge and feed, during one night, as many as may apply to him for such assistance. There are many interesting views about Larissa; but not feeling sufficiently fever-proof, I dared not halt to sketch. During two hours we crossed the level plains; and as the sun was lowering, arrived at pleasant green lanes and park scenery,

---

† A great landowner of Larissa, to whom Lear had been given a letter of introduction by Lord Seaton.

Meteora

below the mighty Olympus. By six we arrived at Baba, which stands at the very gate, as it were, of Tempe, and is certainly one of the loveliest little places I ever beheld. The broad Peneus flows immediately below the village, and is half hidden by the branches of beautiful abeles and plane trees, which dip their branches in the stream. A small mosque, with its minaret, amid spiry cypresses, is the Dervish's abode; and on the opposite side of the river are high rocks and the richest foliage, rejoicing in all the green freshness of spring . . .

The little square room in the Teke, or house of the Dervish, was perfectly clean and neat, and while I ate my supper on the sofas surrounding it the well-behaved Dede Effendi sat smoking in an opposite corner; his son, the smallest possible Dervish, five or six years old, dressed like his father in all points excepting his beard, squatted by his side. For the Dervish is a married man, and his wife, he assures me, has made one or two dishes for my particular taste and is regarding me at this moment through a lattice at the top of the wall.

Towards nine many poor passengers call for lodging and are stowed away in a covered yard by the mosque, each being supplied with a ration of bread and soup.

The Pass of Tempe
Illustration to Tennyson's poem 'To Edward Lear on his Travels in Greece'

19 May 1849   *Baba (Tempe)*

The early morning at Baba is more delightful that can be told. All around is a deep shadow, and the murmuring of doves, the whistling of bee-eaters and the hum of bees fills this tranquil place ... I went onward into Tempe, and soon entered this most celebrated 'vale' – of all places in Greece that which I had most desired to see. But it is not a 'vale', it is a narrow pass – and although extremely beautiful, on account of the precipitous rocks on each side, the Peneus flowing deep in the midst, between the richest overhanging plane woods, still its character is distinctly that of a ravine or gorge ... Well might the ancients extol this grand defile, where the land-scape is so completely different from that of any part of Thessaly, and awakes the most vivid feelings of awe and delight, from its associations with the legendary history and religious rites of Greece.

As it was my intention to pursue the route towards Platamona as far as time would allow, and to return to Baba at evening, I left the gorge of Tempe and crossed the Peneus in a ferry-boat opposite a khan at the eastern extremity of the Pass . . .

In some meadows near a little stream flowing into the Peneus were several camels, which are frequently used about Salonica and Katerina, etc. They were very ragged and hideous creatures, and offered a great contrast to the trim and well-kept animals of our Arabs, which we had so familiarly known in our journey through the desert of Suez and Sinai. But as I returned towards Tempe I perceived a young one among the herd, and I rode a little way towards it spite of the clamorous entreaties of the Ioannina muleteer. I had better have attended to his remonstrances, for the little animal (who resembled nothing so much as a large white muff upon stilts), chose to rush towards us with the most cheerful and innocent intentions, and skipping and jumping after the fashion of delighted kids, thrust himself into the way of our three horses with the most facetious perverseness. One and all took fright, and the muleteer's reared, threw him and escaped. There was much difficulty in recapturing the terrified animal, and when we had done so forth came the little muffy white beast once more, pursuing us with the most profuse antics over the plain and rendering our steeds perfectly unmanageable. To add to our discomfiture, the whole herd of camels, disapproving of the distance to which we were inveigling their young relation, began to follow us with an increasingly quick trot; and we were too glad to ford the stream as quickly as possible and leave our gaunt pursuers and their foolish offspring on the opposite side.

It was evening when, having recrossed the Peneus, I arrived at the Dervish's house in Baba, and the little owls† were piping on every side in that sweet valley.‡ Mr Urquhart says that when he was at Tempe the Dervish roosted in one of the cypress trees; but I cannot say that the respectable Dede Effendi indulged in such a bird-like system of repose. He, the female, and the miniature Dervish, all abide in a little house attached to the mosque, and the good order and cleanliness of his whole establishment very much disarranged all my previously formed ideas of Dervishes in his favour.

† The Strix Passerina (or Scops?) which abounds in these groves, as in the olive woods of Girgenti in Sicily, and southern localities in general: its plaintive piping, so different to the screech or hoot of the larger owls, is a pleasant characteristic of the evening hours.
‡ On a drawing of Baba dated 18 May Lear has written, 'a sort of green quiet', 'Arundel old mill pond', 'O! Little Girgent owl Pipe pipe pipe!'

20 May 1849

On my return to Larissa there is but just time to make one drawing of dark Olympus ere a frightful thunderstorm, with deluges of rain, breaks over the plain and pursues me to the city. It continues to pour all the afternoon, and I amuse myself, as best as I can, in Hassan Bey's house. It is a large mansion, in the best Turkish style, and betokening the riches of its master. It occupies three sides of a walled courtyard, and one of its wings is allotted to the harem, who live concealed by a veil of close lattice work when at home, though I see them pass to and fro dressed in the usual disguise worn out of doors. I watch two storks employed in building on the roof of that part of the building. These birds are immensely numerous in Thessaly, and there is a nest on nearly every house in Larissa. No one disturbs them; and they are considered so peculiarly in favour with the Prophet that the Vulgar believe the conversion of a Christian as being certain to follow their choice of his roof for their dwelling; formerly a Christian so honoured was forced to turn Mussulman or quit his dwelling – so at least they told me in Ioannina, where two pairs have selected the Vice-Consul's house for their abode. It is very amusing to watch them when at work, as they take infinite pains in the construction of what after all seems a very ill-built nest. I have seen them, after twisting and bending a long bit of grass or root for an hour in all directions, throw it away altogether. That will not do after all, they say; and then flying away they return with a second piece of material, in the choice of which they are very particular; and, according to my informants at Ioannina, only make use of one sort of root. When they have arranged the twig or grass in a satisfactory manner they put up their heads on their shoulders and clatter in a mysterious manner with a sound like dice shaken in a box. This clattering at early morning or evening, in this season of the year, is one certain characteristic that these towns are under Turkish government, inasmuch as the storks have all abandoned Greece (modern), for the Greeks shoot and molest them; only they still frequent Larissa, and the plain of the Spercheius, as being so near the frontier of Turkey that they can easily escape thither if necessary. This is foolishness in the Greeks, for the stork is most useful in devouring insects, especially the larva of the locust, which I observed in myriads on the plains near the entrance of Tempe; and I counted as many as seventy storks in one society, eating them as fast as possible, and with great dignity of carriage.

That part of the roof of the harem which is not occupied by storks is covered with pigeons and jackdaws, a humane attention paid to the lower orders of creation being always one of the most striking traits of Turkish character.

Black Stork (Ciconia nigra)
Water-colour study for John Gould's Birds of Europe

The storm continues all night. The air of Larissa is heavy and close, and so much threatens fever, that I resort to quinine in no little quantities.

23 May 1849

Alas! the woes of Thessaly! It is again pouring with rain, and the wind is set in southerly, so that once and for altogether I give up all idea of sailing to Athos.

The horses are ordered, and as soon as Andrea can get about I start at length to return to Ioannina.

As I ride away Volo, its gulf and the scattered villages on the hills of Magnesia seem truly beautiful; but to what purpose should I linger? Tomorrow, and tomorrow, may be equally wet. Mount Athos! Mount Athos! All my toil has been in vain, and I shall now most possibly never see you more!

25 May 1849

The woes of Thessaly continued. In the middle of the night, the roof of Seid Effendi's house being slight, a restless stork put one of his legs through the crevice and could not extricate it; whereon ensued much kicking and screams, and at the summons came half the storks in Thessaly, and all night long the uproar was portentous. Four very wet jackdaws also came down the chimney and hopped over me and about the room till dawn.

*I*n floods and torrents Lear returned to Ioannina and on *30 May he sailed from the village of Philates in Epirus to Corfu. 'So', he concludes his Journal, 'ends my journey in the lands of Greece', possibly the most extensive and eccentric artistic tour ever attempted in the realms of classical antiquity and Turkey in Europe.*

The Spirit of the East

*L*ear's Levantine tour of 1848–9 was the single most fruitful artistic adventure in a life marked by an embarrassment of adventure, confirming him in his commitment to the canons of classical landscape and the conviction that he would ultimately make his mark as the 'Greek topographical painter par excellence'. During the years 1856 to 1863 while he lived on Corfu he made occasional forays into Albania, accompanying friends on shooting and yachting expeditions; in 1857 he made a short tour in Epirus which he spoke of publishing in his 'Zagori Albania' Journal and in 1864 he visited Crete, but during the quiet years on Corfu his travels were chiefly confined to the Ionian islands, with brief, infrequent expeditions to mainland Greece and Turkey. The heroic (or possibly mock-heroic) scope of his early odyssey was never repeated, although after several attempts Lear finally prevailed in his ambition to reach Mount Athos.

In the early days of August 1856 Lear sailed from Corfu to the Albanian coast with Franklin Lushington, and then continued with his servant Giorgio Kokali to retrace his former route through Ioannina, Metsovo, Tempe and Salonica. Travelling conditions had changed drastically since the start of the Crimean War. The British had moved quickly to establish their presence in Turkey in Europe, most large towns now had a British Consul, and Lear found he hardly had need of his bed and pots and skilfully selected roba. In Salonica he found himself 'in the very same room, & everything seems pretty much as it was, save that the black landlady is dead, & people are all 8 years older.' Some aspects of the tour seemed sadly impervious to change; both Giorgio and Lear were stricken with fever and Lear fell down a flight of stairs 'hurting my back', he wrote to Church, 'so much I

Salonica

believed myself to be lamed for life.' His susceptibility to accident seems to have sprung eternal, as did his determination to transcend it.

On 31 August Lear reached Mount Athos, 'the Holy Land of the Greek', an immemorial sacred spot, first as the home of the Greek gods before Olympus, then as a Christian domain dedicated to the Virgin. According to legend, she had landed by mistake on the peninsula after a brief but pleasant visit to Lazarus, Bishop of Cyprus, and claimed the mountain as her own; jealous of her rights, she banished all other female creatures from the place forever, a ban that has been rigidly enforced – and only occasionally infringed – to this day. At first the home of isolated hermits, the monastic communities flourished during the late Middle Ages and remained autonomous even after the fall of Constantinople. Since the nineteenth century this curious, lonely and beautiful site has become a place of pilgrimage for English travellers, especially those of a literary bent. Some Victorian visitors took a particular interest in the Eastern Church and the rights of Christians *in Ottoman lands, an issue that assumed immense and disproportionate political importance during the Crimean War; others, like Robert Curzon, went in quest of Byzantine treasures and a few, such as Lear himself, were lured by landscape – by the wild, roadless country covered in dark forests, the religious retreats perched on precipitous cliffs and the Holy Mountain itself, its white limestone cone shining like a beacon across the north Aegean. During his three weeks on Athos Lear visited the twenty principal monasteries and made a collection of fifty drawings which he hoped to publish with his written account, 'to the benefit obliquely of many of my felly creaturs who will hereafter peeroose my jurnles, and admyer my pigchurs.'*

Letters to Ann Lear

Larissa. 21 August 1856

As I sit in a beautiful room at the English Consul's house here, with sofas all round the walls, matting on the floor, & painted ceilings, & look out on a little court yard where 2 tame cranes are walking up & down – I cannot but think how much easier it is to travel in these parts now than it was in 1848. Moreover, I believe the race of dogs which used to rush & rage & bark are civilised & changed also – or dead – the result being the same, that I have not been bothered by them at all ... I find all the difference in the world here from being able to speak – (even as little as I do –) in Greek ...

I will tell you in a few words, somewhat about Mt. Athos. It is called by the Greeks, *Αγιος Ορος* or 'The Holy Mountain' – & has always been, i.e. from the very early ages, an object of great veneration, & indeed a sort of Holy Land to their form of Christianity ... The high rock of Athos was chosen after the renunciation of Paganism by Constantine as a place of retreat & devotion just as Syria & the Thebaid were. But Athos has never been in the way of war or disturbance, & so the immense monasteries founded by successive emperors have remained undisturbed, & you may conclude are very picturesque. There are 20 principal monasteries, besides 50 or 60 little ones! – I mean to go to all, & draw all, & most probably publish all. Every nation possessing the Greek form of faith has one – Russia a large one, Bulgaria, etc. etc. But the queer part of the story is that no female creature is allowed within the holy ground, let it be woman – no she cat – no hen – no she ass – or mare etc!!!! The common people devoutly believe any woman would die if she crossed the boundary – though Lady Stratford & her daughters went to several,† & tell all sorts of absurd stories.

---

†Another of Lear's friends, Lady Somers, a famous beauty, accompanied a party to Athos, living for two months in a tent. 'A few more such visits', Lear speculated, 'would bust, or go far to bust, the Greek monasticism I think', but a recent guide comments, 'She should have known better'.

It would matter little enough, only one can't get fowls or eggs – so you will imagine me living on fish & fruit during my visit . . . You may be sure I shall send or bring you some recollection of the Holy Mountain . . . most probably a worked cross – for there will be no ladies' dresses!

Salonica. 23 September 1856

One thing you would like at Mt. Athos; there is not a single dog in all the territory –! 60 or 80 miles long – & no dog! but you would be amply repaid for this want by the overwhelming redundance of *Tom Cats.* One day, I observed, hearing a mouse, I wondered there were any left. 'Oh,' said the abbot, 'we have so few cats; there are scarcely 100 left in our Monasteries; but I have sent over to Imbros & Lemnos for 20 score.' Fancy 400 Tom Cats in a boat!!

Quarantine, Corfu. 8 October 1856

Towards dusk I reached Kariess – which is really a beautiful place – at a distance. Here the great peak of the mountain is sublime & I consider the drawings I made hereabouts are some of the finest I possess. The village or town, stands on a hill slope – surrounded by the 21 Parliament houses so to speak, besides a vast number of little villas, as it were, each with a dome chapel. All this I did not see then, as it was dark – but I had leisure enough later. I went first to the 'head of the Holy Mountain' – i.e. the annually chosen Dictator – always sure to be a clever managing man. He made me a tolerably civil welcome – for I had letters from consuls – bishops etc. – & gave me some supper – & a bed; first of all, they bring you on a tray – some sort of sweets, & a glass of spirit; (oh dear! – what a lot of sweets & rhum have I taken in that Holy Mountain!) then coffee; this is the universal routine of all visits. I felt at once on entering Kariess, that it was a place of fever-air, as, later, I had occasion to know.

Next morning the synod of 20 were assembled – & I was put at the head of the room, while my letters were read; a circular was then given to me, to present to all the convents as I chose – & in the afternoon I began my tour by going to Koutloumoushi – close by the town. I hardly know

Mount Athos

how to describe these astonishing places to you; as I said, they resemble a village in a box; high walls surround all; nearly all have a great tower at one end. All have a courtyard more or less large – & this court contains sometimes one, sometimes 2 or 3 churches – a clock tower – a large refectory ... All have a kiosk outside the gates; also a fountain close by. Round 3 or 4 sides of the court are the cells – galleries above galleries of honeycomb arches; very frequently the abbot's house occupies one side – or his, & the strangers' rooms, look out on the best view ...

Next day – after I had got 2 drawings – they lent me 2 mules – & off I set to Pantokratora. I always asked to see the churches – more to please my hosts than myself, – for I can assure you 20 Greek churches – one just like another – are a task – & I listened meekly to the dreadful nonsense stories they told me of this or that picture. One floated from Jerusalem by sea; – one cried when the Turks came; another bled at some apropos time; a 4th – a Pagan having poked his finger at him, held the finger so tight it was obliged to be cut off – & a 5th has a picture which they declare to have been painted by the Almighty himself!!! As it is about only 8 or 900 years old & very ill done – the blasphemy is almost lost in the absurdity of the matter. Oh those candles! & ostrich eggs! – & gold & silver & paintings!! – oh Holy Mountain! what have I not suffered to get drawings of you! – ...

St. Dionysio is stupendously picturesque; it hangs with its walls & towers on the edge of the sea high on a cliff below the vast Athos, & is a terror to look at. Some of the paths to it are as high as Beachy Head above the sea, & merely projecting bits of rock 2 or 3 feet wide – like a cornice; in one place there is a bit of space – & you step literally over the sea below. Here I observe the mules like particularly to scratch themselves, though the rider's outside leg is hanging over the white foam far below. Booh! – I never trust beasts so far as this comes to. St. Gregorio was burned down some years ago – & is just rebuilt – spic, & span new – blue slates & white-wash; it has a little port with boats – & has altogether a civilised look not acceptable to Art, or dovetailing with its brother monasteries' outwardisms.

Simopetra is – by way of atonement – picturesque in the extreme; it looks at a distance like a giant cage; – quite white, but with galleries & interminable stairs of bright scarlet! – I am happy to say I had not to stay at this place – for unless I had had eau de Cologne or some scent, I must have succumbed to its odiferous atmosphere; bah! – I am sick at the thought of it. (All the convents – I should tell you, have very old prints, which they give to travellers: so, besides my own works, I have an antique set; as for sketches, they usually looked at them upside down or sideways, & said 'beautiful! wonderful!')

I had now to see the remaining convents, & to do this, the only way ...

is to return to Kariess – one of the most superb of rides – half way across
the peninsula close below Athos. But unluckily thick clouds came on – &
a pouring rain – & all I saw was dark forests of beech & pine through rain
. . . till near Kariess, when it cleared up & was again fine. Here I went to
the Konak, or Parliament house of St. Paul, by leave of the abbot Sophronia,
& well it was I did so; donkey that I was! – I forgot my own rules &
maxims; for I had got wet in the rain, & yet seeing the finest view of Kariess
as I entered the town, I did not go on to change my dress – but stopped to
draw over a damp ravine. I had hardly got into the house when my dearly
beloved friend Mr. Fever – gripped me – & in the most decided manner!! –
The shaking fit only lasted an hour – & the hot fit attacked my head at
once making me delirious directly – but not till I had taken a vast dose of
physic. I have no fear of fever now as I can doctor it beautifully. Next
morning, I swallowed quinine amain – & soon grew better; Giorgio bought
a cock from an unwilling old monk who used the brute as a clock, & made
me broth – & by common care & lots of quinine I grew well in 3 days –
but you may suppose I took good caution never to move in Kariess again
without warm clothes.

Meanwhile it poured with rain all those days – & I began to believe I
should pass the rest of my life at Kariess – when once more a fine time
arrived, & I, who hate giving up anything once commenced – set off again
to see the rest of the convents – still 9 in number. I did not walk any more
however – firstly because the roads were henceforward tolerably good –
secondly – because I could now sit on horse back, & was anxious to avoid
fatigue so I made a short move to Xeropotamo; – a grand newly restored
convent by the sea, with wide views towards the opposite promontory of
Sithonia; here was a facetious & clever abbot – & a clean one; the rooms
were clean – & he had a musical snuff box – so one felt in a civilised place,
the more that he could talk rationally on various subjects. Indeed I was often
obliged to try all kinds of shuffles to avoid laughing at the strange questions these monks asked; did the Queen of England speak English or Greek?
What city in London was I born in? Are there any cats in England? etc. etc.

Russikon – is the Russian monastery & its pea green domes & gold
crosses make a gorgeous spectacle . . . Zographo – a most splendid (& clean)
pile of building in a deep valley – surrounded by high forest clad hills; its
abbot was a fussy little man, & so frightfully polite I didn't know what to
do. I then crossed the peninsula & went to Kiliandarion – a vast & ancient
convent – built for a thousand monks; – but the air there is very bad.
Esphigmenou is a nice little building – clean, & in a good air, so I resolved
to sleep there on my way back to Salonica – & here let me stop – oh my!
I am so sick of convents!

However, anxious as I was to get out of them, I could not but feel a great pleasure in having done all I had appointed to do – & in possessing some 50 *most valuable drawings*, for I believe no such collection of illustrations has as yet been known in England. From Vatopedi I returned to the odious Kariess once more – to get what luggage I had left there, & to buy some things for little remembrances of one of the most extraordinary places in the world, & one which I never intend to see again – even if I could do so easily. So I bought some of the carved wood crosses – & bone crosses – & spoons – & gourd water jars – & wooden things for marking bread – & beads & a monk's dress – to be of use in painting – & above all 3 of what I thought to be salad mixers – very long handled spoons – with little sharp

Monastery of Philotheo, Mount Athos
Illustration to Tennyson's 'To Edward Lear on his Travels in Greece'

Mount Athos

nobs of wood cut in relief on the – (so believed) bowl of the spoon. Now what do you think these turned out to be? Ma'am – they were flea scratchers! – I thought I must have screamed when an old monk said these are not spoons but are for this – whereon he began to put it to its proper use. After this, I returned to Esphigmenou & slept there; & the next day, passed out of the land of the monks of Mt. Athos the Holy Mountain – never again to return.

As there has been a report of cholera at Constantinople, these idiot Corfiotes have put on a quarantine of 3 days – as if any quarantine ever kept out cholera at all ... However, this quarantine house is very good, & I have a very large good room to myself; & as I am free from all interruption, I can write all or part of my letters, for, as you may suppose there is a pretty budget of them – besides newspapers of 2 months. Frank L. came yesterday in his boat, (having previously sent off a basket of wine, fish, fruit, meat &

Mount Athos

vegetables) & brought me some books – & thus, you see, having my drawings to pen out besides, I am not likely to be very doleful, particularly as I am in such good health.

The Athos Journal has vanished, but Lear's account of his journey survives in these letters to his sister. His detailed notes† on Curzon's Visits to Monasteries in the Levant, possibly made in preparation for this tour, are also of interest. Lear lacked Curzon's antiquarian zeal and his brilliant eye for Byzantine art; his comments on the treasures of Athos, as well as on those of other churches and monasteries he visited in Greece, are ingenuous in the extreme. In

---

† In the Houghton Library at Harvard.

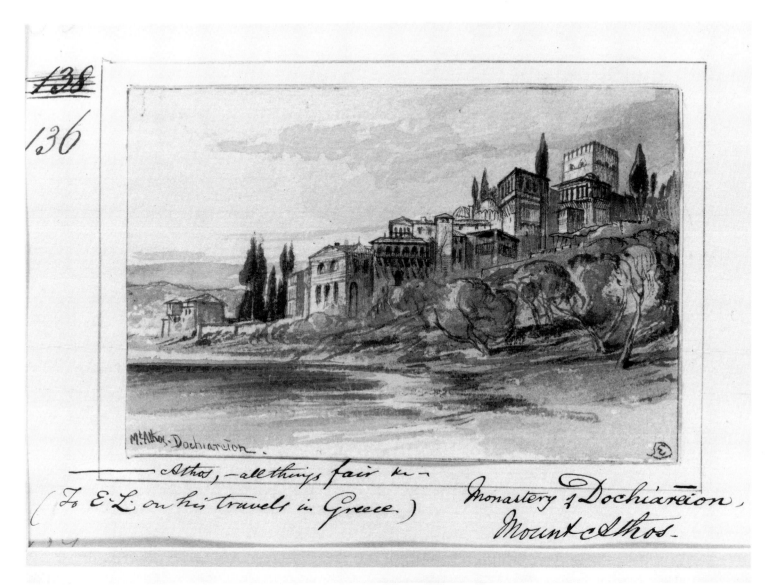

Monastery of Dochiareion, Mount Athos
Illustration to Tennyson's 'To Edward Lear on
his Travels in Greece'

other respects Lear is less parochial than Curzon and a spate of Anglican observers who saw in the Orthodox Church an exemplar of ignorance and idolatry; despite the diverting descriptions he provided for his sister, Lear had a thoughtful, tolerant interest in most varieties of religious experience. Several years after the visit to Athos he set himself the task of translating into Greek an extensive scholarly treatise on the Eastern Church by an old ecclesiastical friend.†

Lear's rare outbursts of rage were normally reserved for the bigotry and sectarianism of his own nation and church; he was also given to occasional criticism of vulgarians, swells and plain women. His tirade against the 'marmalade-masticating

---

† Arthur Penrhyn Stanley, *The Eastern Church*, 1861–2.

Monx' of Athos was atypical of the professional traveller but entirely characteristic of the man who honoured charity and clear thinking.

Letters to Chichester Fortescue

Quarantine Island, Corfu. 9 October 1856

However wondrous and picturesque the exterior & interior of the monasteries, & however abundantly & exquisitely glorious & stupendous the scenery of the mountain, I would not go again to the Ἅγιος Ὄρος [Agios Oros] for any money, so gloomy, so shockingly unnatural, so lonely, so lying, so unatonably odious seems to me all the atmosphere of such monkery. That half of our species which it is natural to every man to cherish & love best, ignored, prohibited and abhorred – all life spent in everlasting repetition of monotonous prayers, no sympathy with ones fellowbeans of any nation, class or age. The name of Christ on every garment and at every tongue's end, but his maxims trodden under foot. God's world and will turned upside down, maimed, & caricatured: – if this I say be Xtianity let Xtianity be rooted out as soon as possible. More pleasing in the sight of the Almighty I really believe, & more like what Jesus Christ intended man to become, is an honest Turk with 6 wives, or a Jew working hard to feed his little old clo' babbies, than these muttering, miserable, mutton-hating, man-avoiding, misogynic, morose, & merriment-marring, monotoning, many-mule-making, mocking, mournful, minced-fish & marmalade masticating Monx. Poor old pigs! Yet one or two were kind enough in their way, dirty as they were: but it is not them, it is their system I rail at.

Corfu. 11 January 1857

Here my boy! give me your eternal thanks for what I am going to suggest to you as a parliamentary motion, to be brought out & spoken on by yourself, to the ultimate benefit of society & to your own postperpetual glorification. As soon as Parliament meets, move that all Sidney Herbert's distressed needlewomen be sent out at once to Mount Athos! By this dodge all the 5000 monks young and old will be vanquished: – distressed needle-babies will ultimately awake the echoes of ancient Acte, & the whole fabric of monkery, not to say of the Greek church will fall down crash & for ever. N.B. Let the needlewomen be all landed at once, 4000 at least, on the South-east side of the peninsula & make a rush for the nearest monastery, that subdued, all the rest will speedily follow.

The tour to Mount Athos marked the end of Lear's travels in the Levant, although he crossed briefly to Albania the following spring. Change, instability and the ubiquitous tourist had diminished the lure of Ottoman lands; as Lear noted in 1866, 'in spite of Lords Stratford and Strangford's nursing, the sick man will be more of an invalid before long I guess — and his dominions will not be good for travelling Topographers.' In the same year Robert Curzon added a disillusioned preface to a new edition of Visits to Monasteries in the Levant, *originally published in 1849; 'Those [Ottoman] countries were ... much better worth seeing at that time than they are now; they were in their original state, each nation retained its particular character, unadulterated by the levelling intercourse with Europeans which always, and in a very short time, exerts so strong an influence that picturesque dress and romantic adventure disappear, while practical utility and a commonplace appearance are so generally disseminated, that in a few years more every country will be alike and travellers will discover that there is nothing to be found in the way of modern manners and customs that they may not see with greater ease in their own houses in London.'*

Greece had also suffered a sea-change in its transformation from a feudal fief to a modern state, and Victorian travellers, like their modern counterparts, had cause to lament the march of progress. Charles Church, who lived into the twentieth century, found in Lear's Athenian drawings the mementoes of a lost land: 'Many of these contain features which have long since disappeared ... the tall brown Venetian watch tower, the Turkish bastion and gateway, the groups of peasants in their native dresses under the pergola of a straw shelter on the plain, the Parthenon standing amid its wilderness of white marble blocks and long grass; all these features belonging to Athens of 60 years ago were represented in the grave and solemn character of Lear's sketches of 1848 — all have disappeared amidst the growth of modern construction.'

The 'Levant Lunatics', those travellers who had ventured beyond the confines of the Grand Tour, were particularly vociferous in their complaints about the advent of mass tourism in the mid-century. It was the age of Cook's Tours, of a booming industry in travel books and of that testament to haut-bourgeois *adventure, Francis Galton's* Art of Travel: Shifts & Contrivances Available in Wild Countries, *with its unintentionally diverting chapters on 'Secreting Jewels', 'Milking Wild Cows', 'Securing Prisoners' and 'Intoxicating Fish'. Lear consoled himself with anecdotes about his compatriots, like the Athenian Mrs Malaprop who transformed the Choragic Monument of Lysicrates into 'The Courageous Monument to Hypocrisy' and his gentle parody of 'The Seven Little Children Who Went Round the World'. These virtuous Victorians travel to exotic lands where they alternately plunder the natives and bestow upon them worthless and futile presents, engage in good works (knitting frocks for fishes) and misguided experiments (trying to churn sea water into butter); the account of their adventures is presented in the spirit of popular contemporary travel books, distinguished by a precise, pedantic, elevated and entirely empty prose.*

In later years Lear kept 'The Spirit of the East' alive in reading and study, writing up his numerous journals and visits with old friends. The Levantine tour of 1848–9 was sometimes associated with regrets for a lost world, sometimes with regrets for his lost youth and always with the discovery of his destiny as a traveller. Long after he had ceased to visit it, Greece remained his inspiration and his goal.

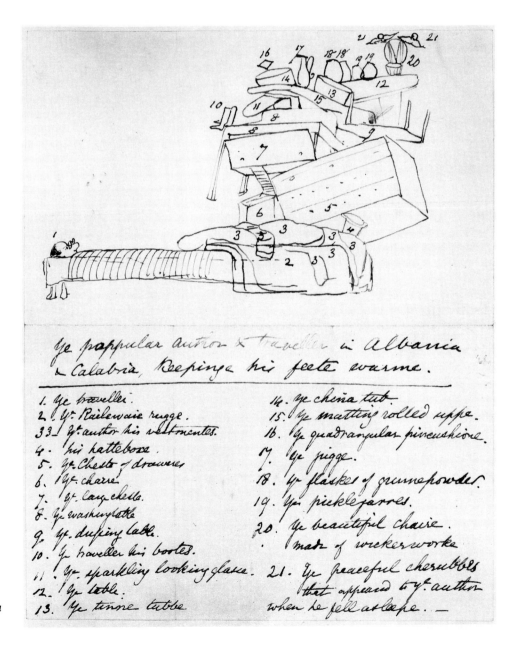

'Ye poppular author &c traveller in Albania & Calabria keppinge his feete warme

*Constantinople and the Golden Horn from
Eyup, oil, 1858*

Tennyson's draft, 'To— on his book about Greece'

TO EDWARD LEAR

ON HIS TRAVELS IN GREECE

Illyrian woodlands, echoing falls
    Of water, sheets of summer glass,
    The long divine Peneïan pass,
The vast Akrokeraunian walls,

Tomohrit, Athos, all things fair,
    With such a pencil, such a pen,
    You shadow forth to distant men,
I read and felt that I was there:

And trust me while I turn'd the page,
    And track'd you still on classic ground,
    I grew in gladness till I found
My spirits in the golden age.

For me the torrent ever pour'd
    And glisten'd – here and there alone
    The broad-limb'd Gods at random thrown
By fountain-urns; – and Naiads oar'd

A glimmering shoulder under gloom
    Of cavern pillars; on the swell
    The silver lily heaved and fell;
And many a slope was rich in bloom

From him that on the mountain lea
    By dancing rivulets fed his flocks
    To him who sat upon the rocks,
And fluted to the morning sea.

Alfred, Lord Tennyson (1853)

Glossary

BEKIR: porter
BEY: a Turkish governor; also a title of rank
BIMBASHI: military commander
BOYOURDI: Turkish passport; general order of introduction to governors and pashas
CADI: Islamic judge
CALIPH: chief civil and religious leader
CAPOTE: long shaggy cloak
CHIBOUQUE: Turkish pipe
COGIA: Muslim elder
DERVISH: member of a Muslim mystical order
DIDASKOLOS: teacher
DOLLAR: Spanish, Austrian or Neapolitan note used by travellers as a standard unit of currency
DRAGOMAN: interpreter, guide
ECONOMO: church steward
EFFENDI: lord, master; Turkish title of respect
ELCHI: ambassador
EMIR: prince
FERINGHI: light outer cloak
FIRMAN: imperial edict; grant, permit
FRANK: any Westerner in the Levant
FUSTANELLA: stiff petticoat of white cotton or linen worn by Greek men
GHEG: northern Albanian
KASTRO: castle or citadel
KAWAS: armed guard

KHAN: inn
KHANJI: innkeeper
KIOSK: pavilion or summer-house
KLEPHT: bandit
LAZARETTO: building used for quarantine
MENZIL: coach road or stage
MILORDOS: any wealthy European traveller
MOLLAH: Muslim religious sage
MUFTI: Muslim priest or judge
NARGILLEH: hubble-bubble, hookah
PALIKARI: member of the Greek or Albanian militia
PAPA (pl. PAPADES): priest
PASHA: officer of high rank; military commander or governor of a province
PASHALIC: the district governed by a pasha
PORTE: the Ottoman court at Constantinople
ROMAIC: vernacular language of modern Greece
SERAGLIO: palace of the Sultan
SERASKIER PASHA: commander-in-chief of army
SKIPETAR: Albanian
SOORUDGI: postilion
TATAR: Tartar guide or courier
TEKE: lodge of a dervish
TESKERE: provincial passport for a traveller and his servants
TOSK: southern Albanian

Constantinople

Select Bibliography

Works and authors cited by Lear in his journals, letters and diaries are marked with an asterisk. The place of publication is London unless otherwise stated. For the most recent standard bibliography on Lear see *Edward Lear*, Royal Academy of Arts, 1985.

Abbey, J. R., *Travels in Aquatint and Lithography*, 1956.

Baggally, John, *Ali Pasha and Great Britain*, Oxford, 1938.

Baillie-Cochrane, Alexander, *In the Days of the Dandies*, 1906.

Beauchamp, Alphonse de, *The Life of Ali Pacha*, 1822.

Beresford, George de la Poer, *Scenes in Southern Albania*, 1855.

Best, J. J., *Excursions in Albania*, 1842.

Bigsby, Robert, *Tribute to the Memory of Scanderbeg the Great*, 1866.

Blake, Robert, *Disraeli's Grand Tour*, 1982.

* Bowen, George Ferguson, *Mount Athos, Thessaly and Epirus*, 1852.

——ed., *Handbook for Travellers in Turkey*, John Murray, 1854.

British Council, *Edward Lear*, Athens, 1964.

Brown, H. A., *A Winter in Albania*, 1888.

Castellan, Georges, *L'Albanie*, Paris, 1980.

* Chirol, M. Valentine, *Twixt Greek and Turk*, 1880.

Christmas, Henry, *The Shores and Islands of the Mediterranean*, 1851.

Church, E. M., *Chapters in an Adventurous Life. Sir Richard Church in Italy and Greece*, Edinburgh, 1895.

* Cockerell, Samuel Pepys, *The Journal of C. R. Cockerell*, 1903.

Cooke, A. B., and Vincent, J. R., eds., *Lord Carlingford's Journal*, Oxford, 1971.

* Curzon, Robert, *Visits to Monasteries of the Levant*, 1849.

Davenport, R. A., *The Life of Ali Pasha*, 1837.

* de Vere, Aubrey, *Picturesque Sketches of Greece and Turkey*, 1850.

* Devereux, W., *Views on the Shores of the Mediterranean*, 1847.

Disraeli, Benjamin, *Contarini Fleming*, 1832

——*The Wondrous Tale of Alroy, or The Rise of Iskander*, 1833.

Dozon, Auguste, *Contes Albanais*, Paris, 1881.

Dupré, Louis, *Voyage à Athènes et à Constantinople*, Paris, 1825.

Ferriman, Z. D., *Some English Philhellenes*, 1917.

Finden's Landscape and Portrait Illustrations of the Life and Work of Lord Byron, 1833.

* Finlay, George, *A History of Greece*, 1856.

——*History of the Greek Revolution*, 1861.

Gennadius Library, *Edward Lear in Greece*, Athens, 1971.

Gettmann, Royal, *A Victorian Publisher. A Study of the Bentley Papers*, Cambridge, 1960.

Glazebrook, Philip, *Journey to Kars*, 1984.

Graves Art Gallery, *Edward Lear: Drawings from a Greek Tour*, Sheffield, 1964.

* Grote, George, *A History of Greece*, 1846.

Grundy, G. B., *The Great Persian War and its Preliminaries*, 1901.

Grylls, R. Glynn, *Trelawny*, 1950.

Gunn, J. A., ed., *Benjamin Disraeli. Letters*, 1982.

Hammond, N. G. L., *Epirus*, 1967.

Haygarth, William, *Greece, a Poem in Three Parts*, 1814.

Hecquard, Hyacinthe, *Histoire et description de la Haute Albanie*, Paris, 1858.

* Hobhouse, John Cam, *A Journey through Albania*, 1813.

——*Recollections of a Long Life*, 1909.

* Holland, Henry, *Travels in the Ionian Isles, Albania, Thessaly, Macedonia & c*, 1815.

Holman-Hunt, William, *Pre-Raphaelitism and the Pre-Raphaelite Brotherhood*, 1905.

* Hughes, Thomas Smart, *Travels in Greece and Albania*, 1820.

Jokai, Maurus, *The Lion of Janina*, 1897.

Joliffe, T. R., *Narrative of an Excursion from Corfu to Smyrna*, 1827.

* Kinglake, Alexander, *Eothen*, 1844.

Knight, E. F., *Albania, A Narrative of Recent Travel*, 1880.

Knight, H. Galley, *Phrosyne*, 1817.

Lane-Poole, Stanley, *The Life of Stratford Canning*, 1888.

* Layard, Austen Henry, *Early Adventures in Persia, Susiana and Babylonia*, 1894.

* Leake, William Martin, *Topography of Athens*, 1821.

——*Travels in the Morea*, 1830.

——*Travels in Northern Greece*, 1835.

* Lewis, J. F., *Constantinople*, 1838.

Longford, Elizabeth, *Byron's Greece*, 1975.

Marchand, Leslie, *Byron*, 1957.

——ed., *Byron's Letters and Journals*, 1973.

Marmullaku, Ramadan, *Albania and the Albanians*, 1975.

Marsden, John Howard, *A Brief Memoir ... of William Martin Leake*, 1864.

Meylan, A., *À travers l'Albanie*, Paris, 1886.

* Milnes, Richard Monckton, *Memoirs of a Tour in Some Parts of Greece*, 1834.

Moore, Clement, *Scanderbeg*, 1850.

* Morier, David, *Photo the Suliot*, 1857.

* Napier, Charles, *The Colonies ...*, 1833.

* Newton, Charles, *Travels and Discoveries in the Levant*, 1865.

Plomer, William, *Ali the Lion*, 1936.

Pollo, Stefanaq, and Puto, Arben, *The History of Albania*, 1981.

Pouqueville, François, *Mémoire sur la vie ... d'Ali Pacha*, Paris, 1820.

——*Travels in Epirus*, 1820.

Rémérand, Gabriel, 'Ali de Tebelen', *Les grandes figures de l'Orient*, Vol. 2, Paris, 1928.

Robinson, Gertrude, *David Urquhart*, Oxford, 1920.

* Senior, Nassau, *A Journal Kept in Turkey and Greece ...*, 1859.

Spencer, Edmund, *Travels in European Turkey*, 1851.

Stackelberg Otto von, *Costumes et usages des peuples de la Grèce moderne*, Rome, 1825.

* Stanley, Arthur Penrhyn, *The Eastern Church*, 1861–2.

* Strangford, Elizabeth, *The Eastern Shores of the Adriatic*, 1863.

* Tennyson, Alfred, Lord, *Poems by Alfred Lord Tennyson*, illus. Edward Lear, 1889.

* Tozer, Henry Fanshawe, *Researches in the Highlands of Turkey*, 1869.

Tregaskis, Hugh, *Beyond the Grand Tour*, 1979.

* Trelawny, Edward, *Recollections of the Last Days of Shelley and Byron*, 1858.

Tsigakou, Fani-Maria, *The Rediscovery of Greece*, 1981.

Turner, William, *A Tour in the Levant*, 1820.

* Urquhart, David, *The Spirit of the East*, 1839.

——*The Turkish Bath*, 1856.

Walker, Mary Adelaide, *Through Macedonia to the Albanian Lakes*, 1864.

* Walpole, Robert, *Memoirs Relating to European and Asiatic Turkey*, 1817–20.

* Walsh, Robert, *Narrative of a Journey from Constantinople to England*, 1823.

* Warburton, Eliot, *The Crescent and the Cross*, 1845.

Ward, Philip, *Albania. A Travel Guide*, Cambridge, 1983.

* Watkin, David, *The Life and Work of C. R. Cockerell*, 1974.

Weber, Shirley Howard, *Voyages and Travels in the Near East during the Nineteenth Century*, Princeton, 1952.

——*Voyages and Travels in Greece and the Near East and Adjacent Regions made Previous to the Year 1801*, Princeton, 1953.

* Williams, Hugh, *Select Views in Greece*, 1829.

Wingfield, W. F., *A Tour in Dalmatia, Albania and Montenegro*, 1859.

* Wordsworth, Christopher, *Greece: Pictorial, Descriptive and Historical*, 1839.

Han at Cucues, Albania

Sources

The author and publisher wish to thank the following for permission to reproduce illustrations:

Ashmolean Museum, Oxford: pp. 123, 133, 139, 153, 154; BBC Hulton Picture Library: p. 63; Blacker-Wood Library of Zoology and Ornithology, McGill University, Montreal: p. 143; Bradford City Art Galleries: p. 59; Bridgeman Art Library, London: p. 149; Christie's: pp. 34, 35, 38; Davis & Long Co., New York: p. 89; Department of Prints and Drawings, British Museum (photography Angelo Hornak): pp. 11, 22, 23, 71, 74, 75: Fine Art Society: front jacket illustration, p. 41 (below); Gennadius Library, Athens: pp. 16 (above), 39 (above), 55, 126, 128, 134; Government Art Collection, London: p. 24; Houghton Library, Harvard University: back jacket illustration, frontispiece, pp. 13, 17, 40 (right), 43 (below), 48 (above), 56, 60 (right), 65, 67, 76, 77, 78, 79, 82, 91, 92, 97, 100, 102, 106, 116, 129, 135, 137, 141, 146, 160 (above), 161; Mary Evans Picture Library: p. 26; Michael Appleby: p. 84; Museum of Art, Rhode Island School of Design: p. 118; Museum of the City of Athens: pp. 19, 122; National Portrait Gallery, London: p. 29; Pierpont Morgan Library, New York: pp. 90, 158 (below); Private collections: pp. 15, 18, 21, 25, 27, 28, 29, 31, 41 (above), 45, 46 (above), 51, 58, 72, 112, 140, 152: Sotheby's: pp. 42, 44, 125.

We would also like to thank the Houghton Library, Harvard University, for permission to reproduce the following quotations: p. 14, lines 9–11 and 14–15; p. 27, lines 23–4; p. 29, line 31; p. 30, lines 3–4, 20–1 and 23–4; p. 37, lines 1–2; p. 41, lines 34–6; p. 123, lines 9–10; p. 142, final footnote.

Index